A BIBLIOGRAPHY OF THE WRITINGS
OF
WILLIAM CARLETON

A BIBLIOGRAPHY OF
THE WRITINGS
OF
WILLIAM CARLETON

Barbara Hayley

COLIN SMYTHE
Gerrards Cross, 1985

Copyright © 1985 by Barbara Hayley

First published in 1985 by Colin Smythe Limited
Gerrards Cross, Buckinghamshire

British Library Cataloguing in Publication Data

Hayley, Barbara
A bibliography of the writings of William Carleton.
1. Carleton, William—Bibliography
I. Title
016.828′91209   Z8145.3/

ISBN 0-86140-188-3

Produced in Great Britain
Set by Crypticks, Leeds, and
printed and bound by Billing & Sons Ltd.,
Worcester

CONTENTS

ACKNOWLEDGEMENTS

I am most grateful to the many librarians without whose assistance this bibliography could not have been compiled. For reasons of space I have listed them at the end of this volume in the section 'Libraries with Significant Carleton Holdings'.

Special thanks are due to the following, who helped beyond the call of duty: Yeatman Anderson III, of the Public Library of Cincinnati and Hamilton County; Vicky Cremin, Trinity College Dublin Library; Ann Drain, Freiberger Library, Case Western Reserve University, Cleveland, Ohio; Michael J. Durkan, Swarthmore College Library; Laird Ellis, William R. Perkins Library, Duke University; Janette Fiore, Michigan State University Library; Richard Heinzkill, University of Oregon Library, Eugene; Betty M. Jarboe, Indiana University; David V. Koch, Southern Illinois University at Carbondale; Margaret MacAnulla, Royal Irish Academy; Norman R. MacDonald, Tacoma Public Library; Stephen Nonack, Library of the Boston Athenaeum; Nora J. Quinlan, Kenneth Spencer Research Library, University of Kansas; Stephen Slovasky, Xavier University Library, Cincinnati; John Withen, British Library Newspaper Library, Colindale; Brooke Whiting, University of California, Los Angeles.

Many friends and colleagues have provided help, encouragement and references; I should like to mention particularly Professor Julia Moynahan and Benedict Kiely. The late Father Frank Morris of Kiltegan and Mrs. W. J. Grier of Belfast volunteered interesting information. Dr. John Kelly helped this work in its infant days as a thesis; Professor A. N. Jeffares approved the thesis and pushed on the work; Colin Smythe provided much bibliographical material as well as publishing the book. My father John Edward Fox did an immense amount of searching and finding. For all the help that I have received from all of these, I am truly thankful.

GENERAL INTRODUCTION

Any reader – or would-be reader – of William Carleton's work will have found his studies impeded by the lack of available books and by the lack of bibliographical evidence to enable him to pursue what books there are. This bibliography is an attempt to correct the sad state of affairs in which an author of acknowledged historical and literary importance is unhonoured, unsung, unavailable and uncatalogued. I hope that it will be of use to the reader who wishes to follow the pattern of Carleton's work and its publication; to the librarian or collector holding in his hand an edition of one of Carleton's books and wondering where or how it fits into his output; and to anyone wishing to follow up a story – its first appearance, its subsequent publishing history, its reception by the critics.

The reader who has been confused by even the titles of Carleton's voluminous output will consider the attempt to make bibliographical sense of it foolhardy. The pitfalls are the apparently infinite permutations and combinations of *Tales and Stories/Tales and Sketches/Traits and Stories* of the *Irish/Irish People/Irish Peasantry*; the multiplication of 'editions'; of 'Fourth Editions' where no second or third exist; of stories revised, recycled and retitled, from collection to collection, edition to edition. The pleasures of the task have outnumbered the perils: the handling of so many beautiful books; the detective exercise of finding them in order to describe them; the tracing of each story from periodical to first edition, and thence through many editions and alterations. The greatest pleasure was the confirmation by all that I saw and read that Carleton is significant not just as an individual writer but as a major figure in the revival of an Irish publishing movement that raised itself from the almost-dead in the 1830s.

Blinded as we are by the splendour of the Yeatsian Irish Literary Revival, we do not see the remarkable achievement of the first Irish literary revival of the 19th century – the first and lost literary revival of the 1830s. This was the period of recovery from the desperate intellectual, social and commercial apathy that had pervaded Ireland after the Act of Union, movingly described in the pages of contemporary periodicals. Irish publishing, which had flourished in the late eighteenth century, died. Irish writers looked to and published in London. The Irish publishing trade virtually disappeared, producing nothing but pamphlets and tracts. There were few bookshops, and only English books and magazines to sell in them. What Irish literary energy remained was dissipated in religious and political disputes – Catholics *versus* Protestants, Unionists *versus* anti-Unionists. Towards 1830, probably as a result of the passing of the Catholic Emancipation Bill, there was a relaxation of this warfare, and the first stirrings of an Irish literary life were seen in periodical and book publication. In the periodicals, at first expensive journals and then good penny magazines, an Irish literary world was created and fostered, and an Irish national consciousness developed. Carleton took part in this movement as a contributor to magazines, and, even more significantly, as the first writer of fiction to publish principally in Ireland. His career parallels the growth of the Irish publishing trade – and the enormous popularity of his work was an influential factor in that growth. The rapid development of Irish publishing and of Carleton's own career can be seen in the progression of *Traits and Stories of the Irish Peasantry* from the slim, anonymous volumes of the *First Series* of 1830 to the lavish 'New Edition' of 1842 published by Curry and Orr in Dublin and London.

The revival of Irish literary life corresponds with Carleton's development from novice minor writer to authoritative voice of Ireland, praised on both sides of the Irish sea and on both sides of the Atlantic as the presenter of Ireland and the Irish to the world. He started with little enough – no education, no experience, no publishing trade, few readers, no literary tradition to learn from. W.B. Yeats said that Carleton's and Banim's novels were

prevented from taking their place as great literature because the literary tradition of Ireland was, when Carleton and Banim wrote, so undeveloped that the novelist, no matter how great his genius, found no fit convention ready to his hand, and no exacting public to forbid him to commingle noisy melodrama with his revelations. (Letter to the Editor of the Dublin *Daily Express. The Letters of W.B. Yeats*, ed. Alan Wade, London, 1954, p.248.)

It was Carleton who, by publishing in Ireland, built up the tradition, created a public, and encouraged other writers such as Banim, Griffin, Lover, to publish in Ireland, so that by 1840 there was a healthy Irish publishing trade selling in England as well as in Ireland.

The value then of a bibliographical study of Carleton seemed self-evident. The difficulties of preparing it were alarming but not insuperable. There had been only one major bibliographical examination of Carleton, by Michael Sadleir in his *XIX Century Fiction*. D.J. O'Donoghue had compiled a list of Carleton's work in his *Life of William Carleton* (London, Downey, 1896, Vol. I, pp. lvii – lxiv), and S.J. Brown had also listed much of Carleton's work in *Ireland in Fiction*, Dublin, 1916. All had remarked on the difficulty of getting hold of books, or specific editions of them. Yeats and D.J. O'Donoghue both wrote many letters to friends and acquaintances with requests for loans of books by Carleton. Michael Sadleir introduced the Carleton section of *XIX Century Fiction* in tones rather forbidding to anyone wishing to pursue the study further:

Although incomplete and containing a few unsatisfactory copies, the following is a really remarkable collection of Carleton's works. His bibliography is complex in the extreme, but nowhere hitherto has the degree of scope and accuracy here reached been achieved. Even the C.B.E.L. (whose Carleton section I myself revised) lacks one or two titles and gives a few incorrect dates which, since that revision, I have been fortunate enough to establish.

Mainly of Irish origin, Carleton's books were frequently of shoddy manufacture, and more or less disintegrated under rough usage – also their supply to the Statutory Libraries was apt to be irregular. Finally his (or his publishers') habit of reissuing stories in different order under new titles and, conversely, giving almost identical titles to quite different collections, has made the identification of genuine First editions baffling and hazardous. (Michael Sadleir, *XIX Century Fiction*, London, 1951. Vol. I, p. 76).

This comment from a great bibliographer excuses any faults or gaps in the present volume; in fact Sadleir was working with his own collection only, whereas I have been able to profit from the generosity of many librarians who allowed me to borrow or see their Carleton holdings, so that I have been able to describe a great many new examples of Carleton's works. I have not concentrated on first editions; for the present bibliography it seemed as important to find the twenty later editions of a novel as to place the first one. Sadleir's work was a splendid foundation on which to build.

Where I would take issue with Sadleir is on the question of the 'shoddy manufacture' of the books themselves. Perhaps he is thinking only of late cheap editions. To me the books are a delight, even the earliest, most unassuming *Traits and Stories*, illustrated by Brooke and Wakeman with running, staggering, jostling, quarrelling peasants: books beautifully laid out, generously leaded, with clear type and lots of space; books like the 1835 first and second series together, bindings intricately blocked; all the variations of the 'New Edition' of *Traits and Stories*, the bindings gilt, shamrocked, cascading with lively figures. This bibliography grew from the sheer pleasure of handling these books; a pity that one's bibliographical delight can be transmitted only in dry transcriptions.

The bibliography contains four sections. The first, properly bibliographical section, is a record of each of Carleton's books in (ideally) all its editions. The second section lists work by Carleton first published in periodicals. The third section contains subsequent printings of Carleton's work, in full or in part, in periodicals and anthologies. By listing these extracts, I hope I shall save others many wild goose chases after early reprints that look like original contributions or undiscovered Carleton stories. The last section lists criticism of Carleton from 1829 to the present; his work was very frequently reviewed not only in the Dublin and London press but in English, Scottish and Welsh local newspapers. Although the reader may find this section surprisingly full, I am sure that many other reviews lie waiting to be disinterred from provincial *Sentinels*, *Guardians* and *Beacons* and, I fear, from more distinguished journals which I have missed.

The index is intended to be a concordance to all the works mentioned in the books. By looking up in the index the name of a novel or collection, one will find its bibliographical number (under which will be listed a description of all its editions), an indication of the number of editions, any change of title and reviews of it listed by the year in which they appeared. By looking up any story, one will find the collections in which it appeared, its first periodical publication, changes of title and criticism.

I have had three principal intentions in laying out this bibliography: first, to show the pattern of publication of Carleton's books, second, to make it possible for the reader to see where any given piece of work fits into that pattern and third, to show the activity around each piece of work. The quantity of the publications, and the amount of interest generated by them are a gauge of Carleton's literary and historical significance.

BIBLIOGRAPHY
OF CARLETON'S BOOKS

INTRODUCTION

Carleton's first modest volume containing the semi-love-story *Father Butler* and the supposedly autobiographical reminiscence *The Lough Dearg Pilgrim* were published in 1829. One year later, he had arrived at the formula that was to make him popular: collections of stories in which an exposition of Irish habits, customs and characteristics was linked to a simple plot. This first *Traits and Stories of the Irish Peasantry* was followed by a second 'series' in 1833. Both of these anonymous collections were well received, going into four and three editions respectively, being published in America in 1833 and 1834, and reissued together in 1836. After collecting almost all his magazine stories into *Tales of Ireland* and *Popular Tales and Legends of the Irish Peasantry* in 1834, Carleton embarked on his first novel, *Fardorougha the Miser*, in 1839, and from then until 1862 produced twelve more novels, mainly to critical and public acclaim. Most of his novels went into seven or more editions; *Willy Reilly* went into at least thirty. Carleton was at his most productive in the 1840s when he produced the 'definitive' collection of *Traits and Stories of the Irish Peasantry* (1842-44), which entailed a great deal of expansion and alteration of twenty stories, and the writing of the *General Introduction*, his best piece of non-fictional prose; a collection of novella-length stories, *The Fawn of Spring Vale etc;* a new major collection of short pieces, *Tales and Sketches . . . of the Irish Peasantry*, and seven novels, *Valentine M'Clutchy, Art Maguire, Rody the Rover, Parra Sastha, The Black Prophet, The Emigrants of Ahadarra* and *The Tithe-Proctor*. In the 1850s and 1860s he continued to produce novels, and many of his earlier books were being republished continually in Britain and in America, in cheap and expensive editions. After his death, publication of his work continued fairly actively until about 1920, after which it virtually ceased until the 1970s.

Carleton had a number of regular publishers and a few who each published only one of his books. His first was Curry, a small Dublin firm which also published the *Christian Examiner*; they brought out

Father Butler. The Lough Dearg Pilgrim in 1829, the first series of
Traits and Stories of the Peasantry in its first two editions (1830 and
1832), and *The Little Chimney Sweep* in 1831. William Frederick
Wakeman, another Dublin Protestant publisher, brought out the
third and fourth editions of the First Series (1834 and 1835), all three
editions of the Second Series (1833, 1834, 1835), *Tales and Legends
of Ireland* (1834 and 1837), and in 1836, with Baldwin and Cradock
of London, the five-volume edition of both series of *Traits and
Stories*. Carleton continued, however, to publish also with Curry –
Tales of Ireland in 1834 and *Fardorougha the Miser* in 1839. It had
become common for Dublin and London firms to publish jointly,
and Curry published the first edition of *The Fawn of Spring Vale*
with Longman Orme in 1841 and the second edition with Routledge
in 1843. It was Curry, in conjunction with Orr of London, who
brought out the ambitious 'New Edition' of *Traits and Stories of the
Irish Peasantry* in parts in 1842 and in two volumes in 1843 and 1844.

From 1845 onwards, Carleton's most regular publisher was quite
unlike Curry or Wakeman: he was James Duffy, the editor of
numerous Roman Catholic magazines, and the foremost Irish
publisher of missals, catechisms and other religious-educational
material. Duffy took account of the general trend towards less
expensive fiction and started several cheap series such as 'Tales for
Ireland' and 'Duffy's Library of Ireland', which included a number of
Carleton titles. His first Carleton publications, however, were large
and richly illustrated: *Tales and Sketches . . . of the Irish Peasantry*
and *Valentine M'Clutchy*, both in 1845. Also in 1845, but in cheap
editions, Duffy published *Art Maguire, Parra Sastha* and *Rody the
Rover*. With offices in London and Dublin, he published *The Evil
Eye* in 1860, *The Double Prophecy* and *Redmond Count O'Hanlon*
in 1862. Duffy seems to have believed in pushing several works of an
author at the same time – it is noticeable that he published five new
Carleton titles in 1845 and two in 1862. He also kept reissuing his
books over a long period, in many 'editions' – *Rody the Rover* until
after 1905, *Parra Sastha* until after 1875, *Valentine M'Clutchy* until
1869. Duffy published late editions of Carleton as well as new titles
– the fourth edition of *Fardorougha the Miser* in 1846, the second
edition of *Willy Reilly* in 1857, and late editions of *Red Hall* which he
retitled *The Black Baronet*, in 1858, 1875 and n.d. In 1869, the year
of Carleton's death, Duffy published, in London and Dublin, three
selections of Carleton's short stories, from various earlier collections:
The Poor Scholar . . . and other Irish Tales; *Barney Brady's Goose*

. . . *and other Irish Tales*; *Tubber Derg . . . and other Irish Tales*, which each went into five editions.

Another regular publisher of Carleton's work was Simms and M'Intyre of Belfast, who used a new story by Carleton, *The Black Prophet*, in 1847 to launch their new 'Parlour Library' series – a new venture in the production of inexpensive but attractive books with illustrated board backs, in tune with the movement towards cheaper fiction. Their choice itself gives an indication of Carleton's popularity; the book proved so successful that Simms and M'Intyre were able to place themselves as a London firm for its second edition that same year. They also reissued it in 1848 and 1849. Other new Carleton titles in the Parlour Library were *The Emigrants of Ahadarra* (1848, reissued 1851 and 1857) and *The Tithe Proctor* (1849); a late edition of *Fardorougha the Miser* also appeared in the series (1848).

Several London firms published one Carleton first edition only: The Office of the Illustrated London Library brought out *The Squanders of Castle Squander* in 1852; in the same year, Saunders and Otley published the first edition of *Red Hall or the Baronet's Daughter*; in 1855 Hope brought out the first edition of *Willy Reilly* which was to be republished by tens of other firms in its long lifetime; in 1862 Ward, Lock published the only edition of *The Silver Acre*. After Carleton's death they republished stories from it in *The Fair of Emyvale* and they also published two late editions of *The Squanders of Castle Squander* and of *Traits and Stories of the Irish Peasantry*.

There were of course many publishers who did not deal directly with Carleton, but who took over his books by buying the copyright or the sheets from other publishers. They included Philip Dixon Hardy, the staunchly Unionist magazine proprietor and editor (of the *National Magazine*, the *Dublin Penny Journal* and others). He published selections of Carleton stories from previous collections – *Alley Sheridan and other Stories* (1857) and *Characteristic Sketches of Ireland and the Irish* (1840) – with a succession of different London publishers for five editions before selling it to Milner of Halifax who published the next five. Tegg of London often took over late copyright from other publishers: they published *Traits and Stories of the Irish Peasantry* from the 'Fifth Edition' (1864) to the 'Eleventh Complete Edition' (after 1869), and also a one-volume edition in 1870. Routledge published *Traits and Stories* in several arrangements of their own; they took over *The Tithe Proctor* and the *Emigrants of Ahadarra* from Simms and M'Intyre; they published

Denis O'Shaughnessy going to Maynooth by itself in 1845, and made several new combinations of *Jane Sinclair*, *The Clarionet*, *The Dead Boxer* and *Phil Purcel* with other stories. Routledge published most of these books in London and New York, linking the British and American publication of Carleton's work.

After Carleton's death, Simpkin and Marshall of London, who had published several Carleton works with Duffy, published for the first time, with Sealy Bryers of Dublin, Carleton's novel *The Redhaired Man's Wife* (1889). They also joined Hamilton Adams and Morison of Glasgow in publishing *Amusing Irish Tales*, abridged from *Tales and Sketches of the Irish Peasantry*, (1889, 1892 and n.d.). The most impressive productions at the end of the century were D.J. O'Donoghue's edition of *Traits and Stories of the Irish Peasantry* from Dent, London, in 1896, and his edition of Carleton's *Life* for Downey, London, in the same year. Briefer selections of Carleton's work were offered by Putnam, New York and London, edited by W.B. Yeats (1904), Blackie (edited by Tighe Hopkins, 1905), and The Talbot Press, edited by Darrell Figgis (1918). In the 1960s, the New English Library brought out a selection from *Traits and Stories* (1962), and McGibbon and Kee published Patrick Kavanagh's edition of Carleton's *Life* (1968); in the 1970s, the Irish University Press reprinted *The Black Prophet* in facsimile (1972) and Mercier published four volumes of *Traits and Stories* edited by Maurice Harmon (1973).

Carleton publishing in America followed a slightly different course, with a particular strength in the last quarter of the nineteenth century. Readers of this bibliography may be surprised to see how much of Carleton's work appeared in America, from how many different publishing houses. Carleton's work was taken up very early by American publishers. By 1835, up to which year all Carleton's books had been anonymous, American firms had already republished two editions of *Father Butler* (Philadelphia, Latimer, 1834 and 1835), an edition of the First Series of *Traits and Stories* (Philadelphia and Baltimore, Carey and Hart, 1833), and the Second Series divided into two two-volume collections (Philadelphia, Carey and Hart, 1833 and 1834). Carey and Hart published *Fardorougha the Miser* within a year of its first publication, and all Carleton's subsequent novels were taken up by American publishers. The 'New Edition' of *Traits and Stories of the Irish Peasantry* was published by Wilson and Hawkins in 1861. Twenty-seven of the thirty editions of *Willy Reilly* were published in America. It was the

New York firm of Collier who brought out the nearest thing to a *Complete Works*, and Sadlier of New York and Montreal also produced a fine set of ten volumes as 'Carleton's Works'. Around the turn of the century there were several beautiful American editions of Carleton's work, such as Niccolls's *Traits and Stories of the Irish Peasantry* (Boston, 1911). From the beginning, there were also many cheap editions in 'Pocket', 'Seaside' or 'Holiday Library' series from houses such as Munro and Houghton Mifflin.

This sequence was partially dictated by the state of publishing in America in the nineteenth century. Before the passing of the International Copyright Act of 1891 and the Copyright Code of 1909, American publishers were free to pirate any European writer's work without paying the author or the European publisher. In order to forestall this, American firms could, however, legitimately buy the sheets of the book from the European publisher, and publish the book from them, often even from advance sheets, a procedure that protected both the legitimate American publisher and the European one. The Carey and Hart editions of both series of *Traits and Stories* and of *Fardorougha the Miser* mentioned above are from the sheets of the Curry, Dublin, editions, as are many other early transatlantic editions of Carleton's work, whereas many multiple late editions such as the twenty-seven *Willy Reilly*s may have been pirated.

Carey and Hart, who first introduced Carleton to American readers with the two series of *Traits and Stories* in 1833 and 1834, also published assorted collections of his stories: *Neal Malone and other Tales of Ireland* in 1839, and *The Battle of the Factions and other Tales of Ireland, Phelim O'Toole's Courtship and The Poor Scholar* and *Phil Purcel and other Tales of Ireland* in 1845. In 1847 they brought out Carleton's novel *Parra Sastha* with *O'Sullivan's Love* and Lever's *Knight of Gwynne*.

Three American houses who published a great deal of Carleton's fiction were D. and J. Sadlier, P.F. Collier and P.J. Kenedy, all recently founded by Irishmen, and all emphatically Roman Catholic. They naturally did not publish Carleton's early anti-Catholic stories, but the strong Irish interest of his later, milder work was well suited to the large number of Irish who formed a high proportion of the Catholic population of America, which rose from just over three million in 1860 to just under nine million in 1890.

The firm of D. & J. Sadlier, which did much to create a specific Catholic reading market in America, was founded in 1838 by Dennis Sadlier from Co. Tipperary. Based first in New York and later in

Montreal as well, it specialised in devotional and educational works and in handsome Bibles and missals, and published *The Catholic Directory* and *The Tablet*. Over four decades, they published Carleton's *Valentine M'Clutchy* (1846, 1854, 1876 and undated editions), *Art Maguire* (1846 and n.d.), *The Tithe Proctor* (1873 and n.d.), *Jane Sinclair etc.* (1872 and n.d.), *The Evil Eye* and *Redmond Count O'Hanlon* (1875), and late editions of *The Black Baronet* and *Fardorougha the Miser*. It was these ten volumes that Sadlier reissued in 1879 in a handsome uniform set with 'Carleton's Works' on the spine, though not on the title pages, which were all laid out just as they had been in the individual volumes. They were heavily advertised in the trade press as a set though the volumes were still for sale separately. Sadlier also published *Traits and Stories of the Irish Peasantry* as 'Two Volumes in One' in 1860 with two later undated editions, and a *Tales and Stories of the Irish Peasantry* of their own selection, which they later retitled *The Poor Scholar and Other Stories* (1880 and subsequent editions).

Also straight from Ireland, and specialising in Catholic and Irish titles, was Peter Fenelon Collier of New York, who published a more comprehensive *Works of William Carleton* than anyone else ever attempted. It appeared in 1881, 1882 and 1892 in a variety of two- and three-volume editions. The stories in the collection were designated 'Unabridged'; it was not a truly *Complete* works, as it left out a number of well-known pieces; it also included by mistake several stories not by Carleton. Its curious bibliographical history is detailed at [76a].

Kenedy of New York was the oldest Roman Catholic publishing house in America, founded by P.J. Kenedy from Co. Kilkenny. Its list resembled that of Duffy in Dublin, including lives of the Saints, apologias, school textbooks, catechisms, missals, and novels dealing with Catholic life. It had several cheap fiction series, including an 'Irish Fireside Library'. In 1896 Kenedy published Carleton's *Redmond Count O'Hanlon*, *The Evil Eye* and *The Black Prophet*.

As I have mentioned, Routledge published simultaneously in Great Britain and America, and from 1857 to 1895 they had several titles in various editions – *The Emigrants of Ahadarra* and *The Tithe Proctor*, *Jane Sinclair*, *Neal Malone and other Tales*, *The Clarionet, the Dead Boxer and other Tales* and *Phil Purcell the Pig-Driver and other Irish Stories*. In 1877 they brought out four-series and two-series arrangements of *Traits and Stories*.

Also available to the American reader were the Walter Scott

edition of Yeats's *Stories from Carleton* (1889) and later, the Dent/ Macmillan edition of *Traits and Stories of the Irish Peasantry* edited by D.J. O'Donoghue in 1896.

Carleton's American publishers also included long-established family firms such as Scribner, Appleton and Putnam. Some houses would publish a few Carleton titles, as did Donaho of Boston (*Parra Sastha*, 1865, *The Black Baronet*, 1869, *Willy Reilly*, n.d.) Others would publish only one, as did Wilson and Hawkins (*Traits and Stories of the Irish Peasantry*, 'A New Edition', 1862), Peterson (*Rody the Rover*, n.d.), Ross Wilkinson (*Poor Scholar*, 1847), Jones in Boston (*The Dead Boxer*, n.d.) and Adam Stevenson in Toronto, who published a selection of *Traits and Stories of the Irish Peasantry* (1871). *Willy Reilly* alone was published by Moore of Boston (1856), Munro of New York (1880), Belford Clarke of Chicago (1885), The Mercantile Publishing Co. (1888), Allison (1889), The New York Publishing Co, The New York American News Company, Crowell, Fenno, Burt, Caldwell, Potter and others.

The last distinguished new edition of Carleton was produced by Niccolls of Boston in 1911: this was the lavish 'Celtic Edition', with gilt title plate, in 1,000 numbered copies. After it American interest in Carleton seems to have declined just as sharply as that in the British Isles, with only a few isolated reprints. A recent development however has been the admirable Garland Series of facsimile reprints of early editions of Carleton including the first and second series of *Traits and Stories*, *Father Butler. The Lough Dearg Pilgrim*, five novels, *Tales of Ireland*, *Tales and Sketches* . . ., and the D.J. O'Donoghue edition of Carleton's *Life*, thereby making available many volumes which are difficult to find in their original editions.

A note on this section.

This bibliographical section is arranged so that the first appearance of a book gives it its place in the chronological order, and its number. Subsequent appearances of the book follow immediately, with a letter to distinguish the order of publication. So Carleton's first book, *Father Butler. The Lough Dearg Pilgrim* is numbered [1], its first edition from Curry, Dublin in 1829 being [1a], its second edition from Curry in 1839 being [1b]. When *Father Butler* is published without the *Lough Dearg Pilgrim* by Latimer, Philadelphia, in 1834, it has a new number with the chronological placing [7a], and the next edition of that book, published by Latimer in 1835, is [7b].

The general term 'edition' is used as Carleton's publishers used it, that is, for a separate, distinctive book, for a new publishing effort, and for what we would properly call issues or impressions. This usage is to help the reader trying to identify or place a book: the 1842 collection of *Traits and Stories of the Irish Peasantry*, for example, had got to its 'Tenth Complete Edition' by 1869, according to its title page, although in fact the 'editions' were reimpositions from the stereotypes of the original partwork of 1842. The term on the title page seemed the clearest to keep to. For the bibliographical convolutions of the title *Traits and Stories of the Irish Peasantry*, see note below: it is the most confusing example of what made Carleton's bibliography seem 'baffling and hazardous' to Sadleir, the 'habit of reissuing stories in different order under new titles and conversely giving almost identical titles to quite different collections'.

I hope that the listing system of this bibliography has circumvented the hazards. Where a collection of stories varies in title, but is the same collection, all new 'editions' and issues are grouped together at the same number: *Tales and Sketches of the Irish Peasantry*, retitled *Tales and Stories of the Irish Peasantry* and again retitled *Tales of Ireland*, for example, are all together in order of publication at [18a-h]. Where the title is the same, but the stories are different, the collections have different numbers according to the date of their publication. The tale of *The Poor Scholar*, for example, appears with different companions under the title *The Poor Scholar and other Tales of Irish Life*, and the two collections are to be found at [42a-b] and [46e-f]. *The Clarionet and other Stories* and *Jane Sinclair and other Stories* go through similar variations. I have given cross-references where confusion might arise.

Where a novel is clearly the principal feature of a book, but an accompanying short piece of 'filling' varies, I have ignored the makeweight in the numbering. *Art Maguire*, for example, has a variety of short companion pieces in various editions, without any indication of the fact on the title page, so it seems more practical for the searcher to look for it under the main heading *Art Maguire*. Similarly, *Parra Sastha* has *Observations on Farming* by Martin Doyle at the end of its first edition, no companion in its second edition, and *Rose Moan* in most other editions, with the editions numbered by the publisher without reference to this fact.

In almost all cases I have numbered only volumes that I have seen. I have not, for example, left gaps for a second and third edition where I have seen only a first and a fourth, as it seems clear that publishers often jumped from one edition to another. *Rody the*

Rover, for example, apparently went from its first to its fourth edition in the same year, and I have seen nothing to indicate that there really was a second or a third edition. (Nor have I found a fifth edition after the fourth – but there were two 'sixth editions' [20a-d]). I have not counted advertisements as sufficient evidence that a book appeared, there being many a slip between prospectus and public (I have in my possession a magnificent prospectus for Carleton's *Chronicles of Ballymacruiskeen* incorporating numerous specific details of character, incident and plot, to be published by Duffy, which I am pretty sure did not materialise). I have not numbered books listed as appearing in a series or as 'companions to this volume' when I have not seen them – I have, however, mentioned them. In only a few cases have I given a book the 'benefit of the doubt' – *The Little Chimney Sweep*, for example, was given a book review, so I have assumed that it was published [3a], though even here the element of doubt persists as the story had been printed in instalments in the *Christian Examiner*, which reviewed it. I have marked entries which I have not seen: †.

Several books and editions are nowhere available to be seen. Promising entries in library catalogues are disappointing when pursued: the books turn out to be different collections after all, or wrongly dated, or sometimes, alas, not in the library at all, missing presumed stolen or never there in the first place. I have excluded such references. I think I have explored all sources except private collections, but should be delighted to be told of any editions that I have missed.

As well as title page, contents and pagination I have included any notable features such as engraved title pages. There are too many variants in binding to make it useful to describe them, though it would have been a pleasure to give details of the distinctive, attractive and often witty bindings which embellished these books.

In the heading to each item, I have used the term 'First Edition' where the edition was a first book publication (as *The Tithe Proctor* [31a]) but not where it was merely a new combination of stories (as *The Clarionet* [34a]). Other terms such as 'Second Edition', 'Third Edition Corrected', 'Ninth Complete Edition', 'Author's Copyright Edition', I have taken direct from the title page of the book described. The term 'American Edition' is given by me, to mark the many transatlantic publications of Carleton's work.

After each entry I have given the number of the edition in Sadleir's *XIX Century Fiction*, (Cambridge University Press, 1951),

S.J. Brown's *Ireland in Fiction,* Dublin and London, Maunsel, 1919 and the page-reference to D.J. O'Donoghue's Bibliography of Carleton's Works (*Life of William Carleton*), if they have mentioned it.

A note on Traits and Stories of the Irish Peasantry.

The title *Traits and Stories of the Irish Peasantry* covers an inordinate number of books. It was originally used for Carleton's second book, an anonymous collection of eight stories published by Curry in Dublin in 1829. This then had a 'second edition corrected', Curry, Dublin 1832 [2b], still anonymous. In 1833 an American edition appeared from Carey and Hart, Philadelphia [2d] which uses the term 'First Series' as a second series had appeared in 1833. The same eight stories appeared in a 'third edition, corrected' from Wakeman, in 1834 [2d], still anonymous, and *not* called 'first series'. In 1835 Wakeman brought them out in a 'fourth edition, corrected' [2e], with Carleton's name and the term *First Series* on the title page.

The 'Second Series' of eleven stories was published by Wakeman, Dublin, in 1833 [4a]. Its second edition, also Wakeman, was published in 1834 [4b] with alterations and cuts, especially in 'An Essay on Irish Swearing'. A 'third edition' from Wakeman in 1835 [4c] was in fact a reissue of the first edition and had none of the alterations of the second. All three of these editions were anonymous. (The second series was split into two parts by Carey and Hart, Philadelphia, for publication in 1833 and 1834 ([5a] and [6a]).

The fourth edition of the first series [2e] and the second edition of the second series [4b] were often bound together as a matching set. As a logical extension of this, Wakeman brought out a five-volume collection of the first and second series together in 1836 [10a]. This was composed of [2e] and [4b], and was designated 'fourth edition' on the title page, though it is the first collected edition of the *Traits and Stories of the Irish Peasantry*.

To these nineteen stories, reduced to eighteen by the merging of the 'Geography of an Irish Oath' and the 'Essay on Irish Swearing', Carleton added two more in 1842 to make the full *Traits and Stories of the Irish Peasantry* for the 'New Edition' which first appeared in 1842 as a partwork [15a] which ran until 1844, and was published in book form, Volume I in 1843 and Volume II in 1844 [15b]. This can be said to be the 'definitive' edition of *Traits and Stories of the Irish Peasantry* as it is the last in which Carleton took any active part. It ran to 'Eleven Complete Editions' from various publishers over the following forty years, with an American edition in 1865 [15b].

Up to this point, the lines of development of *Traits and Stories of the Irish Peasantry* are easy enough to follow; the subsequent use of the name to cover various permutations of Carleton's work is somewhat confusing. Briefly, the name was used

a) for the contents of the two volumes of the 'New Edition' bound together, either with the phrase 'Complete in One Volume' (Ward, Lock, n.d. [59a]) or without (Tegg etc. n.d. [58a])

b) for the 'New Edition' with a piece or two omitted (Lovell, n.d. [59b])

c) for the 'New Edition' with additional material (Maxwell Vickers, n.d. [63a])

d) for a totally new grouping of the stories (for example, Routledge took Carleton's original first and second series and divided them into four series [62a-e])

e) as the title of any collection of Carleton's stories, however small (for example, Adam Stevenson, 1871 [55a] gives no indication that its three stories are not the full collection)

f) where it appears to be the title of the book but is actually being used as a superscription to the main title of one or more stories (for example, *Traits and Stories of the Irish Peasantry. Dominick, the Poor Scholar*, Lovell, n.d. [74a]).

The index shows collections using the title in any way, listed together under *Traits and Stories of the Irish Peasantry*, with publisher and date and an identifying phrase such as 'Complete in One Volume'. Fuller descriptions of interesting editions of the collection will be found above their entries in the chronological bibliography.

BIBLIOGRAPHY

Father Butler. The Lough Dearg Pilgrim

[1a] First edition, Dublin, Curry, 1829 (1 vol., pp. iv + 302)

FATHER BUTLER. | THE | LOUGH DEARG PILGRIM. |
BEING | SKETCHES OF IRISH MANNERS. | [short rule] |
DUBLIN: | WILLIAM CURRY, JUN. AND CO | 9, UPPER
SACKVILLE-STREET | [short rule] | 1829.

Contains 'Notice to the Reader'; 'Father Butler'; 'The Lough Dearg
Pilgrim'. This is No. [503] in Michael Sadleir's *XIX Century Fiction*,
No. 317 in S.J. Brown's *Ireland in Fiction*, and is listed on p. lviii of
D.J. O'Donoghue's 'Bibliography of Carleton's Writings' in his *Life
of William Carleton*, Vol. I, pp. lvii-lxiv. Brown and O'Donoghue
misspell 'Dearg' as 'Derg'.

An American edition of *Father Butler* appeared in 1834, with a
second impression in 1835 (Philadelphia, Latimer). These did not
include the 'Lough Dearg Pilgrim', so are separately classified [7a]
and [7b].

[1b]   'Second Edition', Dublin, Curry, 1839 (1 vol., pp. [iv] + 230)

FATHER BUTLER. | THE | LOUGH DEARG PILGRIM. | BY
| WILLIAM CARLETON, | Author of "Traits and Stories of the
Irish Peasantry," | "Tales of Ireland," &c. | SECOND EDITION. |
DUBLIN | WILLIAM CURRY, JUN. AND COMPANY, | 9,
UPPER SACKVILLE-STREET. | MDCCCXXXIX.

Contains 'Preface'; 'Father Butler'; 'The Lough Dearg Pilgrim'.
This is the first edition to name the author. O'Donoghue p. lix.

[1c]   Another edition (reprint), New York and London, Garland,
1979 (1 vol., pp. *8* + iv + 302 + *8*)

Father Butler | The Lough Dearg Pilgrim | *William Carleton* |

23

Garland Publishing, Inc., New York and London | 1979

With Garland Series title page and reprint title page of [1a]
Reprint of [1a] (Garland Reprint No. 33)

Traits and Stories of the Irish Peasantry, First Series

[2a]   First edition, Dublin, Curry, 1830 (2 vols., pp. xii + 276; iv + 304)

TRAITS AND STORIES | OF THE | IRISH PEASANTRY. | WITH ETCHINGS BY W.H. BROOKE, ESQ. | IN TWO VOLUMES | VOL. [I] | DUBLIN: | WILLIAM CURRY, JUN. AND COMPANY, | 9, UPPER SACKVILLE STREET. | 1830.

Contains (Vol. I:) 'Preface'; 'Ned M'Keown – Introductory'; 'The Three Tasks, or the Little House under the Hill; A Legend'; 'Shane Fadh's Wedding'; 'Larry M'Farland's Wake'; 'The Battle of the Factions'; (Vol. II:) 'The Funeral and Party Fight'; 'The Hedge School, and the Abduction of Mat Kavanagh'; 'The Station'.
Sadleir No. [518]; D.J. O'Donoghue p. lix.

[2b]   'Second edition, corrected', Dublin, London, Edinburgh, Curry &c, 1832 (1 vol., pp. viii + 568)

TRAITS AND STORIES | OF | THE IRISH PEASANTRY. | WITH SIX ETCHINGS. | SECOND EDITION, CORRECTED. | DUBLIN: | WILLIAM CURRY, JUN. AND COMPANY, | 9, UPPER SACKVILLE-STREET; | SIMPKIN AND MARSHALL, LONDON: AND OLIVER AND | BOYD, EDINBURGH. | 1832.

Contains same preface and stories as [2a]; 'The Funeral and Party Fight' is now retitled 'The Party Fight and Funeral', a change not noted by Sadleir until 1836. Sadleir No. [518a].

[2c]   American edition, Philadelphia and Baltimore, Carey & Hart, 1833 (2 vols., pp. [viii] + 208; [ii] + 216)

TRAITS AND STORIES | OF | THE IRISH PEASANTRY. | [short rule] | IN TWO VOLUMES. | VOL. [I.] | [short rule] | FIRST SERIES. | [short decorative rule] | PHILADELPHIA: | E.L.

CAREY & A. HART – CHESNUT STREET. | BALTIMORE: | CAREY, HART & CO. | 1833.

Preface and stories as [2b]. This is the first use of the term 'First Series', the second series having appeared in this year. See [4a] below.

[2d] 'Third edition, corrected', Dublin and London, Wakeman &c., 1834 (2 vols., pp. xii + 340; iv + 372)

TRAITS AND STORIES | OF | THE IRISH PEASANTRY. | WITH SIX ETCHINGS, AND ENGRAVINGS ON WOOD, BY | W.H. BROOKE, ESQ., A.R.H.A. | VOL. [I.] | THIRD EDITION, CORRECTED. | DUBLIN: | WILLIAM FREDERICK WAKEMAN, | 9, D'OLIER-STREET; | SIMPKIN AND MARSHALL, AND RICH. GROOMBRIDGE, | LONDON. | [short rule] | MDCCCXXXIV.

Contains 'Preface to the First Edition' and same stories as [2b]. Sadleir No. [518b].

[2e] 'Fourth edition, corrected', Dublin & London, Wakeman &c., 1835 (2 vols., pp. x + [340]; iv + 372)

TRAITS AND STORIES | OF THE | IRISH PEASANTRY, | FIRST SERIES. | IN TWO VOLUMES. | BY WILLIAM CARLETON. | WITH | SIX ETCHINGS, AND ENGRAVINGS ON WOOD, BY | W.H. BROOKE, ESQ. A.R.H.A. | VOL. [I.] | FOURTH EDITION, CORRECTED. | DUBLIN: | WILLIAM FREDERICK WAKEMAN, | 9, D'OLIER STREET; | SIMPKIN AND MARSHALL, AND RICH. GROOMBRIDGE, | LONDON. | [short rule] | MDCCCXXXV.

This is a reissue of [2d], with the author's name used for the first time for *Traits and Stories*, or any other work. The collection has a new dedication to John Birney, and the wood engravings have been taken out of the text and displayed on separate sheets. The pagination of Vol. I is inaccurate; there are two uncounted, unnumbered pages between pages 192 and 193. This is the first Irish or English edition to use the term 'First Series'. These two volumes were sometimes bound in a 'set' to match the three volumes of the Second Series, second edition [4b].

Sadleir No. [518a].

A 'First Series' of *Traits and Stories of the Irish Peasantry* was published by Routledge, London and New York, 1877 [64a], but this is not the same collection; it contains four stories from Carleton's *Second Series* [4a].

[2f]   Another edition (reprint), New York and London, Garland, 1979 (2 vols., pp. *8* + xii + [276]; *10* + 304 + *8*)

Traits and Stories | of the Irish Peasantry | *William Carleton* | *in two volumes* | Volume [I] | *Garland Publishing, Inc., New York & London* | 1979

With Garland Series title page and reprint title pages of [2a]

Reprint of [2a] (Garland Reprint No. 34)

The Little Chimney Sweep

†[3a]   Dublin, Curry, 1831.

[*The Little Chimney Sweep*, an affecting narrative. With authentic Facts illustrative of the sufferings of Climbing Boys. Dublin, Curry, 1831.]

This is reviewed in the *Christian Examiner*, Vol. XI, No. 74, August 1831, p. 632: 'Our readers will recognise the narrative . . . not unworthy of the pen of WILTON'. It is clearly the book version of the 'History of a Chimney Sweep' from the *Christian Examiner*, Vol. XI, No. 70, April 1831, pp, 276-291. I have found no example of the book, nor any reference to it in Sadleir, Brown or O'Donoghue.

Traits and Stories of the Irish Peasantry, Second Series.

[4a]   First edition, Dublin and London, Wakeman &c., 1833 (3 vols., pp. viii + 472; iv + 476; iv + 448)

TRAITS AND STORIES | OF THE | IRISH PEASANTRY. | [short rule] | SECOND SERIES. | [short rule] | IN THREE VOLUMES. | VOL. [I] | DUBLIN: | WILLIAM FREDERICK WAKEMAN. | SOLD IN LONDON, | BY W. SIMPKIN AND R.

MARSHALL, AND BY R. GROOMBRIDGE, | 6, PANYER-ALLEY, PATERNOSTER-ROW | [short rule] | 1833.

Contains: (Vol. I:) 'Preface'; 'The Midnight Mass'; 'The Donagh; or the Horse Stealers'; 'Phil Purcel, the Pig-Driver'; 'An Essay on Irish Swearing'; 'The Geography of an Irish Oath'; (Vol. II:) 'The Lianhan Shee'; 'The Poor Scholar'; 'Wildgoose Lodge'; 'Tubber Derg, or the Red Well'; (Vol. III:) 'Denis O'Shaughnessy going to Maynooth'; 'Phelim O'Toole's Courtship'.
Sadleir no. [519]; D.J. O'Donoghue p. lix.

[4b]   Second edition, Dublin and London, Wakeman &c., 1834 (3 vols., pp. vi + 364; iv + 376; iv + 344)

TRAITS AND STORIES | OF | THE IRISH PEASANTRY. | [short rule] | SECOND SERIES. | [short rule] | IN THREE VOLUMES. | VOL. [I.] | SECOND EDITION. | DUBLIN: | WILLIAM FREDERICK WAKEMAN. | SOLD IN LONDON, | BY W. SIMPKIN AND R. MARSHALL, AND BY R. GROOMBRIDGE, | 6, PANYER-ALLEY, PATERNOSTER-ROW. | [short rule] | 1834.

Contains same stories as [4a] but 'The Geography of an Irish Oath' now precedes 'An Essay on Irish Swearing'. Text considerably altered, particularly by the omission of oaths from 'An Essay on Irish Swearing'.
Sometimes bound to form a 'set' with *First Series*, fourth edition, 1834 [2e].
Sadleir No. [519a].

[4c]   Third edition, Dublin & London, Wakeman &c., 1835 (3 vols., pp. x + 472; vi + 476; iv + 448)

TRAITS AND STORIES | OF | THE IRISH PEASANTRY. | SECOND SERIES. | THIRD EDITION, | WITH TWENTY-ONE ETCHINGS AND ENGRAVINGS ON WOOD, FROM THE DESIGNS | OF W.H. BROOKE, ESQ. F.S.A. | IN THREE VOLUMES. | VOL. [I.] | DUBLIN: | WILLIAM FREDERICK WAKEMAN. | SOLD IN LONDON, | BY W. SIMPKIN AND R. MARSHALL, AND BY R. GROOMBRIDGE, | 6, PANYER-ALLEY, PATERNOSTER-ROW. | [short rule] | 1835.

This is a reissue of the first edition [4a] with the Brooke illustrations from the second edition [4b]. The text, which had been altered and cut for [4b] now reappears complete.

[4d]   Another edition (reprint), London and New York, Garland, 1979 (3 vols., pp. *8* + viii + [472]; *[10]* + [476]; *12* +[448] + *8*

Traits and Stories | of the Irish Peasantry | Second Series | *William Carleton* | *in three volumes* | Volume [I] | *Garland Publishing, Inc., New York & London* | 1979

With Garland Series title page and reprint title pages of [4a] Reprint of [4a] (Garland Reprint No. 35)

The 'Second Series' published by Routledge, London and New York, 1877, was not an edition of this collection; it lacked four of the stories, which were included in a companion 'First Series'. See [65a] below. The *Second Series* was split up by its first American publishers, Carey and Hart, into two 2-volume editions, published in 1833 and 1834. These were similar editions to their *First Series*, 1833 [2c], but there is no reference to the fact that together they form Carleton's *Second Series*.

[5a]   *Traits and Stories of the Irish Peasantry*, American edition of 5 stories from the *Second Series*, Philadelphia and Baltimore, Carey & Hart, 1833 (2 vols., pp. [200]; [200])

TRAITS AND STORIES | OF THE | IRISH PEASANTRY. | IN TWO VOLUMES. | VOL. [I.] | [Gothic:] **Philadelphia:** | E.L. CAREY & A. HART, CHESNUT STREET. | [Gothic:] **Baltimore:** | CAREY, HART & Co. | [short dotted rule] | 1833.

Contains (Vol. I:) 'The Donagh, or the Horse-Stealers'; 'Phil Purcel, the Pig-driver'; 'The Poor Scholar'; (Vol. II:) 'Phelim O'Toole's Courtship'; 'The Geography of an Irish Oath'.

Variant: Philadelphia and Boston.
Title page as above except '**Boston:** | ALLEN & TICKNOR.' for '**Baltimore:** | CAREY, HART & Co.'

[6a]   *Traits and Stories of the Irish Peasantry*, American edition of 6 stories from the *Second Series*, Philadelphia and Baltimore, Carey

& Hart, 1834 (2 vols., pp. [iv] + [13-220]; 204)

TRAITS AND STORIES | OF | THE IRISH PEASANTRY. | [short rule] | IN TWO VOLUMES. | VOL. [I.] | [short rule] | PHILADELPHIA: | E.L. CAREY & A. HART, CHESNUT STREET. | BALTIMORE: | CAREY, HART, & CO. | [short rule] | 1834.

Contains (Vol. I:) 'The Midnight Mass'; 'The Lianhan Shee'; 'Tubber Derg, or The Red Well'; (Vol. II:) 'An Essay on Irish Swearing'; 'Wildgoose Lodge'; 'Denis O'Shaughnessy going to Maynooth'.

Father Butler

[7a]   American edition, Philadelphia, Latimer, 1834 (1 vol., pp. iv + [5-218])

FATHER BUTLER, | OR | SKETCHES OF IRISH MANNERS. | [short decorative rule] | PHILADELPHIA: | PUBLISHED BY THOMAS LATIMER. | [short rule] | 1834.
Variant: 'Philadelphia:' for 'PHILADELPHIA:'
Contains 'Preface'; 'Father Butler'. This is the first appearance of 'Father Butler' without 'The Lough Dearg Pilgrim' (See [1a] and [1b] above.)

[7b]   American edition, Philadelphia, Latimer, 1835 (1 vol., pp. iv + [5-218])

FATHER BUTLER, | OR | SKETCHES OF IRISH MANNERS. | [short decorative rule] | PHILADELPHIA: | PUBLISHED BY THOMAS LATIMER. | [short rule] | 1835.

Another impression of [7a].

Tales of Ireland

[8a]   Dublin and London, Curry &c., 1834 (1 vol, pp. [xiv] + 366)

TALES OF IRELAND. | BY THE AUTHOR OF | "TRAITS AND STORIES OF THE IRISH PEASANTRY." | DUBLIN | WILLIAM CURRY, JUN. AND COMPANY | SIMPKIN AND MARSHALL, LONDON. | M.DCCC.XXXIV.

Contains: 'Preface'; 'The Death of a Devotee'; 'The Priest's Funeral'; 'Neal Malone'; 'The Brothers'; 'The Illicit Distiller'; 'The Dream of a Broken Heart'; 'Lachlin Murray and the Blessed Candle'.
Sadleir No. [516]; Brown No. 319; D.J. O'Donoghue p. lix.

These stories were rearranged and the collection retitled *Neal Malone and other Tales of Ireland* for an American edition, Philadelphia, Carey & Hart, 1839. See [12a] below.

[8b]　Another edition (reprint), New York and London, Garland, 1979 (1 vol., pp. *8* + [xiv] + 366 + *8*)

Tales of Ireland | William Carleton | *Garland Publishing, Inc., New York & London* | 1979

With Garland Series title page and reprint title page of [8a]

Reprint of [8a] (Garland Reprint No. 36)

[with others] **Popular Tales and Legends of the Irish Peasantry**

[9a]　First edition, Dublin, Wakeman, 1834 (1 vol., pp. vi + 406)

POPULAR TALES AND LEGENDS | OF THE IRISH PEASANTRY | WITH ILLUSTRATIONS BY SAMUEL LOVER ESQ. R.H.A. | DUBLIN | WILLIAM FREDERICK WAKEMAN | [short rule] | 1834.

Contains two Carleton stories, 'Laying a Ghost' and 'Alley Sheridan, or the Runaway Marriage', attributed to 'the author of "Traits and Stories of the Irish Peasantry" ', and stories by Mrs. Hall and 'Denis O'Donoho'. First book publication of the Carleton pieces.
Sadleir No. [508].

[9b]　Second edition, Dublin, Wakeman, 1837 (1 vol., pp. vi + 406)

POPULAR TALES AND LEGENDS | OF THE IRISH PEASANTRY | WITH ILLUSTRATIONS BY SAMUEL LOVER ESQ. R.H.A. | DUBLIN | WILLIAM FREDERICK WAKEMAN | SOLD IN LONDON BY SIMPKIN & MARSHALL & RICHARD GROOMBRIDGE, & BY FRAZER & CO EDINBURGH | 1837

Traits and Stories of the Irish Peasantry, First and Second Series together.

[10a] 'Fourth edition', London and Dublin, Baldwin & Cradock, Wakeman, 1836 (5 vols., pp. x + [342]; iv + [372]; xii + 364; iv + 376; iv + 342)

TRAITS AND STORIES | OF THE | IRISH PEASANTRY. | [vignette of crowd, pillar, harpist] | BY WILLIAM CARLETON. | WITH ILLUSTRATIONS BY W.H. BROOKE, ESQ. A.R.H.A. | IN FIVE VOLUMES. | VOL. [I.] | FOURTH EDITION. | [short rule] | BALDWIN AND CRADOCK, LONDON: | WILLIAM F. WAKEMAN, DUBLIN. | [short rule] | 1836.

Contains (Vol. I:) 'Dedication to John Birney'; 'Preface to the First Edition'; 'Ned M'Keown'; 'The Three Tasks, or The Little House under the Hill'; 'Shane Fadh's Wedding'; 'Larry M'Farland's Wake'; 'Battle of the Factions'; (Vol. II:) 'The Party Fight and Funeral'; 'The Hedge School, and the Abduction of Mat Kavanagh'; 'The Station'; (Vol. III:) 'Preface to the Second Edition'; 'The Midnight Mass'; 'The Donagh; or, the Horse-stealers'; 'Phil Purcel, the Pig-driver'; 'The Geography of an Irish Oath'; 'An Essay on Irish Swearing'; (Vol. IV:) 'The Lianhan Shee'; 'The Poor Scholar'; 'Wildgoose Lodge'; 'Tubber Derg, or the Red Well'; (Vol. V:) 'Denis O'Shaughnessy going to Maynooth'; 'Phelim O'Toole's Courtship'.

These five volumes are reissues of the fourth edition of the *First Series* [2e] (Vols. I and II) and the second edition of the *Second Series* [4b] (Vols. III, IV and V). Vol. I has the 2 unnumbered uncounted pages of [2e]. There is no mention that this is the first collected edition of both series of *Traits and Stories*, and the collection is designated 'fourth edition' in accordance with its first series volumes.

Sadleir No. [520].

This collection of the stories from the first and second series was superseded by the lavish 'New Edition' of *Traits and Stories of the Irish Peasantry* from Curry and Orr in 1842-44 [15a/b], which contained 'Neal Malone' and 'The Lough Derg Pilgrim' as well as the stories from the first and second series, with 'An Essay on Irish Swearing' and 'The Geography of an Irish Oath' combined into one story. The first and second series stories reappeared together in

1877, when Routledge published an incomplete 'Complete Edition'. In this and subsequent variations ([61a-c], [62a-e]) they disregard the 'New Edition', by now in its eleventh edition, although they themselves had published editions of it in 1852, 1854 and 1856.

Fardorougha the Miser/The Miser

[11a]   First edition, Dublin, Curry, 1839 (1 vol., pp. xii + 468)

FARDOROUGHA THE MISER; | OR | THE CONVICTS OF LISNAMONA. | BY | WILLIAM CARLETON, | Author of "Tales of Ireland," "Traits and Stories of the Irish Peasantry," | "Father Butler," &c. &c. | DUBLIN | WILLIAM CURRY, JUN. AND COMPANY, | 9, UPPER SACKVILLE-STREET. | 1839.

Contains dedicatory letter to James M'Cullagh, Preface, novel. Sadleir No. [502]; Brown No. 320; O'Donoghue p. lix. This edition contains a notice of *The Chronicles of Ballymacruiskeen* 'preparing for immediate Publication, in monthly parts, with the Lives, Deaths, Marriages, and other Misfortunes of its Inhabitants'. This notice was to appear in several other editions of *Fardorougha the Miser* but there is no record of its ever having reached publication, no review or reference in any magazine or publisher's list.

[11b]   American edition, Philadelphia, Carey & Hart, 1840 (2 vols., pp. x + [202]; [viii] + [172]) [as *The Miser*)

THE MISER; | OR, | THE CONVICTS OF LISNAMONA. | BY | WILLIAM CARLETON, | AUTHOR OF "NEIL MALONE," "TRAITS AND STORIES OF THE IRISH | PEASANTRY," "FATHER BUTLER," &C. &C. | IN TWO·VOLUMES. | [VOL. [I.] | PHILADELPHIA: | CAREY & HART. | [short dotted rule] | 1840.

[11c]   'Second edition', Dublin, Curry, 1841 (1 vol., pp. viii + 468)

FARDOROUGHA THE MISER; | OR | THE CONVICTS OF LISNAMONA. | BY | WILLIAM CARLETON, | Author of "Tales of Ireland," "Traits and Stories of the Irish Peasantry," | "Father Butler," &c. &c. | Second Edition | DUBLIN | WILLIAM CURRY, JUN. AND COMPANY, | 9, UPPER SACKVILLE-STREET. | 1841.

This is [11a] with preliminaries reduced.

[11d]   Another 'second edition', Dublin and London, Curry, Longman, Orme, 1841 (1 vol., pp. viii + 468)

FARDOROUGHA THE MISER; | OR | THE CONVICTS OF LISNAMONA. | BY | WILLIAM CARLETON, | Author of "Tales of Ireland," "Traits and Stories of the Irish Peasantry," | "Father Butler," "The Fawn of Spring-vale,' &c. &c. | SECOND EDITION. | DUBLIN | WILLIAM CURRY, JUN. AND COMPANY. | LONGMAN, ORME, AND CO., LONDON. | 1841.

[11e]   'Fourth edition', Dublin, Duffy, 1846 (1 vol., pp. viii + 468)

FARDOROUGHA THE MISER; | OR, THE | CONVICTS OF LISNAMONA. | BY | WILLIAM CARLETON. | Fourth edition | DUBLIN: | PUBLISHED BY JAMES DUFFY, | 23, ANGLESEA STREET. | 1846.

O'Donoghue p. lxi

[11f]   Another fourth edition, 'carefully revised and corrected', Dublin, Duffy, 1846 (1 vol., pp. [xii] + [360])

FARDOROUGHA | THE MISER; | OR, THE | CONVICTS OF LISNAMONA. | BY | WILLIAM CARLETON, | Author of "Traits and Stories of the Irish Peasantry," "Valentine M'Clutchy," | "The Broken Pledge," "Rody the Rover," "Paddy Go Easy," | &c., &c., &c. | FOURTH EDITION, CAREFULLY REVISED AND CORRECTED. | DUBLIN: | JAMES DUFFY, 10, WELLINGTON-QUAY. | [short rule] | MDCCCXLVI.

[11g]   'Parlour Library' edition, London and Belfast, Simms & M'Intyre, 1848 (1 vol., pp. xvi + 296)

[within rule frame:] FARDOROUGHA THE MISER; | OR, THE | CONVICTS OF LISNAMONA. | BY | WILLIAM CARLETON, | Author of "Traits and Stories of the Irish Peasantry," | "The Black Prophet," &c. &c. | WITH | AN INTRODUCTION, | WRITTEN FOR THE PRESENT EDITION. | [short rule] | LONDON: | SIMMS AND M'INTYRE, | PATERNOSTER ROW, AND DONEGALL STREET, BELFAST. | [short rule] | 1848.

Contains new introduction, novel. Parlour Library half-title (No. XXI).
Sadleir No. [502a].

[11h]   Another edition, London and New York, Routledge, 1857 (1 vol., pp. xvi + 296)

FARDOROUGHA | THE | MISER. | BY WILLIAM CARLETON, | AUTHOR OF | "TRAITS AND STORIES OF THE IRISH PEASANTRY;" | ETC. ETC. | [Gothic:] **With an Introduction,** | WRITTEN FOR THIS EDITION. | LONDON: | G. ROUTLEDGE AND CO., FARRINGDON STREET; | AND 18, BEEKMAN STREET, NEW YORK. | 1857.

†[11i]   American edition, New York, Haverty, 1868

Publishers' Weekly, New York, lists *Fardorougha the Miser; or, the Convicts of Lisnamona* (boards, 50 cents), from P.M. Haverty, 218, Sixth Avenue, New York, in 1868. I cannot trace this.

†[11j]   American edition, New York, Routledge, 1875

Publishers' Trade-List Annual, New York, lists *Fardorougha the Miser* as one of the '*Novels and Tales* of William Carleton in 5 Vols.' published by George Routledge & Sons, 416 Broome Street, New York, in 1875. The others are *The Tithe Proctor* [31d], *The Clarionet* [57a], *The Emigrants [of Ahadarra]* [30d], and *Jane Sinclair, Neal Malone,* etc. [33c]. I have not seen *Fardorougha the Miser*; possibly a reissue of [11h].

[11k]   'Irish Novelists' Library' edition, London, Downey, n.d. [1895] (1 vol., pp. xiv + [280])

[within rule frame, shamrocks, celtic cross and sun; in panel, ornamental caps:] THE IRISH NOVELISTS' LIBRARY | [within inner rule frame:] FARDOROUGHA | THE MISER | OR THE | CONVICTS OF LISNAMONA | BY | WILLIAM CARLETON | AUTHOR OF 'TRAITS AND STORIES OF THE | IRISH PEASANTRY' | ETC. | [device] | [within outer frame, ornamental caps:] DOWNEY & Co | 12 YORK St. COVENT GARDEN | LONDON

Two unnumbered uncounted pages between pages 8 and 9.
O'Donoghue p. lxiv.

[11l]   American edition, New York and Montreal, Sadlier, n.d.
[1875] [1 vol., pp. [2] + 444]

FARDOROUGHA, | THE MISER; | OR, | THE CONVICTS OF
LISNAMONA | By WILLIAM CARLETON, | Author of
"Valentine McClutchy," "Tales and Stories of the Irish | Peasantry,"
"Jane Sinclair," "Art Maguire," "Willy Reilly," | "The Emigrants of
Ahadarra," "The Tithe Proctor," | "The Black Prophet," "Black
Baronet," &c. | NEW YORK: | PUBLISHED BY D. & J.
SADLIER & CO., | 31 BARCLAY STREET, | MONTREAL: –
COR. NOTRE DAME AND ST. FRANCIS XAVIER STS.

One of 10 volumes published by Sadlier in 1875 as the *Works* of
William Carleton, though not in fact complete, and without indication
on the volumes that they are part of a set.

[11m]   American edition, Boston, New York, etc., Littell etc.,
n.d. (1 vol., pp. [2] + [102])

FARDOROUGHA: | THE MISER. | [short rule] | [Gothic:]
A Tale. | [short rule] | BOSTON: | PUBLISHED BY E.
LITTELL & CO. | NEW YORK: DEWITT & DAVENPORT,
STRINGER & TOWNSEND, LONG & BROTHER. |
PHILADELPHIA: GETZ, BUCK & CO. | BALTIMORE:
BURGESS & TAYLOR.

No author's name.

[11n]   Another edition (reprint), New York and London, Garland,
1979 (1 vol., pp. *8* + x + 468 + *8*)

Fardorougha | the Miser | *William Carleton* | *Garland Publishing,
Inc., New York & London* | 1979

With Garland Series title page and reprint title page of [11a].

Reprint of [11a] (Garland Reprint No. 37)

Neal Malone and other Tales of Ireland

[12a]   American edition, Philadelphia, Carey and Hart, 1839 (2 vols., pp. xii + [13-196]; 212)

NEAL MALONE, | AND OTHER | TALES OF IRELAND. | BY | W.H. CARLETON, | AUTHOR OF | "TRAITS AND STORIES OF THE IRISH PEASANTRY." | IN TWO VOLUMES. | VOL. [I.] | [short rule] | PHILADELPHIA: | E.L. CAREY & A. HART. | [short dotted rule] | 1839.

Contents as *Tales of Ireland* [8a], rearranged. (Vol. I:) 'Preface'; 'Neal Malone'; 'Death of a Devotee'; 'The Priest's Funeral'; 'The Illicit Distiller'; (Vol. II:) 'The Brothers'; 'The Dream of a Broken Heart'; 'Lachlin Murray and the Blessed Candle'.

The initials 'W.H.' were sometimes used on American title pages, whereas Irish and English publishers used 'W.' or 'William' Carleton.

[with others] **Characteristic Sketches of Ireland and the Irish/Tales and Stories of Ireland.**

[13a]   First edition, Dublin and London, Hardy & Walker; Ball, Arnold, 1840 (1 vol., pp. [vi] + [300])

CHARACTERISTIC SKETCHES | OF | IRELAND AND THE IRISH. | BY | CARLETON, LOVER, AND MRS. HALL. | WITH ETCHINGS BY KIRKWOOD. | "Ye Modern Scotch and English writers, | Novel, Romance and Poem enditers, | You're challenged now – both great and small – | C. L. and H. against you all." | DUBLIN: HARDY & WALKER, 4, LR. SACKVILLE-ST., | LONDON: BALL, ARNOLD, AND CO. | 1840.

Contains Carleton's 'The Horse Stealers'; 'Owen M'Carthy'; 'Squire Warnock'; 'The Abduction'; 'Sir Turlough', that is, 'The Donagh', 'Tubber Derg', 'The Hellfire Club', 'Alley Sheridan' and 'Sir Turlough, or the Church-yard Bride'.

Sadleir incorrectly lists the first edition as P.D. Hardy, 1845, [13e] below.

There does not appear to have been a second edition or a third edition; there are two 'fourth editions':

[13b]   'Fourth edition', Dublin, Hardy, 1842 (1 vol., pp. [iv] + 288)

CHARACTERISTIC SKETCHES | OF IRELAND AND THE
IRISH | by CARLETON, LOVER AND MRS. HALL: | with six
etchings. | Fourth Edition | Dublin: | P. D. Hardy, 4 Lr. Sackville-
Street | 1842.

[13c]   Another 'fourth edition', Dublin, Manchester, Liverpool,
Hardy, Johnson, 1844 (1 vol., pp. [iv] + 288)

CHARACTERISTIC SKETCHES | OF | IRELAND AND THE
IRISH. | BY | CARLETON, LOVER, AND MRS. HALL. |
WITH SIX ETCHINGS. | [verse as [13a]] | FOURTH EDITION.
| DUBLIN: | PHILIP DIXON HARDY AND SONS: | 22, UPPER
SACKVILLE-STREET. | MANCHESTER: S. JOHNSON AND
SON, 3, OLDHAM-STREET; | AND, 48, CHURCH-ST.,
LIVERPOOL. | 1844.

[13d]   Another edition, Dublin, Hardy, 1844 (1 vol., pp. [iv] +
288)

CHARACTERISTIC SKETCHES | OF IRELAND AND THE
IRISH | by | CARLETON, LOVER AND MRS. HALL: | with six
etchings. | DUBLIN: | P. D. HARDY & SONS, 4 Lr. Sackville-
Street | 1844.

[13e]   Another edition, Dublin and London, Hardy, Groombridge,
1845 (1 vol., pp. [4] + 288)

CHARACTERISTIC SKETCHES | OF | IRELAND AND THE
IRISH. | BY | CARLETON, LOVER, AND MRS. HALL. |
WITH ETCHINGS BY KIRKWOOD. | [verse as [13a]] | DUBLIN:
P. D. HARDY & SONS, 23, UPPER SACKVILLE-ST. |
LONDON: R. GROOMBRIDGE & SONS. | 1845.

Sadleir's No. [496], incorrectly given as first edition.

[13f]   Another edition, Halifax, Milner, 1846 (1 vol., pp. [iv] +
288)

CHARACTERISTIC SKETCHES | OF IRELAND AND THE
IRISH. | BY | CARLETON, LOVER & MRS. HALL | [verse as
[13a]] | HALIFAX: | WILLIAM MILNER | 1846.

[13g]   Another edition, Halifax, Milner & Sowerby, 1849 (1 vol., pp. [iv] + 288)

CHARACTERISTIC SKETCHES | OF IRELAND AND THE IRISH. | BY | CARLETON, LOVER & MRS. HALL. | [verse as [13a]] | HALIFAX: | MILNER & SOWERBY | 1852.

Sadleir No. [496a]

[13h]   Another edition, retitled *Tales and Stories of Ireland*, Halifax, Milner & Sowerby, 1852 (1 vol., pp. iv + 288)

TALES AND STORIES OF IRELAND. | BY CARLETON, LOVER AND MRS. HALL | [verse as [13a]] | HALIFAX: | MILNER & SOWERBY | 1852.

Contains same stories as *Characteristic Sketches of Ireland and the Irish*.

[13i]   Another edition, London, Milner, n.d. (1 vol., pp. [6] + 280)

TALES | AND | STORIES | OF | IRELAND. | BY | CARLETON, LOVER, AND MRS. HALL. | WITH ETCHINGS BY KIRKWOOD. | [verse as [13a]] | LONDON: | MILNER AND COMPANY, LIMITED, | PATERNOSTER ROW.

[Engraved title plate: in red rule frame, [Gothic:] TALES AND STORIES | of | Ireland | BY | CARLETON, LOVER, AND | MRS. S. C. HALL. | WITH ETCHINGS BY KIRKWOOD. | [short decorative rule] | LONDON | *MILNER AND COMPANY,* | PATERNOSTER ROW.]

[13j]   Another edition, London, Milner, n.d. (1 vol., pp. 280)

TALES | AND | STORIES | OF | IRELAND. | BY | CARLETON, LOVER, AND MRS. HALL. | WITH ETCHINGS BY KIRKWOOD. | [verse as [13a]] | LONDON: | MILNER AND COMPANY, | PATERNOSTER ROW.

Fawn of Spring-Vale/Jane Sinclair &c.

[14a]   First edition, *The Fawn of Spring-Vale, The Clarionet, and*

other Tales, Dublin and London, Curry, Longman Orme, 1841 (3 vols., pp. [xii] + [368]; iv + [352]; iv + 328)

[Vol. I:] THE FAWN OF SPRING-VALE, | THE CLARIONET, | AND OTHER TALES. | BY WILLIAM CARLETON, | Author of "Fardorougha the Miser," – "Traits and Stories of the | Irish Peasantry," &c. | IN THREE VOLUMES. | VOL. I. | JANE SINCLAIR; OR THE FAWN OF SPRING-VALE | LHA DHU; OR THE DARK DAY. | DUBLIN | WILLIAM CURRY, JUN. AND COMPANY. | LONGMAN, ORME, AND CO., LONDON | 1841.

[Vol. II:] as Vol. I except 'VOL. II. | THE CLARIONET – THE DEAD BOXER.'

[Vol. III:] As Vol. I except 'VOL. III. | THE MISFORTUNES OF BARNEY BRANAGAN. | RESURRECTIONS OF BARNEY BRADLEY.'

Contains (Vol. I:) 'Preface'; 'Jane Sinclair; or the Fawn of Spring-Vale'; 'Lha Dhu; or the Dark Day'; (Vol. II:) 'The Clarionet'; 'The Dead Boxer'; (Vol. III:) 'The Misfortunes of Barney Branagan'; 'Resurrections of Barney Bradley'. These stories had all appeared in the *Dublin University Magazine.*

Sadleir No. [504]; Brown No. 321; O'Donoghue p. lix

[14b]   Reissued as *Jane Sinclair; or, the Fawn of Spring Vale,* Dublin and London, Curry, Routledge, 1843 (3 vols., pp. [xii] + [368]; iv + [352]; iv + 328)

JANE SINCLAIR; | OR, THE | FAWN OF SPRING VALE, | THE CLARIONET, | AND OTHER TALES. | BY WILLIAM CARLETON, | AUTHOR OF "TRAITS AND STORIES OF THE IRISH PEASANTRY," ETC. | IN THREE VOLUMES. | VOL. [I.] | DUBLIN: | WILLIAM CURRY, JUN. AND COMPANY; | GEORGE ROUTLEDGE, LONDON. | 1843.

Contents as [14a]. Sadleir No. [504a]; mentioned in Brown (No. 330) but dated [1849].

[14c]   Another edition (reprint), New York and London, Garland, 1979 (3 vols., pp. *6* + [xii] + [368]; *12* + [352]; *10* + 328 + *8*)

The Fawn | of Spring-Vale | *William Carleton* | *in three volumes* |
Volume [I] | *Garland Publishing, Inc.*, *New York & London* | 1979

With Garland Series title page and reprint title pages of [14a]

Reprint of [14a] (Garland Reprint No. 38)

There are other collections of stories with the title *Jane Sinclair; or,
the Fawn of Spring Vale* (New York and Montreal, Sadlier 1872
[56a-b]) or with the name *Jane Sinclair* in combination with another
title, as *Jane Sinclair; or the Fawn of Spring-Vale and The Dark Day*,
London, Routledge, 1849 [32a]; *Jane Sinclair, Neal Malone &c*,
Routledge, 1850 [33a-b], later retitled *Jane Sinclair, Neal Malone
and other Tales*, London and New York, Routledge n.d. [33c]. The
other stories in the collection also appeared in various permutations,
such as *The Clarionet, the Dead Boxer and Barney Branagan* [34a],
or *Barney Branagan, Fawn of Spring Vale, Barney Bradley, & other
Tales* [26a].

Traits and Stories of the Irish Peasantry, complete – 'A New
Edition'.

The most widely known collection of *Traits and Stories of the Irish
Peasantry*, and the last for which Carleton himself seems to have
prepared the text, is the 'New Edition' of 1842/44. It consists of the
stories from the *First* and *Second Series*, with two additional tales –
'Neal Malone', which had previously appeared in *Tales of Ireland*
[8a] and *Neal Malone and other Tales of Ireland* [12a], and 'The
Lough Derg Pilgrim', which had already appeared with 'Father
Butler' [1a-b]. The stories are in a new order, the two series no
longer kept separate as they had been in the collection of 1836 [10a],
which had been simply a reissue of the fourth edition of the *First
Series* and the second edition of the *Second Series*. 'An Essay on
Irish Swearing' and 'The Geography of an Irish Oath' are combined
under the latter title, the former piece, expurgated, serving as an
introduction. There are numerous revisions of style (especially in
the presentation of dialect) and of content (including additions,
excisions and rearrangement).

This collection was announced in the *Publishers' Circular* (Vol.
V, No. 117, 1 August 1842, p. 240) as 'a New Edition of all the early

Productions and most of the recent Tales of this celebrated Author', and indeed the only new piece in it is the 'General Introduction,' or 'Autobiographical Introduction' as it is called in the list of contents. This is one of Carleton's most significant and lucid essays. The autobiographical part of it contains an account of Ireland's literary and publishing history from the Act of Union of 1800 up to the time of writing (1842), with Carleton's opinions of contemporary writers, and his views of Irish life and character.

The form of these *Traits and Stories* most familiar to readers of Carleton today is that of the two volumes lavishly decorated and spaciously set, with illustrated title headings and tailpieces, woodcut illustrations within the text, engraved and tinted title plates and frontispieces, and thirty-six etched plates from illustrations by eight eminent artists – a handsome publication that ran to nearly twenty 'editions', or more precisely new impressions. But their first appearance was as a shilling part-work in paper covers, that came out over the twenty-five months from August 1842 to June 1844, overlapping with the publication of the book, the first volume of which appeared late in 1843, the second early in 1844. The parts are not complete in themselves; they are from the same plates as the book, and usually consist of two gatherings from it, which often results in a part ending in mid-sentence. The publishers promise an engraved title-head and tailpiece in each part and give 'an extra sheet of letter-press' on two occasions when the length of the story would preclude a new heading. The 'General Introduction' is divided (in the middle of a sentence) between parts I and II.

[15a]   *Traits and Stories of the Irish Peasantry*, in parts, Dublin and London, Curry, Orr, August 1842 – June 1844 (23 vols., pp. [48]; [32]; [32]; [32]; [32]; [32]; [48]; [32]; [32]; [32]; [32]; [60]; [48]; [32]; [48]; [32]; [32]; [32]; [48]; [48]; [32]; [32]; [46])

[within rule frame:] PART I. AUGUST. PRICE 1s | [within an inner rule frame, elaborate rectangular pattern of interwoven shamrocks, harpist top centre; in rounded ornamental caps:] TRAITS | AND | [curved:] STORIES | OF | THE | [spiky caps:] IRISH PEASANTRY | BY | [curved hollow caps:] WILLIAM CARLETON | [in oval, cottage scene, people around table] | WILLIAM CURRY, JUNR., SACKVILLE STREET, DUBLIN; | AND WM. S. ORR & CO.,

AMEN CORNER, PATERNOSTER ROW, | LONDON. | [outside inner rule frame, within outer rule frame:] Bradbury & Evans, [square bracket] MDCCCXLII. [square bracket] Printed by

All covers as Part I except for part no., date, and price of '2S' where double issue. I give collation for comparison with the book edition.

Vol. I, August 1842, contains pp. [i]-xvi of 'General Introduction'; pp. [1]-22, 'Ned M'Keown'; pp. [23]-32 of 'The Three Tasks' (coll. $b^8B - C^8$).

Part II, Sept. 1842, contains pp. xvii-xxiv of 'General Introduction'; pp. 33-50 of 'The Three Tasks'; pp. [51]-64 of 'Shane Fadh's Wedding' (coll. $c^4D - E^8$).

Part III, Oct. 1842, contains pp. 65-83 of 'Shane Fadh's Wedding'; pp. [84]-96 of 'Larry M'Farland's Wake' (coll. $F - G^8$) [Note: signature from F onwards now has 'VOL. I.']

Part IV, Nov. 1842, contains pp. 97-114 of 'Larry M'Farland's Wake'; pp. [115]-128 of 'The Battle of the Factions' (coll. $H - I^8$)

Part V, Dec. 1842, contains pp. 129-144 of 'The Battle of the Factions'; pp. [145]-160 of 'The Station' (coll. $K - L^8$)

Part VI, Jan. 1843, contains pp. 161-180 of 'The Station'; pp. [181]-192 of 'The Party Fight and Funeral' (coll. $M - N^8$).

Part VII, Feb. 1843, contains pp. 193-235 of 'The Party Fight and Funeral'; pp. [236]-240 of 'The Lough Derg Pilgrim' (coll. $O - Q^8$). (A slip tipped in between cover and page 193 explains the length of this part: 'Several of the Tales in the "TRAITS AND STORIES" being found to extend beyond the limits of a Part, the Publishers have determined to give an additional sheet of letter-press, as an equivalent, where that occurs, rather than depart from the plan laid down, of giving two etchings and a head and tail piece to each Story. The present Part is the first instance in which this has been found necessary, but it will recur more than once in the course of publication.')

Part VIII, March 1843, contains pp. 241-270 of 'The Lough Derg Pilgrim'; pp. [271]-272 of 'The Hedge School' (coll. $R - S^8$).

Part IX, April 1843, contains pp. 273-304 of 'The Hedge School' (coll. $T - U^8$). (Note: this part does not contain 'an additional sheet of letter-press' as promised in Part VI, although it has no head or tail piece since the same story continues throughout the part.)

Part X, May 1843, contains pp. 305-324 of 'The Hedge School'; pp. [325]-336 of 'The Midnight Mass' (coll. $X - Y^8$).

Part XI, June 1843, contains pp. 337-368 of 'The Midnight Mass' (coll. $Z - AA^8$). (Note: no 'extra sheet of letter-press'.)

Parts XII and XIII (double part, price 2s.), July 1843, contains pp. 369-380 of 'The Midnight Mass'; pp. [381]-406, 'The Donagh; or, the Horse-stealers'; pp. [407]-427, 'Phil Purcel, the Pig-driver'; p. [428], blank (coll. $BB - DD^8 EE^8 - EE7, EE8$).

Part XIV, Aug. 1843, contains pp. [1]-48 of 'The Geography of an Irish Oath' (coll. $B - D^8$). (Note: signature now 'VOL. II').

Part XV, Sept. 1843, contains pp. 49-74 of 'The Geography of an Irish Oath'; pp. 75-80 of 'The Lianhan Shee' (coll. $E - F^8$).

Part XVI, Oct. 1843, contains pp. 81-96 of 'The Lianhan Shee'; pp. [97]-128 of 'Going to Maynooth' (coll. $G - I^8$).

Part XVII, Nov. 1843, contains pp. 129-160 of 'Going to Maynooth' (coll. $K - L^8$). (Note: no title-head or tail-piece.)

Part XVIII, Dec. 1843, contains pp. 161-187 of 'Going to Maynooth'; pp. 188-192 of 'Phelim O'Toole's Courtship' (coll. $M - N^8$).

Part XIX, Jan. 1844, contains pp. 193-224 of 'Phelim O'Toole's Courtship' (coll. $O - P^8$). (Note: no title-head or tail piece.)

Part XX, Feb. 1844, contains pp. 225-256 of 'Phelim O'Toole's Courtship'; pp. 257-272 of 'The Poor Scholar' (coll. $Q - S^8$).

Part XXI, March 1844, contains pp. 273-320 of 'The Poor Scholar' (coll. $T - X^8$). (Note: no title-head or tail-piece, although there is an extra gathering.)

Part XXII, April 1844, contains pp. 321-348 of 'The Poor Scholar'; pp. 349-352 of 'Wildgoose Lodge' (coll. $Y - Z^8$).

Part XXIII, May 1844, contains pp. 353-362 of 'Wildgoose Lodge'; pp. 363-384 of 'Tubber Derg; or, the Red Well' (coll. $AA - BB^8$).

Parts XXIV and XXV (double part, price 2s.), June 1844, contains pp. 385-414 of 'Tubber Derg; or, the Red Well'; pp. 415-430, 'Neal Malone' (coll. CC – DD^8 EE^8 – EE8).

Book edition:

[15b]   'A New Edition', Dublin and London, Curry, Orr, 1843/44 (2 vols., pp. *8* + xxiv + [428]; pp. [*8*] + 430)

[Vol. I:] TRAITS AND STORIES | OF | THE IRISH PEASANTRY. | BY | WILLIAM CARLETON. | [short decorative rule] | [Gothic:] **A New Edition.** | WITH AN AUTOBIOGRAPHICAL INTRODUCTION, EXPLANATORY NOTES, | AND | NUMEROUS ILLUSTRATIONS ON WOOD AND STEEL, | *By Harvey, Phiz, Franklin, Macmanus, Gilbert, and other Artists of Eminence.* | VOLUME I. | WILLIAM CURRY, JUN., AND Co., DUBLIN; | AND WILLIAM S. ORR AND Co., LONDON. | MDCCCXLIII.

[Vol. II:] As Vol. I except 'eminence' for 'Eminence'. 'II.' for 'I.' and 'MDCCCXLIV.' for 'MDCCCXLIII.'

Vol. I has a yellow-tinted lithographic frontispiece of Carleton seated (after C. Grey's engraving for 'Our Portrait Gallery', *Dublin University Magazine*, Vol. XVII, No. 97, January 1841; Vol. II of 'Prillisk, the birth place of William Carleton' by Macmanus. Both volumes have a yellow-tinted lithographic title plate as follows: [within elaborate frame simulating curved and pierced metal, mainly in hollow lettering:] TRAITS AND STORIES | OF THE | [set in curve, shaded deep yellow and white:] IRISH PEASANTRY. | BY | WILLIAM CARLETON, | *WITH AN* | AUTOBIOGRAPHICAL INTRODUCTION, | [Gothic:] **Illustrative Notes & Graphic Illustrations,** | ON WOOD AND STEEL, | *BY* | PHIZ, HARVEY, MAC MANUS & FRANKLIN. | VOL. [I.] | [short rule] | [Gothic:] **Dublin:** | PUBLISHED BY W$_M$. CURRY, JUN$_R$. & Co. SACKVILLE STR$_T$. | AND W.S. ORR & Co. PATERNOSTER ROW, | LONDON. [Vol. II has beneath the frame: Russell & Mitchell, Litho. | *Lovell's Court, P.N. Row.* The shading on 'IRISH PEASANTRY.' is not present in Vol. II.]

Contents: Vol. I: 'General Introduction'; 'Ned M'Keown'; 'The Three Tasks'; 'Shane Fadh's Wedding'; 'Larry M'Farland's Wake';

'The Battle of the Factions'; 'The Station'; 'The Party Fight and Funeral'; 'The Lough Derg Pilgrim'; 'The Hedge School'; 'The Midnight Mass'; 'The Donagh, or the Horse-stealers'; 'Phil Purcel, the Pig-Driver'; (Vol. II:) 'Geography of an Irish Oath'; 'The Lianhan Shee'; 'Going to Maynooth'; 'Phelim O'Toole's Courtship'; 'The Poor Scholar'; 'Wildgoose Lodge'; 'Tubber Derg; or, the Red Well'; 'Neal Malone'.

This is much more ornate than previous editions of either series, having 36 'illustrative etchings' on steel, numerous wood engravings within the type area, impressive illustrated title headings often taking up half the page, a tailpiece to every story, and a tinted lithographic title plate and frontispiece in both volumes. As well as the artists named on the title page, Wrightson, Griffiths, Sibson and Lee appear in the list of illustrations and other artists' signatures are visible on the title headings.

This edition was the parent of nine numbered 'editions' or more properly impressions with edition numbers, as well as many un-numbered and undated impressions of the two volumes. After many changes of publisher, Ward, Lock incorporated the two volumes into one. As time went on and blocks became worn, new title headings replaced some of the original ones, necessitating new typesetting where the illustration had extended into the type area. When tailpiece blocks wore out, however, they were often replaced with irrelevant illustrations, probably from stock, and later not replaced at all.

As well as such new impressions, called 'editions', groups of stories from this parent edition were reissued with the title page of the full edition, so that there are, confusingly, two 'Fifth editions', one from Routledge in 1856 of the first five stories only [37b], one from Tegg in 1864 of all the stories [15f], both entitled *Traits and Stories of the Irish Peasantry*. Many similar cases present problems of classification and listing for the bibliographer, and of identification and finding for the reader. I have classified such issues, and other editions entitled *Traits and Stories of the Irish Peasantry*, according to the year of the first publication, as is usual in this Bibliography, but I have also listed them here where they might appear to belong, with a cross-reference to their proper chronological placing. The index lists all editions under *Traits and Stories of the Irish Peasantry*.

[15c] *Traits and Stories of the Irish Peasantry*, 'A New Edition', London, Routledge, 1852.

This is a new impression of [15a] by a new publisher. Title page as [15b] except 'LONDON: | GEORGE ROUTLEDGE & CO., FARRINGDON STREET. | 1852.' for 'WILLIAM CURRY . . . MDCCCXLIII.'

Sadleir No. [520a], though he dates it 'about 1850'.

[15d] *Traits and Stories of the Irish Peasantry*, 'Fourth Edition', London, Routledge, 1854.

Another impression of [15a]. Title page as [15c] except 'Fourth Edition.' for 'A New Edition.', '1854.' for '1852.'

The tinted lithographic title plates and frontispieces are usually absent; frontispiece of Vol. I replaced by engraving used in [10a]; that of Vol. II no longer tinted.

[*Traits and Stories of the Irish Peasantry*, 'Fifth Edition', London and New York, Routledge, 1856 (5 stories only).

This is a reissue of the first 5 stories only of [15a] and is classified as [37b] below. The title page is as [15b] except for publishers' names and addresses and date, with no indication that there are only 5 stories out of 20. Sadleir mentions in a note to No. [519] ([4a] above) that the first five stories in the Second Series 'were issued in 1854 as a volume in Routledge's New Series'.]

[15e] American edition, 'A New Edition', New York, Wilson & Hawkins, 1862 (2 vols., pp. [*4*] + [xxiv] + [428]; [*8*] + 430)

TRAITS AND STORIES | OF | THE IRISH PEASANTRY. | BY | WILLIAM CARLETON. | [Gothic:] **A New Edition,** | WITH AN AUTOBIOGRAPHICAL INTRODUCTION, EXPLANATORY NOTES, | AND | NUMEROUS ILLUSTRATIONS ON WOOD AND STEEL, | *By Harvey, Phiz, Franklin, Macmanus, Gilbert, and other Artists of eminence.* | VOLUME [I.] | NEW YORK: | PUBLISHED BY WILSON & HAWKINS, | 172, FEDERAL-STREET, BROADWAY. | 1862.

Contents as [15b]. Dedication to Butt now dated 1854. Title pages of Vols. I and II both have 'eminence'.

[15f] 'Fifth edition', London, Tegg, 1864 (2 vols., pp. [*4*] + xxiv + [428]; [*4*] + 430)

TRAITS AND STORIES | OF | THE IRISH PEASANTRY. | BY | WILLIAM CARLETON. | *FIFTH EDITION,* | WITH AN INTRODUCTION, EXPLANATORY NOTES, | AND | NUMEROUS ILLUSTRATIONS, | By HARVEY, GILBERT, PHIZ, FRANKLIN, MACMANUS, &c. | VOLUME [I.] | LONDON: WILLIAM TEGG. | 1864.

[15g] 'Sixth Edition', London, Tegg, 1865 (2 vols., pp. [*6*] + xxiv + [428]; [*4*] + 430)

Title page as [15f] except '*SIXTH EDITION*,' for '*FIFTH EDITION*,', '1865.' for '1864.'

[15h] 'Seventh Edition', London, Tegg, 1867 (2 vols., pp. [*8*] + xxiv + [428]; [*4*] + 430)

[Vol. I:] TRAITS AND STORIES | OF | THE IRISH PEASANTRY. | BY | WILLIAM CARLETON. | [vignette of jaunting car] | *SEVENTH EDITION*, | WITH AN INTRODUCTION, EXPLANATORY NOTES, | AND | NUMEROUS ILLUSTRATIONS, | By HARVEY, GILBERT, PHIZ, FRANKLIN, MACMANUS, &c. | VOLUME I. | LONDON: WILLIAM TEGG. | 1867.

Vol. II as Vol. I except vignette of man with stick riding pony, 'VOLUME II.' for 'VOLUME I.'

Contents as [15b] except new illustrations in text, replacing worn blocks; these are probably from stock as they are often unconnected with the story. Some worn tailpieces omitted and not replaced. New title head illustrations make new typesetting necessary at the beginning of some stories.

[15i] 'Eighth Edition', London, Tegg, 1868 (2 vols., pp. [*4*] + xxiv + [428]; [*4*] + 430)

Title page as [15h] except '*EIGHTH EDITION*.' for '*SEVENTH*

EDITION,', '1868.' for '1867.'

[15j] 'Ninth Complete Edition', London, Tegg, 1869 (2 vols., pp. [*8*] + xxiv + [*428*]; [*6*] + 430)

TRAITS AND STORIES | OF | THE IRISH PEASANTRY. | BY | WILLIAM CARLETON. | [vignette as [15g] | *NINTH COMPLETE EDITION.* | WITH THE AUTHOR'S LAST CORRECTIONS, AN INTRODUCTION, | EXPLANATORY NOTES, | AND | NUMEROUS ILLUSTRATIONS, | BY HARVEY, GILBERT, PHIZ, FRANKLIN, MACMANUS, &C. | VOLUME [I.] | LONDON: WILLIAM TEGG. | 1869.

This title page profits from Carleton's death in January 1869 by mentioning 'the author's last corrections' – factual but misleading, as Carleton had made his last corrections in 1842, and the text is still as [15a].

[15k] 'Tenth Complete Edition', London, Tegg, 1869 (2 vols, pp. [*6*] + xxiv + [*428*]; [*4*] + 430)

As [15j] except '*TENTH COMPLETE EDITION.*' for '*NINTH COMPLETE EDITION*'.

[Another impression in the year of Carleton's death.

The Canadian edition of *Traits and Stories of the Irish Peasantry*, Toronto, Adam Stevenson, 1871, 'From the Tenth English Edition' is not the full collection, so is classified as [55a] below.]

[15l] 'Eleventh Complete Edition', London, Tegg, n.d. (2 vols., pp. [*4*] + xxiv + [*428*]; [*4*] + 430)

As [15k] except '*ELEVENTH COMPLETE EDITION.*' for '*TENTH COMPLETE EDITION.*', date omitted.

†[15m] American edition, New York, Appleton, 1875

The *Publishers' Trade-List Annual* for 1875 lists a 2-volume *Traits and Stories of the Irish Peasantry* from D. Appleton & Co, 549 & 551 Broadway, New York, which I have not seen.

†[15n]   American edition, New York, Worthington, 1875 (Library Edition)

The *Publishers' Trade-List Annual* for 1875 also lists a 2-volume *Traits and Stories of the Irish Peasantry* from R. Worthington & Co., 750 Broadway, New York ('Library Edition'), which I have not seen.

These two-volume 'editions' derive directly from the 'New Edition' of 1843/44. There were many other editions of *Traits and Stories* in various degrees of completeness; they have been entered in their chronological places in the bibliography. (See particularly [58a-63a] and index.)

Valentine M'Clutchy, the Irish Agent

[16a]   First edition, Dublin, London and Edinburgh, Duffy etc., 1845 (3 vols., pp xii + 300; *4* + 318; *4* + 336)

VALENTINE M'CLUTCHY, | THE IRISH AGENT; | OR, | CHRONICLES OF THE CASTLE CUMBER PROPERTY. | BY WILLIAM CARLETON, | AUTHOR OF "TRAITS AND STORIES OF THE IRISH PEASANTRY," | "FARDOROUGHA, THE MISER," "JANE SINCLAIR," &c. &c. | QUI CAPIT ILLE FACIT. | IN THREE VOLUMES. | VOL. [I.] | DUBLIN: | PUBLISHED BY JAMES DUFFY, | 23, ANGLESEA STREET. | LONDON: CHAPMAN AND HALL, 186, STRAND. | EDINBURGH: OLIVER AND BOYD. | 1845.

Contains 'Preface' and novel.
Sadleir No. [521], Brown No. 323, O'Donoghue p. lx.

[16b]   American edition, New York, Sadlier, 1846 (1 vol., pp. 408)

VALENTINE M'CLUTCHY, | THE IRISH AGENT; | OR, | CHRONICLES OF THE CASTLE CUMBER PROPERTY. | BY WILLIAM CARLETON, | AUTHOR OF "TRAITS AND STORIES OF THE IRISH PEASANTRY," "FARDOROUGHA, THE | MISER," "JANE SINCLAIR," &C. &C. | QUI CAPIT ILLE FACIT. | [short decorative rule] | NEW YORK: | PUBLISHED BY D. & J. SADLIER, | 45 GOLD STREET | [short rule] | 1846. Contains 'Preface' and novel.

[16c]   Another edition, Dublin, Duffy, 1847 (1 vol., pp. xii + 468)

VALENTINE M'CLUTCHY, | THE IRISH AGENT; | OR, | THE CHRONICLES OF CASTLE CUMBER; | TOGETHER WITH | THE PIOUS ASPIRATIONS, PERMISSIONS, VOUCHSAFEMENTS, AND OTHER | SANCTIFIED PRIVILEGES OF | SOLOMON M'SLIME, A RELIGIOUS ATTORNEY. | BY WILLIAM CARLETON, | AUTHOR OF "TRAITS AND STORIES OF THE IRISH PEASANTRY," "FARDOROUGHA, THE | MISER," "RODY THE ROVER," "ART MAGUIRE," "PADDY GO EASY," &c., &c. | QUI CAPIT ILLE FACIT. | WITH TWENTY ILLUSTRATIONS, BY PHIZ. | DUBLIN: | PUBLISHED BY JAMES DUFFY, | 10, WELLINGTON QUAY. | MDCCCXLVII.

Contains Preface, dated 1846, and novel.
Sadleir No [521a] and [521b]; O'Donoghue dates this edition as preface, 1846 (p. lxi).

[16d]   Another edition, Dublin, Duffy, 1848 (1 vol., pp. viii + 468)

Title page as [16c] except 'AND | OTHER', 'FARDAROUGHA, THE MISER | "RODY, THE ROVER,"', '7, WELLINGTON-QUAY. | MDCCCXLVIII.'

[16e]   Another edition, Dublin, Duffy, 1854 (1 vol., pp. viii + 468)

Title page as [16d] except 'MDCCCLIV.' for 'MDCCCXLVIII.' Variant title page '1854.' for 'MDCCCLIV.'

[16f]   American edition, New York, Sadlier, 1854 (1 vol., pp. [viii] + 408)

[In double rule frame:] VALENTINE M'CLUTCHY, | THE IRISH AGENT; | OR, | THE CHRONICLES OF CASTLE CUMBER, | TOGETHER WITH | THE PIOUS ASPIRATIONS, PERMISSIONS, VOUCHSAFEMENTS, AND | OTHER SANCTIFIED PRIVILEGES OF | SOLOMON M'SLIME, A RELIGIOUS ATTORNEY. | BY WILLIAM CARLETON, | Author of "Traits and Stories of the Irish Peasantry," "Fardorougha, the Miser," | "Rody the Rover," "Art Maguire," "Paddy Go Easy," &c., &c., | QUI CAPIT ILLE FACIT. | NEW YORK: | PUBLISHED BY D. & J. SADLIER, | 164 WILLIAM STREET. | 1854.

[16g] Another edition, Dublin, Duffy, 1857 (1 vol., pp. viii + 468)

Title page as [16e] except '1857.' for '1854.'

[16h] Another edition, Dublin, Duffy, 1859 (1 vol., pp. [xii] + [13 – 444])

VALENTINE M'CLUTCHY, | THE IRISH AGENT, | AND | SOLOMON M'SLIME, | HIS RELIGIOUS ATTORNEY. | BY WILLIAM CARLETON, | AUTHOR OF "WILLY REILLY," "THE BLACK BARONET," "RODY THE ROVER," | "PADDY GO EASY," "ART MAGUIRE," ETC., ETC. | [scene with man and woman seated in room, he leaning on her chair] | "Eliza," said Solomon, "Eliza, I have often had an intention of asking | you to allow me the privilege and the pleasure, Eliza, of some serious | conversation with you. It is a trying world, a wicked world, and to – to a | girl – so charming a girl as you are, Eliza –" | DUBLIN: | PUBLISHED BY JAMES DUFFY, | 7 WELLINGTON-QUAY. | 1859.

[16i] 'Fourth edition', Dublin and London, Duffy, 1869 (1 vol., pp. xii + [13-444])

Title page as [16h] except '[Gothic:] **Fourth Edition.**' above illustration, and 'DUBLIN: | JAMES DUFFY, 15, WELLINGTON-QUAY. | LONDON: 22, PATERNOSTER-ROW. | 1869

[16j] Another 'fourth edition', Dublin, Duffy, 1869 (1 vol., pp. 444)

VALENTINE McCLUTCHY, | THE IRISH AGENT, | AND | SOLOMON McSLIME, | HIS RELIGIOUS ATTORNEY. | *Fourth Edition.* | DUBLIN: | JAMES DUFFY | [short rule] | 1869.

[16k]   'Eighth edition, Dublin, Duffy, n.d. (1 vol., pp. xii + [13-444])

VALENTINE M'CLUTCHY, | [Gothic:] **The Irish Agent,** | AND | SOLOMON M'SLIME, | HIS RELIGIOUS ATTORNEY, | BY | WILLIAM CARLETON, | Author of *"Willy Reilly," "The Black Baronet," "Rody the Rover,"* | *"Paddy-go-Easy," "Art Maguire,"* etc., etc. | [Gothic:] **Eighth Edition.** | [illustration and caption as [16h]] | [Gothic:] **Dublin:** | JAMES DUFFY AND CO., LIMITED | 14 & 15 WELLINGTON QUAY.

[16l]   American edition, New York and Montreal, Sadlier, 1876 (1 vol., pp. [xlviii] + [7-408])

VALENTINE M'CLUTCHY, | THE IRISH AGENT; | OR, | THE CHRONICLES OF CASTLE CUMBER. | TOGETHER WITH | THE PIOUS ASPIRATIONS, PERMISSIONS, VOUCHSAFEMENTS, | AND SANCTIFIED PRIVILEGES OF | SOLOMON M'SHINE, | A RELIGIOUS ATTORNEY. | BY | WILLIAM CARLETON. | WITH | A BIOGRAPHICAL SKETCH OF THE AUTHOR, | BY JOHN SAVAGE, LL.D. | [short rule] | *Qui Capit, Ille Facit.* | [short rule] | NEW YORK: | D. & J. SADLIER & CO., 31 No, BARCLAY STREET. | MONTREAL: NO. 275 NOTRE-DAME STREET. | [short rule] | 1876.

Biographical introduction, novel.
'Solomon M'Slime' is here altered to 'Solomon M'Shine'.

This is one of a ten-volume 'set' of Carleton's *Works* from Sadlier – though not all his books are included.

[16m]   American edition, New York, Sadlier, n.d. (1 vol., pp. [xlviii] + [7-408)]

Title page as [16i] except 'NEW YORK: | D. & J. SADLIER & CO. | 33 BARCLAY STREET AND 38 PARK PLACE.

[16n]   Another edition, London, Lea, n.d. (1 vol., pp. [viii] + 468)

VALENTINE McCLUTCHY, | THE IRISH AGENT. | BY | WILLIAM CARLETON, ESQ. | [short rule] | WITH STEEL ENGRAVINGS BY PHIZ. | [short rule] | LONDON: HENRY LEA, 22, WARWICK LANE. | PATERNOSTER ROW.

This edition must have been published at some time as a part-work: Trinity College Dublin has a copy with imprint on spine of gatherings 'London: Published by HENRY LEA, 2A Warwick Lane – PRICE ONE PENNY.'

[16o]   Another edition (reprint), New York and London, Garland, 1979 (1 vol., pp. 6 + viii + 468 + 6)

Valentine M'Clutchy, the Irish Agent | *William Carleton* | *Garland Publishing, Inc., New York & London* | 1979

With Garland Series title page and reprint title page of [16c]

Reprint of [16c] (Garland Reprint No. 40)

Denis O'Shaughnessy Going to Maynooth

[17a]   London, Routledge, 1845 (1 vol., pp. [2] + 200)

DENIS O'SHAUGHNESSY | GOING TO | MAYNOOTH. | [short rule] | BY | WILLIAM CARLETON, | AUTHOR OF TRAITS AND STORIES OF THE IRISH PEASANTRY. | [short rule] | WITH ILLUSTRATIONS | LONDON: | GEORGE ROUTLEDGE. | [short rule] | 1845.

Tales and Sketches/Tales and Stories

[18a]   First edition, Dublin, Duffy, 1845 (1 vol., pp. [xii] + [394])

TALES AND SKETCHES, | ILLUSTRATING THE | CHARACTER, USAGES, TRADITIONS, | SPORTS AND PASTIMES | OF | THE IRISH PEASANTRY. | BY WILLIAM CARLETON, | Author of "Traits and Stories of the Irish Peasantry," | "Fardorougha, the Miser," "Jane Sinclair," | "Valentine M'Clutchy," &c. | DUBLIN: | PUBLISHED BY JAMES DUFFY, | 23, ANGLESEA-STREET. | [short rule] | 1845.

Contains: 'Dedication to Charles Gavan Duffy', 'Preface', 'Mickey M'Rorey, the Irish Fiddler'; 'Buckramback, the Country Dancing-Master'; 'Mary Murray, the Irish Match-Maker'; 'Bob Pentland; or, The Gauger Outwitted'; 'The Fate of Frank M'Kenna'; 'The Rival Kempers'; 'Frank Martin and the Fairies'; 'A Legend of Knockmany'; 'Rose Moan, the Irish Midwife'; 'Talbot and Gaynor, the Irish Pipers'; 'Frank Finnegan, the Foster-Brother'; 'Tom

Gressiey, the Irish Senachie'; 'The Castle of Aughentain; or, A Legend of the Brown Goat. Narrated by Tom Gressiey, the Irish Senachie'; Barney M'Haigney, the Irish Prophecy Man'; 'Moll Roe's Marriage; or, the Pudding Bewitched'; 'Barney Brady's Goose; or, Dark Doings at Slathbeg'; 'Condy Cullen; or, the Exciseman Defeated'; 'A Record of the Heart; or, The Parents' Trial'; 'The Three Wishes; an Irish Legend'; 'The Irish Rake'; 'Stories of Second-Sight and Apparition'.

These stories had appeared in the *Irish Penny Journal*, 1840-41. Sadleir No. [515], Brown No. 331.

This collection appears again in the same year, 1845, with a curious discrepancy between the title page, which is as [18a], and the title plate, which is dated 1846, and gives the title as *Tales and Stories of the Irish Peasantry*. This engraved title plate, an etched frontispiece and 6 new plates were all by Phiz. A new head title above the title of the first story reads 'TALES AND STORIES | OF | THE IRISH PEASANTRY.'

[18b]   Another edition, Dublin, Duffy, 1845, with title plate *Tales and Stories of the Irish Peasantry*, 1846 (1 vol., pp. [xii] + [394])

Title page as [18a].

engraved title plate [surrounded by groups of peasants in various occupations, with elves, fairies, animals, etc., drawn wood-like caps. in curved lines:] TALES AND STORIES | OF THE IRISH PEASANTRY | BY | WILLIAM CARLETON. | [drawn italic caps:] *DUBLIN.* | [drawn caps:] PUBLISHED BY JAMES DUFFY. | 10, Wellington Quay. | 1846.

Sadleir No. [515a i]; O'Donoghue p. lx.

[18c]   Another edition, Dublin, Duffy, 1849 (1 vol., pp. [x] + [394])

Title page as [18a] except '10, WELLINGTON QUAY. | [short rule] | 1849.' for '23, ANGLESEA-STREET. | [short rule] | 1845.'

No 'Preface'. Title plate as [18b].
Sadleir No. [515a] n.ii; O'Donoghue p. lxi.

[18d]   Another edition, Dublin, Duffy, 1851 (1 vol., pp. [viii] + [394])

Title page as [18a] except publisher's address and date: '7, WELLINGTON QUAY.] | [short rule] | 1851.'

Contents as [18c]; Title plate as [18b].

[18e]   Another edition, Dublin, Duffy, 1854 (1 vol., pp. [viii] + [394])

Title page as [18d] except '1854.' for '1851.' Type worn, giving ' "Jane Sinclair,' for ' "Jane Sinclair," '.

[18f]   Another edition, Dublin, Duffy, 1855 (1 vol., pp. [iv] + [394])

Title page as [18e] except '1855.' for '1854.'

[18g]   Another edition, Dublin, Duffy, 1860 (1 vol., pp. [iv] + [394])

Title page as [18f] except '1860.' for '1855.'
O'Donoghue p. lxii.

An incomplete version of this edition, from the same plates but omitting the last story, 'Second Sight and Apparition', was published by Henry Lea [n.d.], entitled *Irish Life and Character; or, Tales and Stories of the Irish Peasantry*. See [79a] below.

[18h]   Another edition (reprint), London and New York, Garland, 1980 (1 vol., pp. *8* + [xii] + [394] + *6*)

Tales and Sketches | Illustrating the Character | of the Irish Peasantry | *William Carleton* | *Garland Publishing, Inc., New York & London* | 1980

With Garland Series title page and reprint title page of [18a].

Reprint of [18a] (Garland Reprint No. 39)

[*Tales and Stories of the Irish Peasantry*, New York, Sadlier, 1860, is not the same collection, although it contains several of the same stories. See [46a] below.]

Art Maguire

[19a]   First edition, Dublin, Duffy, 1845 (1 vol., pp. [xii] + 252)

ART MAGUIRE; | OR, | THE BROKEN PLEDGE. | A NARRATIVE. | BY WILLIAM CARLETON, | Author of "Traits and Stories of the Irish Peasantry," "The Miser," | "Jane Sinclair," "Sports and Pastimes of the Irish People," | "Valentine M'Clutchy," &c. &c. | DUBLIN: | PUBLISHED BY JAMES DUFFY, | 23, ANGLESEA STREET. | 1845.

Contains 'Dedication to Father Matthew' [*sic*]; 'Preface'; 'Art Maguire'. Half title 'Tales for the Irish People'. The story is a revised and extended version of 'The Broken Oath', which had appeared in the *Christian Examiner* in June and July 1828.
Sadleir No. [492]; Brown No. 326.

[19b]   American edition, New York and Montreal, Sadlier, 1846 (1 vol., pp. 318)

[Within rule frame:] ART MAGUIRE; | OR, THE BROKEN PLEDGE. | A NARRATIVE. | BY WILLIAM CARLETON, | AUTHOR OF "TRAITS AND STORIES OF THE IRISH PEASANTRY," | "THE MISER," "JANE SINCLAIR," "SPORTS AND PASTIMES | OF THE IRISH PEOPLE," "VALENTINE M'CLUTCHY." | ETC., ETC. | [short rule] | New York: | D. & J. SADLIER & CO., Publishers, | 31 BARCLAY STREET, | Montreal: 275 Notre Dame Street. | 1846.

Contents as [19a].

[19c]   American edition, New York and Montreal, Sadlier, n.d. (1 vol., pp. viii + 214)

Title page as [19b] except no date.

Contents as [19b].

[19d]   Another edition, Dublin and London, Duffy, Simpkin Marshall, 1847 (1 vol., pp. viii + 214)

ART MAGUIRE; | OR, | THE BROKEN PLEDGE. | A NARRATIVE. | BY WILLIAM CARLETON, | Author of "Traits and Stories of the Irish Peasantry," "The Miser," | "Jane Sinclair,"

"Sports and Pastimes of the Irish People," | "Valentine M'Clutchy," &c &c. | DUBLIN: | PUBLISHED BY JAMES DUFFY, | 10, WELLINGTON-QUAY. | LONDON: SIMPKIN, MARSHALL AND CO. | STATIONERS' HALL COURT | 1847.

Contents as [19a].

[19e]   Another edition, Dublin and London, Duffy, n.d. (1 vol., pp. viii + [9-254])

ART MAGUIRE; | OR, | THE BROKEN PLEDGE. | A NARRATIVE. | BY WILLIAM CARLETON, | Author of "Traits and Stories of the Irish Peasantry," "The Miser," | "Jane Sinclair," "Sports and Pastimes of the Irish People," | "Valentine M'Clutchy," &c., &c. | DUBLIN: | PUBLISHED BY JAMES DUFFY & SONS, | 15 WELLINGTON QUAY, | AND 1A, PATERNOSTER ROW, LONDON.

Contains 'Dedication to Father Mathew' (sic); 'Preface'; 'Art Maguire'; 'The Castle of Aughentain; or, a legend of the Brown Goat, Narrated by Tom Gressiey, the Irish Senachie'.

[19f]   Another edition, Dublin, Duffy, n.d. (1 vol., pp. viii + 254)

Title page as [19e] except [Gothic:] '**Dublin:** | JAMES DUFFY AND CO., LIMITED, | 15 WELLINGTON QUAY.' as publisher's address.

Contains 'Dedication', 'Preface', 'Art Maguire', 'Tom Gressiey, the Irish Senachie', 'The Castle of Aughentain (narrated by Tom Gressiey, the Irish Senachie'.

†[19g]   American edition, New York, Sadlier, Household Library, 1878.

Art Maguire; or, the Broken Pledge, a Household Library paperback, was published by D. & J. Sadlier & Co., 31 Barclay St., New York. *Publishers' Weekly* 1878, entry 345. I cannot find any example of this edition.

Rody the Rover

[20a]   First edition, Dublin, Duffy, 1845 (1 vol., pp. iv + 240)

RODY THE ROVER; | OR, | THE RIBBONMAN. | BY WILLIAM CARLETON, | AUTHOR OF "TRAITS AND STORIES OF THE IRISH | PEASANTRY," "VALENTINE M'CLUTCHY," | "ART MAGUIRE," ETC. ETC. | DUBLIN: | PUBLISHED BY JAMES DUFFY, | 23, ANGLESEA-STREET. | 1845.

Contains author's 'Preface'; 'Rody the Rover'.
Sadleir No. [512]; Brown No. 324; O'Donoghue p. lx.

In the same year Duffy published a 'fourth edition'; I have not found any example of a second or third edition, nor of a fifth edition after the 'fourth edition' – there are, however, two 'sixth editions'.

[20b]   'Fourth edition', Dublin, Duffy, 1845 (1 vol., pp. viii + 244)

RODY THE ROVER; | OR, | THE RIBBONMAN. | BY WILLIAM CARLETON, | AUTHOR OF "TRAITS AND STORIES OF THE IRISH | PEASANTRY," "VALENTINE M'CLUTCHY," | "ART MAGUIRE," ETC. ETC. | FOURTH EDITION. | DUBLIN: | PUBLISHED BY JAMES DUFFY, | 23, ANGLESEA-STREET. | 1845.

Contents as [20a].

[20c]   'Sixth edition', Dublin, Duffy, 1859 (1 vol., pp. [2] + [iv] + [vii-viii] + 244)

RODY THE ROVER; | OR, | THE RIBBONMAN. | BY WILLIAM CARLETON, | AUTHOR OF "TRAITS AND STORIES OF THE IRISH PEASANTRY," | "VALENTINE M'CLUTCHY," | ART MAGUIRE, ETC., ETC. | SIXTH EDITION. | DUBLIN: | PUBLISHED BY JAMES DUFFY, | 7, WELLINGTON-QUAY. | 1859.

[20d]   Another 'sixth edition', Dublin and London, Duffy, 1864 (1 vol., pp. viii + 244)

RODY THE ROVER; | OR, | THE RIBBONMAN. | BY WILLIAM CARLETON, | AUTHOR OF "TRAITS AND STORIES OF THE IRISH | PEASANTRY," "VALENTINE M'CLUTCHY," | ART MAGUIRE, ETC., ETC. | SIXTH

EDITION. | DUBLIN: | JAMES DUFFY, 15, WELLINGTON QUAY; | AND 22, PATERNOSTER-ROW, LONDON. | 1864

[20e]   Another edition, Dublin, Duffy, 1905 (1 vol., pp. [240])

RODY THE ROVER; | OR, | THE RIBBONMAN. | BY | WILLIAM CARLETON, | *Author of* | [Gothic:] **"Traits and Stories of the Irish Peasantry," "Valentine** | [Gothic:] **M'Clutchy," "Art Maguire,"** etc. | [short decorative twisted rule] | [Gothic:] **Dublin:** | JAMES DUFFY & CO., Ltd., | 15 Wellington Quay. | 1905.

[20f]   Another edition, Dublin, Duffy, n.d. (1 vol., pp. [240])

[Ornamental caps:] RODY THE ROVER; | OR, | [ornamental caps:] THE RIBBONMAN. | BY WILLIAM CARLETON, | AUTHOR OF "TRAITS AND STORIES OF THE IRISH PEASANTRY," | "VALENTINE M'CLUTCHY," "ART MAGUIRE," | ETC., ETC., ETC. | [short decorative rule] | [Gothic:] **Dublin:** | JAMES DUFFY AND CO., Limited, | 15 Wellington Quay.

[20g]   Another edition [New York, Peterson], n.d.

THE LIFE AND ADVENTURES | OF | RODY THE ROVER; | THE | RIBBONMAN OF IRELAND. | BY | WILLIAM CARLETON. | AUTHOR OF THE "TRAITS AND STORIES OF THE IRISH PEASANTRY," | "VALENTINE McCLUTCHY," "ART MAGUIRE," | "O'SULLIVAN'S LOVE," ETC. | [short wavy rule] | COMPLETE AND UNABRIDGED EDITION. | [short wavy rule]

No publisher's name, but published by Peterson, New York.

Parra Sastha

[21a]   First edition, Dublin, Duffy, 1845 (1 vol., pp. xvi + 198)

PARRA SASTHA; | OR, | THE HISTORY OF | PADDY GO-EASY | AND | HIS WIFE NANCY. | BY WILLIAM CARLETON, | AUTHOR OF "TRAITS AND STORIES OF THE IRISH PEASANTRY," "VALEN | TINE M'CLUTCHY," "ART

MAGUIRE; OR, THE BROKEN | PLEDGE," "RODY THE ROVER," ETC., ETC. | DUBLIN: | PUBLISHED BY JAMES DUFFY, | 23, ANGLESEA-STREET. | 1845.

Contains 'Preface', 'Parra Sastha' and 'Observations on Farming' by an unnamed author [Martin Doyle].
Sadleir No. [506]; Brown No. 322 but entitled *Paddy Go Easy and his Wife Nancy*; O'Donoghue p. lx.

[21b] 'Second edition', Dublin and London, Duffy, Simpkin and Marshall, 1846 (1 vol., pp. [xvi] + [13-228])

PARRA SASTHA; | OR, | THE HISTORY OF | PADDY GO-EASY | AND | HIS WIFE NANCY. | BY WILLIAM CARLETON, | AUTHOR OF "TRAITS AND STORIES OF THE IRISH PEASANTRY" – "VALEN- | TINE M'CLUTCHY" – "ART MAGUIRE; OR, THE BROKEN | PLEDGE" – "RODY THE ROVER," ETC., ETC. | SECOND EDITION. | DUBLIN: | PUBLISHED BY JAMES DUFFY, | 10, WELLINGTON QUAY. | LONDON: SIMPKIN, MARSHALL AND CO. | STATIONERS' HALL COURT. | 1846.

Contains 'Preface to the First Edition', 'Preface to the Second Edition', novel.

[21c]   American edition, Boston, Donahoe, 1865 (1 vol., pp. 264)

PARRA SASTHA; | OR, THE | HISTORY OF PADDY GO-EASY | AND | HIS WIFE NANCY. | BY WILLIAM CARLETON, | AUTHOR OF | "Willy Reilly and his Dear Coleen Bawn," "The Black | Baronet," "The Evil Eye," &c. &c. | [short decorative rule] | BOSTON: | PUBLISHED BY PATRICK DONAHOE. | 1865.

Duffy claimed 15 editions for the novel, but I have not seen the third to the eleventh editions.

[21d] 'Twelfth edition', Dublin and London, Duffy, 1875 (1 vol., pp. xiv + [236])

PARRA SASTHA; | OR, | THE HISTORY OF | PADDY GO-EASY | AND | HIS WIFE NANCY. | TO WHICH IS ADDED ROSE MOAN, | THE IRISH MIDWIFE. | BY | WILLIAM

CARLETON, | AUTHOR OF "TRAITS AND STORIES OF THE IRISH PEASANTRY" – "VALENTINE | M'CLUTCHY" – "ART MAGUIRE; OR, THE BROKEN PLEDGE" – | "RODY THE ROVER," ETC. ETC. | [Gothic:] **Twelfth Edition.** | DUBLIN: | PUBLISHED BY JAMES DUFFY & SONS, | 15, WELLINGTON QUAY; | AND PATERNOSTER ROW, LONDON. | 1875.

Contains 'Parra Sastha', 'Rose Moan'.

[21e]   *Parra Sastha* and *Rose Moan*, 'Thirteenth Edition', Dublin, Duffy, n.d. (1 vol., pp. [xvi] + [236])

PARRA SASTHA; | OR, | THE HISTORY OF | PADDY GO-EASY | AND | HIS WIFE NANCY. | TO WHICH IS ADDED | ROSE MOAN, | THE IRISH MIDWIFE. | BY | WILLIAM CARLETON, | AUTHOR OF "TRAITS AND STORIES OF THE IRISH PEASANTRY" – "VALENTINE | M'CLUTCHY" – "ART MAGUIRE; OR, THE BROKEN PLEDGE" – | "RODY THE ROVER," ETC. ETC. | [Gothic:] **Thirteenth Edition.** | [Gothic:] **Dublin:** | JAMES DUFFY AND CO., LIMITED, 14 & 15 WELLINGTON QUAY.

Contains 'Dedication to the People of Ireland'; 'Preface'; 'Preface to the Second Edition'; 'Parra Sastha'; 'Rose Moan'.

[21f]   'Fourteenth edition', Dublin, Duffy, n.d. (1 vol., pp. [xvi] + [236])

PARRA SASTHA; | OR | THE HISTORY OF | PADDY GO-EASY | AND | HIS WIFE NANCY. | TO WHICH IS ADDED | ROSE MOAN, | THE IRISH MIDWIFE. | BY | WILLIAM CARLETON, | AUTHOR OF "TRAITS AND STORIES OF THE IRISH PEASANTRY" – "VALENTINE | M'CLUTCHY" – "ART MAGUIRE; OR, THE BROKEN PLEDGE" – | "RODY THE ROVER," ETC. ETC. | [short rule] | [Gothic:] **Fourteenth Edition.** | [short rule] | DUBLIN: | JAMES DUFFY AND CO., LIMITED, | 15 WELLINGTON QUAY.

[21g]   Fifteenth edition, Dublin, Duffy, n.d. (1 vol., pp. [xvi] + [236])

PARRA SASTHA; | OR, | THE HISTORY OF | PADDY GO-EASY | AND | HIS WIFE NANCY. | TO WHICH IS ADDED |

ROSE MOAN, | THE IRISH MIDWIFE. | BY | WILLIAM CARLETON, | AUTHOR OF "TRAITS AND STORIES OF THE IRISH PEASANTRY" – "VALENTINE M'CLUTCHY" – "ART MAGUIRE; OR, THE BROKEN PLEDGE" – | "RODY THE ROVER," ETC., ETC. | [short rule] | [Gothic:] **Fifteenth Edition.** | [short rule] | [Gothic:] **Dublin:** | JAMES DUFFY AND CO., LTD., | 15 WELLINGTON QUAY.

'Parra Sastha' also appeared in 1847 in an edition of Lever's *The Knight of Gwynne*, Philadelphia, Carey and Hart, with 'O'Sullivan's Love'. This is classified as [28a] below.

In 1845, Carey and Hart of Philadelphia published the following sets of Carleton stories in uniform editions. They have a selection of the Phiz illustrations of the 'New Edition' of 1842/3/4 [15a/b]. The title plate of each collection has a Phiz illustration, sometimes with caption, and a variety of ornamental lettering, curved and straight. The pagination starts late.

[22a]   *The Battle of the Factions and other Tales of Ireland*, Philadelphia, Carey & Hart, 1845 (1 vol., pp. [9-104])

[engraved title plate:] [top and left hand side, title head illustration of *Traits and Stories* 1842 [15a], men fighting, women grieving over man's body] THE | [ornamental caps. in curve:] BATTLE | of the | [different ornamental caps:] FACTIONS | *and other Tales of Ireland* | BY | [hollow caps:] WILLIAM CARLETON. | [short decorative rule] | PHILADELPHIA | CAREY & HART. | 1845.

Contains 'The Battle of the Factions'; 'The Geography of an Irish Oath'; 'Neal Malone'; 'The Donagh; or, the Horse-Stealers'; 'The Station'.

[23a]   *Phelim O'Toole's Courtship and The Poor Scholar*, Philadelphia, Carey & Hart, 1845 (1 vol., pp. [17-98])

[hollow caps:] PHELIM O'TOOLES [sic] | [ornamental caps:] COURTSHIP | AND | [striped caps:] THE POOR SCHOLAR | BY | [checked caps:] WILLIAM CARLETON. | [man and girl on potato bin] | [twiglike caps:] PHELIM O'TOOLE'S COURTSHIP. | [double and single line caps:] PHILADELPHIA. | CAREY & HART. | 1845.

Contains 'Phelim O'Toole's Courtship'; 'The Poor Scholar'.

[24a] *Phil Purcel, and other Tales of Ireland*, Philadelphia, Carey & Hart, 1845 (1 vol., pp. [9-78])

[ornamental caps. in curve:] PHIL PURCEL, | and | other Tales of Ireland, | BY | [shaded caps:] WILLIAM CARLETON. | [in double rule frame, 2 men and dressed dog playing cards] | Jack Magennis playing at "Five and Ten" with the "dark looking" gentleman. | PHILADELPHIA. | CAREY & HART. | 1845.

Contains 'Phil Purcel'; 'Ned M'Keown'; 'The Three Tasks'; 'Shane Fadh's Wedding'; 'Larry M'Farland's Wake'.

The Black Prophet

[25a] 'Parlour Library' edition, Belfast, Simms & M'Intyre, 1847 (1 vol., pp. [2] + [iv] + [5-320])

[Within rule frame:] THE | BLACK PROPHET: | A TALE OF IRISH FAMINE. | BY WILLIAM CARLETON, | AUTHOR OF | "TRAITS AND STORIES OF THE IRISH PEASANTRY," | "FARDOROUGHA THE MISER," ETC. | BELFAST: | SIMMS AND M'INTYRE. | [short rule] | 1847.

Variant title page, London and Belfast: Publisher's name and address: 'LONDON: | SIMMS AND M'INTYRE, | ALDINE CHAMBERS, PATERNOSTER ROW; | AND DONEGALL-STREET, BELFAST. | [short rule] | 1847.'

No. I of the Parlour Library series. Contains 'Dedication to Lord John Russell'; 'Author's Preface'; novel.
Sadleir No. [495], inaccurately subtitled 'A Tale of the Irish Famine'. O'Donoghue p. lxi.

[25b] Another edition, London and Belfast, Simms & M'Intyre, 1847 (1 vol,. pp. [xii] + [5-456])

THE | BLACK PROPHET: | A TALE OF IRISH FAMINE. | BY WILLIAM CARLETON, | AUTHOR OF | "TRAITS AND STORIES OF THE IRISH PEASANTRY," | FARDOROUGHA THE MISER," ETC. | WITH SIX ILLUSTRATIONS BY W.

HARVEY, | ENGRAVED BY DICKES. | LONDON: | SIMMS
AND M'INTYRE, | ALDINE CHAMBERS, PATERNOSTER
ROW; AND | DONEGALL STREET, BELFAST. | [short rule] |
1847.

Variant title page has ' | ALDINE CHAMBERS, PATERNOSTER
ROW; | AND DONEGALL-STREET, BELFAST. | [short rule] |
1847.'

[Engraved title plate:] alarmed peasants, man dying | THE |
BLACK PROPHET | A TALE OF | IRISH FAMINE | BY |
WILLIAM CARLETON | [buried pot, spade, pick].

Contains 'Dedication to Lord John Russell', 'Author's Preface',
novel.

This is the 'illustrated first edition' that Sadleir lists as [495b], copy
III; although published in the same year as the Parlour Library
edition [25a] above, it is a different edition, with different typesetting
etc.

[25c]   American edition, New York, Burgess Stringer, 1847 (1
vol., pp. [224])

[Within wavy rule frame:] THE | [hollow caps:] BLACK
PROPHET: | A TALE OF IRISH FAMINE. | BY WILLIAM
CARLETON. | [Gothic:] **New-York:** | BURGESS, STRINGER
AND COMPANY, 200 BROADWAY. | [short rule] | 1847

[25d]   Another edition, London and Belfast, Simms & M'Intyre,
1848 (1 vol., pp. [*4*] + [iv] + [5-320]) (Parlour Library)

[Within rule frame:] THE | BLACK PROPHET: | A TALE OF
IRISH FAMINE. | BY WILLIAM CARLETON, | AUTHOR OF |
"TRAITS AND STORIES OF THE IRISH PEASANTRY," | '[sic]
FARDOROUGHA THE MISER," ETC. | LONDON: | SIMMS
AND M'INTYRE, | ALDINE CHAMBERS, PATERNOSTER
ROW; | AND DONEGALL-STREET, BELFAST. | [short rule] |
1848.

Contents as [25a].

[25e]   Another edition, London and Belfast, Simms & M'Intyre,

1849 (1 vol., pp. [*4*] + [iv] + [5-320]) (Parlour Library)
As [25d] except '1849.' for '1848.'

[25f] Another edition, London, Thomas Hodgson, 1854 (1 vol., pp. 320)

[Within rule frame:] THE | BLACK PROPHET: | A TALE OF IRISH FAMINE. | BY WILLIAM CARLETON, | AUTHOR OF | "TRAITS AND STORIES OF THE IRISH PEASANTRY," | 'FARDOROUGHA THE MISER," ETC. | LONDON: | THOMAS HODGSON, 13, PATERNOSTER ROW. | [short rule] | 1854.

Still 'Parlour Library', but now published by Hodgson.

[25g] American edition, New York and Montreal, Sadlier, n.d. [1875] [1 vol., pp. 580)

THE | BLACK PROPHET: | A TALE OF | IRISH FAMINE. | BY WILLIAM CARLETON, | Author of "Valentine M'Clutchy," "Tales and Stories of the Irish | Peasantry," "Fardorougha, the Miser" "The Evil Eye," | "Art Maguire," "The Tithe Proctor," &c., &c. | NEW YORK: | D. & J. SADLIER & CO., 31 BARCLAY STREET, | MONTREAL: | COR. NOTRE DAME AND ST. FRANCIS XAVIER STS. | [short rule]

This is one of the 10 volumes of Sadlier's *Works* of Carleton, 1875.

[25h] American edition, New York, Kenedy, 1896 (1 vol., pp. [*6*] + 518)

THE | BLACK PROPHET: | A TALE OF | THE IRISH FAMINE. | BY WILLIAM CARLETON, | Author of "Willy Reilly," "Valentine M'Clutchy," "Tales and Stories | of the Irish Peasantry," "Fardorougha, the Miser," "The Evil Eye," | "The Tithe Proctor," "Jane Sinclair," "Emigrants of Ahad- | arra," "The Poor Scholar," "The Black Baronet," etc. | [short rule] | NEW YORK: | P.J. KENEDY, | EXCELSIOR PUBLISHING HOUSE, | 5 BARCLAY STREET. | 1896.

Story only, without preface etc. Verso of title page has 'Copyright: | D. & J. SADLIER & CO. | 1885.'

[25i]   Another edition, London, Lawrence and Bullen, 1899 (1 vol., pp. xvi + 408)

The Black Prophet | A TALE OF IRISH FAMINE | By | WILLIAM CARLETON | AUTHOR OF "TRAITS AND STORIES OF THE IRISH | PEASANTRY," "FARDOROUGHA THE MISER," ETC. | WITH AN INTRODUCTION BY | D. J. O'DONOGHUE | AND ILLUSTRATIONS BY J. B. YEATS | [Lawrence and Bullen device] | LONDON | LAWRENCE & BULLEN LTD. | 16 HENRIETTA STREET COVENT GARDEN | 1899

Contains Dedication and Author's Preface as [25a] and introduction by D. J. O'Donoghue. Brown No. 327. He also mentions a New York edition of 1899 from Sadlier, misspelt as 'Sadleir'.

[25j]   'Irish Novels Series', Shannon, Irish University Press, 1972 (1 vol., pp. [xx] + [v-xvi] + 408)

IRISH NOVELS SERIES | general editor: A. Norman Jeffares | The Black Prophet | *A Tale of Irish Famine* | by | WILLIAM CARLETON | *Introduction by* | Timothy Webb | [shamrock device] | IRISH UNIVERSITY PRESS | *Shannon Ireland*

A facsimile reprint of [25i] omitting 2 prelim. leaves; contents as [25i], with 'Introduction' by Timothy Webb.

[25k]   Another edition (reprint), New York and London, Garland, 1979 (1 vol., pp. *8* + iv + [5-320] + *8*)

The Black Prophet | *William Carleton* | *Garland Publishing Inc., New York & London* | 1979

With Garland Series title page and reprint title page of [25a].

Reprint of [25a] (Garland Reprint No. 41).

[26a]   *Barney Branagan, Fawn of Spring Vale, Barney Bradley, and other Tales*, 'Three Volumes in One', London, Routledge, 1847 (1 vol., pp. [xii] + [368]; [352]; [328])

BARNEY BRANAGAN, | FAWN OF SPRING VALE, | BARNEY BRADLEY, | AND OTHER TALES. | BY | WILLIAM CARLETON, | AUTHOR OF "TRAITS AND STORIES OF

THE IRISH PEASANTRY." | [short rule] | THREE VOLUMES IN ONE. | [short rule] | LONDON: | GEORGE ROUTLEDGE, | SOHO SQUARE. | 1847.

This is a new presentation of the stories in [14a], with a new overall title, and abbreviated titles for several stories. Contains '[The Misfortunes of] Barney Branagan', 'Fawn of Spring Vale', '[The Resurrections of] Barney Bradley', 'Lha Dhu', 'The Clarionet,' 'The Dead Boxer'.

The Poor Scholar

[27a]   American edition, New York, Ross Wilkinson, 1847 (1 vol., pp. 56)

THE POOR SCHOLAR. | [vignette of man walking with bundle, from title heading of [15a] | A PATHETIC STORY OF IRISH LIFE. | BY WILLIAM CARLETON. | AUTHOR OF "THE BLACK PROPHET," "THE MISER," "TRAITS AND STORIES OF | THE IRISH PEASANTRY," &C. &C. | [Gothic:] **New York:** | ROSS WILKINSON, 105 NASSAU STREET. | [short rule] | 1847.

Contains 'The Poor Scholar' alone.

[With another:] **The Knight of Gwynne, Parra Sastha and O'Sullivan's Love**

[28a]   American edition of Lever's *Knight of Gwynne*, with *Parra Sastha* and 'O'Sullivan's Love', Philadelphia, Carey and Hart, 1847 (1 vol., pp. 226 + [104])

THE | KNIGHT OF GWYNNE; | A TALE OF THE TIME OF THE UNION. | BY CHARLES LEVER, | AUTHOR OF "HARRY LORREQUER," "CHARLES O'MALLEY," ETC. | WITH TWO ILLUSTRATIONS BY "PHIZ." | PHILADELPHIA: | PUBLISHED BY CAREY AND HART. | 1847.

Contains Lever's *Knight of Gwynne*; Carleton's *Parra Sastha* and 'O'Sullivan's Love'. Only the Lever story appears on the title page, and the pagination is separate for each author's work, so it is possible that the Carleton section had been published elsewhere. New York Public Library has the text of 'O'Sullivan's Love' but no title page.

[With others:] **Art Maguire, or the Broken Pledge, and the Lives of Curran and Grattan**

[29a]   Dublin, Duffy, 1848 (1 vol., pp. [viii] [9] 10-214 [2] [iv] [5] 6-232)

ART MAGUIRE; | OR, | THE BROKEN PLEDGE, | AND THE | LIVES OF CURRAN & GRATTAN. | BY WILLIAM CARLETON, | THOMAS DAVIS, | AND | DANIEL OWEN MADDEN, ESQRS. | DUBLIN: | JAMES DUFFY, 10, WELLINGTON-QUAY. | 1848.

Contains *Art Maguire*; *The Life of the Right Hon. J. P. Curran* by Thomas Davis; *A Memoir of the Life of the Right Hon. Henry Grattan* by D. O. Madden. The general title page is shown above; there is a further 'title page' dated 1846 for the lives of Curran and Grattan:

THE LIFE | OF | THE RIGHT HON. J. P. CURRAN. | BY THOMAS DAVIS, M.R.I.A. | AND | A MEMOIR OF THE LIFE OF | THE RIGHT HON. HENRY GRATTAN, | BY D. O. MADDEN, | OF THE INNER TEMPLE. | WITH ADDENDA, AND LETTER IN REPLY TO LORD CLARE. | DUBLIN: | PUBLISHED BY JAMES DUFFY, | 10, WELLINGTON-QUAY. | LONDON: SIMPKIN, MARSHALL AND CO. | STATIONERS' HALL COURT. | 1846.

The Emigrants of Ahadarra

[30a]   'Parlour Library' edition, London and Belfast, Simms & M'Intyre, 1848 (pp. viii + [310])

[Within rule frame:] THE | EMIGRANTS OF AHADARRA: | A TALE OF IRISH LIFE. | BY | WILLIAM CARLETON, Esq. | AUTHOR OF "TRAITS AND STORIES OF THE IRISH PEASANTRY," | "FARDOROUGHA THE MISER," "THE BLACK PROPHET," ETC. | [short rule] | "LUCUS A NON LUCENDO." | [short rule] | But soon a wonder came to light | That showed the rogues they lied, — | The man recovered of the bite, | The dog it was that died. — Goldsmith. | LONDON: | SIMMS AND M'INTYRE, | PATERNOSTER ROW, AND DONEGALL STREET, BELFAST. | [short rule] | 1848.

Contains 'Preface', novel, Parlour Library No. XI.
O'Donoghue dates this edition 1847 (p. lxi) but Sadleir (No. [499]) dates its publication January 1, 1848.

[30b]   Another edition, London and Belfast, Simms & M'Intyre, 1851 (1 vol., pp. viii + [310])

[Within rule frame:] THE | EMIGRANTS OF AHADARRA: | A TALE OF IRISH LIFE. | BY WILLIAM CARLETON, | AUTHOR OF "TRAITS AND STORIES OF THE IRISH PEASANTRY;" | "THE BLACK PROPHET;" "THE TITHE PROCTOR;" | "FARDOROGHA [sic] THE MISER;" ETC. | [short rule] | "LUCUS A NON LUCENDO." | [short rule] | "But soon a wonder came to light | That showed the rogues they lied: | The man recovered of the bite, | The dog it was that died." — GOLDSMITH. | LONDON: | SIMMS AND M'INTYRE, | PATERNOSTER ROW; AND DONEGALL STREET, BELFAST. | [short rule] | 1851.

Contents as [30a]. Parlour Library.

[30c]   As *The Emigrants*, London and New York, Routledge, 1857 (1 vol., pp. viii + [310])

THE EMIGRANTS: | [Gothic:] **A Tale of Irish Life.** | BY WILLIAM CARLETON, | AUTHOR OF | "THE TITHE-PROCTOR;" "FARDOROUGHA THE MISER, | ETC. | [Verse as [30b]] | LONDON: | GEORGE ROUTLEDGE AND CO., FARRINGDON STREET; | AND 18, BEEKMAN STREET, NEW YORK. | 1857.

Contents as [30a].

[30d]   Another edition, *The Emigrants*, London and New York, Routledge, n.d. [1875] (1 vol., pp. viii + [310])

THE EMIGRANTS: | [Gothic:] **A Tale of Irish Life.** | BY WILLIAM CARLETON, | AUTHOR OF | "THE TITHE-PROCTOR," "FARDOROUGHA THE MISER," | ETC. | [verse as [30b]] | LONDON: | GEORGE ROUTLEDGE AND SONS | THE BROADWAY, LUDGATE. | NEW YORK: 416, BROOME STREET.

Contents as [30a].

This is one of Routledge's set of 5 volumes of Carleton's *Novels and Tales*, 1875.

[30e]   American edition, New York and Montreal, Sadlier, n.d.
[1875] (1 vol., pp. 516)

THE | EMIGRANTS | OF | AHADARRA. | BY WILLIAM
CARLETON, | Author of "Valentine McClutchy," "Tales, and
Stories of the Irish | Peasantry," "The Evil Eye," "Art Maguire,"
"Willy Reilly," | "Fardorougha, the Miser," "The Tithe Proctor," |
"The Black Prophet," "Black Baronet," &c. | NEW YORK: | D. &
J. SADLIER & CO., 31 BARCLAY STREET. | MONTREAL: –
COR. NOTRE DAME AND ST. FRANCIS XAVIER STS. |
[short rule]

Contains novel only.

One of Sadlier's set of ten volumes of Carleton's *Works*, 1875.

[30f]   American edition, New York, Sadlier, n.d. (1 vol., pp. 516)

THE | EMIGRANTS | OF | AHADARRA. | By WILLIAM
CARLETON, | Author of "Valentine McClutchy," "Tales, and
Stories of the Irish | Peasantry," "The Evil Eye," "Art Maguire,"
"Willy Reilly," | "Fardorougha, the Miser," "The Tithe Proctor,"
| "The Black Prophet," "Black Baronet," &c. | NEW YORK:
| D. & J. SADLIER & CO., | 33 BARCLAY STREET and 38 PARK
PLACE.

Novel only. No date on title page but 'Copyright, D. & J. Sadlier &
Co., 1885.' on verso. This is Brown No. 328.

[30g]   Another edition (reprint), New York and London, Garland,
1979 (1 vol., pp. *6* + viii + [310] + *8*)

The Emigrants | of Ahadarra | *William Carleton* | *Garland Publishing,
Inc., New York & London* | 1979

With Garland Series title page and reprint Parlour Library and [30a]
title pages.

Reprint of [30a] (Garland Reprint No. 42).

The Tithe Proctor

[31a]   First edition, London and Belfast, Simms & M'Intyre, 1849 (1 vol., pp. xvi + 288) – 'Parlour Library'.

[Within rule frame:] THE | TITHE PROCTOR: | A NOVEL. | BEING A TALE OF THE TITHE REBELLION IN IRELAND. | BY | WILLIAM CARLETON, Esq. | AUTHOR OF | "TRAITS AND STORIES OF THE IRISH PEASANTRY," | "THE EMIGRANTS OF AHADARRA," ETC. | [short rule] | LONDON: | SIMMS AND M'INTYRE, | PATERNOSTER ROW, AND DONEGALL STREET, BELFAST. | [short rule] | 1849.

Contains 'Author's Preface'; novel; *The Hand and Word* (by Gerald Griffin, here not named). Parlour Library Series, No. XXIV. Sadleir No. [517], Brown No. 329, O'Donoghue p. lxi.

[31b]   Another edition, London and New York, Routledge, 1857 (1 vol., pp. [xx] + [21-284])

THE | TITHE-PROCTOR: | [Gothic:] **A Novel.** | BY | WILLIAM CARLETON, Esq., | AUTHOR OF | "TRAITS AND STORIES OF THE IRISH PEASANTRY," | "THE EMIGRANTS," ETC. | LONDON: | G. ROUTLEDGE AND CO., FARRINGDON STREET. | AND 18, BEEKMAN STREET, NEW YORK. | 1857.

Contains 'Preface'; 'Introduction'; novel; not *The Hand and Word*.

[31c]   American edition, New York and Montreal, Sadlier, 1873 (1 vol., pp. xiv + (5-432])

THE TITHE-PROCTOR: | A NOVEL. | BY | WILLIAM CARLETON, | Author of "Valentine McClutchy," "Traits and Stories of the Irish | Peasantry," "Rody the Rover," "Art Maguire," "Willy Reilly," | "Fardorougha, the Miser," "Paddy Go Easy," | "The Black Prophet," "Black Baronet," | "Jane Sinclair," "The Emigrants | of Ahadarra," &c. | NEW YORK: | D. & J. SADLIER & CO., 31 BARCLAY STREET. | MONTREAL: COR. NOTRE DAME AND ST. FRANCIS XAVIER STS. | [short rule] | 1873.

Contents as [31b].

[31d] Another edition, London and New York, Routledge, n.d. (1 vol., pp. [xx] + [21-284])

THE | TITHE-PROCTOR: | [Gothic:] **A Novel.** | BY | WILLIAM CARLETON, Esq., | AUTHOR OF | "TRAITS AND STORIES OF THE IRISH PEASANTRY," | "THE EMIGRANTS," ETC. | LONDON: | GEORGE ROUTLEDGE AND SONS, | THE BROADWAY, LUDGATE. | NEW YORK: 416, BROOME STREET.

[31e] American edition, New York and Montreal, Sadlier, n.d. [1875] (1 vol., pp. xiv + [5-432])

Title page as [31c] except no short rule or date.
This is a volume of Sadlier's 10-vol. set of Carleton's *Works*, 1875.

[31f] Another edition, London and New York, Routledge, n.d. [1875] (1 vol., pp. [xx] + [21-284])

THE | TITHE-PROCTOR | BY | WILLIAM CARLETON | AUTHOR OF | "TRAITS AND STORIES OF THE IRISH PEASANTRY" | LONDON | GEORGE ROUTLEDGE AND SONS | THE BROADWAY, LUDGATE | NEW YORK: 416 BROOME STREET

This is one volume of Routledge's 5-volume set of Carleton's *Novels and Tales*, 1875.

[31g] Another edition, London and New York, Routledge, n.d. (1 vol., pp. [xx] + [21-284]

Title page as [31f].

This is from the same stereos as [31f], but whereas the 1875 5-volume set was 'bound in flexible cloth', this has board covers with a pasted paper cover with illustration and wording 'PRICE ONE SHILLING | THE TITHE PROCTER' [sic]. (The 1875 set cost $3·75, or presumably 75c each.) The verso of the title page lists as 'Shilling Novels' the same titles as the 1875 set, that is, *The Clarionet, Fardorougha, The Emigrants, Jane Sinclair* and *The Tithe-Proctor*.

[31h] Another edition (reprint), New York and London, Garland,

1979 (1 vol., pp. *6* + xvi + [264] + *8*)

The Tithe Proctor | *William Carleton* | *Garland Publishing, Inc.,* *New York & London* | 1979

With Garland Series title page and reprint Parlour Library title page and title page of [31a].

Reprint of greater part of [31a], without *The Hand and Word.* (Garland Reprint No. 43).

Jane Sinclair; or, the Fawn of Spring-Vale; and The Dark Day

[32a]   London, Routledge, 1849 (1 vol., pp. [2] + 198)

JANE SINCLAIR; | OR, | THE FAWN OF SPRING-VALE; | AND | THE DARK DAY. | BY | WILLIAM CARLETON, | AUTHOR OF "TRAITS AND STORIES OF THE IRISH | PEASANTRY," "THE CLARIONET," &c. &c. | LONDON: | GEORGE ROUTLEDGE AND CO., SOHO SQUARE. | 1849.

Contains 'Jane Sinclair'; 'The Dark Day'. These two stories had constituted Vol. I of *The Fawn of Spring-Vale*, 1839 [14a], as 'The Fawn of Spring-Vale' and 'Lha Dhu, or the Dark Day'.

Jane Sinclair, Neal Malone &c. &c./and Other Tales

[33a]   *Jane Sinclair, Neal Malone &c. &c.,* London, Routledge, 1850 (1 vol., pp. [2] + [284])

JANE SINCLAIR. | NEAL MALONE. | &C. &C. | BY | WILLIAM CARLETON, | AUTHOR OF "TRAITS AND STORIES OF THE IRISH PEASANTRY," | "THE CLARIONET," &C. &C. | LONDON: | GEORGE ROUTLEDGE AND CO., SOHO SQUARE. | 1850.

Contains 'Jane Sinclair'; 'Lha Dhu'; 'Barney Bradley'; 'Neal Malone'; 'Wildgoose Lodge'.

[33b]   Another edition, London, Routledge, 1854 (1 vol., pp. [2] + [284])

Title page as [33a] except '1854.' for '1850.'

Contents as [33a].

[33c]   As *Jane Sinclair, Neal Malone and Other Tales*, London and New York, Routledge, n.d. [1875] (1 vol., pp. [2] + [284])

JANE SINCLAIR | NEAL MALONE | *AND OTHER TALES* | BY WILLIAM CARLETON | AUTHOR OF "TRAITS AND STORIES OF THE IRISH PEASANTRY" | LONDON | GEORGE ROUTLEDGE AND SONS | THE BROADWAY, LUDGATE | NEW YORK: 416 BROOME STREET

Contents as [33a].

This is one of the 5 volumes of Routledge's 5-volume set of Carleton's *Novels and Tales*, 1875.

The Clarionet, The Dead Boxer, and Barney Branagan

[34a]   London, Routledge, 1850 (1 vol., pp. [256])

THE CLARIONET, | THE DEAD BOXER, | AND BARNEY BRANAGAN. | BY | WILLIAM CARLETON, | AUTHOR OF "TRAITS AND STORIES OF THE IRISH PEASANTRY," | &C. &C. | LONDON: | GEORGE ROUTLEDGE AND CO., SOHO SQUARE. | 1850.

Contains 'The Clarionet'; 'The Dead Boxer'; 'Barney Branagan'. O'Donoghue p. lxi; mentioned by Brown in *Fawn of Springvale* entry, No. 321.

[34b]   Another edition, London, Routledge, 1852 (1 vol., pp. [256])

THE CLARIONET, | THE DEAD BOXER, | AND | BARNEY BRANAGAN. | BY | WILLIAM CARLETON, | AUTHOR OF "TRAITS AND STORIES OF THE IRISH PEASANTRY," ETC. ETC. | LONDON: | GEORGE ROUTLEDGE AND CO., FARRINGDON STREET. | 1852.

See also a volume with the same title, but including 'Wildgoose Lodge', published by Routledge in 1875 as part of their 5-volume *Novels and Tales of William Carleton* [57a] below.

The Squanders of Castle Squander

[35a]   First edition, London, Illustrated London Library, 1852 (2 vols., pp. vi + 326; [iv] + [312])

THE SQUANDERS | OF | CASTLE SQUANDER. | BY | WILLIAM CARLETON, Esq. | Author of "Traits and Stories of the Irish Peasantry," "The Black Prophet," &c. &c. | IN TWO VOLUMES. | VOL. [I.] | LONDON: | OFFICE OF THE ILLUSTRATED LONDON LIBRARY, | 227, STRAND. | [short rule] | 1852.

Contains 'Author's Preface'; novel. 'Illustrated Family Novelists' Series.
Sadleir No. [514]; Brown No. 333; O'Donoghue p. lxi.

[35b]   Another edition, London, Ward, Lock and Tyler, n.d. (1 vol., pp. iv + 414)

THE SQUANDERS | OF | CASTLE SQUANDER. | BY | WILLIAM CARLETON, Esq. | AUTHOR OF "TRAITS AND STORIES OF THE IRISH PEASANTRY," | "THE BLACK PROPHET," &c. | [Ward, Lock and Tyler device] | LONDON: | WARD, LOCK, AND TYLER, | WARWICK HOUSE, PATERNOSTER ROW.

Contents as [35a].

[35c]   Another edition, London, Ward Lock, n.d. (1 vol., pp. [iv] + [312])

THE SQUANDERS | OF | CASTLE SQUANDER. | BY | WILLIAM CARLETON, Esq. | AUTHOR OF "TRAITS AND STORIES OF THE IRISH PEASANTRY," | "THE BLACK PROPHET," &c. | WARD, LOCK, AND CO. | LONDON: WARWICK HOUSE, SALISBURY SQUARE, E.C. | NEW YORK: BOND STREET.

Contents as [35a].

[35d]   Another edition, London, Lea, n.d. (1 vol., pp. [iv] + 414)

THE SQUANDERS | OF | CASTLE SQUANDER. | BY | WILLIAM CARLETON, Esq. | Author of "Traits and Stories of the Irish Peasantry," "The Black Prophet," &c. | LONDON: | HENRY LEA, 22, WARWICK LANE, | PAAERNOSTER [sic] ROW.

Contents as [35a].

Red Hall or the Baronet's Daughter/The Black Baronet

[36a]   First edition, London, Saunders & Otley, 1852 (3 vols., pp. [iv] + 308; [iv] + 316; [iv] + [320])

RED HALL | OR | THE BARONET'S DAUGHTER. | BY | WILLIAM CARLETON, ESQ. | AUTHOR OF "STORIES OF THE IRISH PEASANTRY," ETC. | IN THREE VOLUMES. | VOL. [I.] | LONDON | SAUNDERS AND OTLEY, CONDUIT STREET. | 1852.

Contains novel only.

Sadleir No. [510]; Brown No. 333A; O'Donoghue p. lxi.

[36b]   Another edition, London, Saunders & Otley, 1854 (3 vols., pp. [2] + 308; [2] + 316; [2] + [320])

RED HALL: | OR, | THE BARONET'S DAUGHTER. | BY | WILLIAM CARLETON, ESQ. | AUTHOR OF "STORIES OF THE IRISH PEASANTRY," ETC. | IN THREE VOLUMES. | VOL. [I.] | LONDON: | SAUNDERS AND OTLEY, CONDUIT STREET. | 1854.

Contents as [36a].

[36c]   Retitled *The Black Baronet*: Dublin, Duffy, 1858 (1 vol., pp. [xii] + [5-476])

THE | BLACK BARONET; | OR, | THE CHRONICLES OF BALLYTRAIN. | BY WILLIAM CARLETON, | AUTHOR OF "WILLY REILLY." "VALENTINE M'CLUTCHY," "RODY THE ROVER," | "TALES AND STORIES OF THE IRISH PEASANTRY," ETC., ETC. | [engraving of marriage scene] | " 'Doctor Sombre," said his lordship, 'do NOT proceed with the ceremony until | I shall have spoken to Miss Gourlay's father. | If it be necessary that I should | speak more plainly, I say I forbid the banns." | [Gothic:] **Dublin:** | JAMES DUFFY AND CO., LTD., | 14 & 15 WELLINGTON QUAY. | 1858.

Contains author's 'Preface' dated October 26, 1857; novel.
Sadleir dates this 1858 (No. [494]); Brown dates it [1856]; O'Donoghue dates it 1857 (p. lxii) and mentions 'another edition' in 1858.

[36d]   American edition, Boston, Donahoe, 1869 (1 vol., pp. [*4*] + viii + [9-480])

THE | BLACK BARONET; | OR, | [Gothic:] **The Chronicles of Ballytrain.** | BY WILLIAM CARLETON, | AUTHOR OF "WILLY REILLY," "VALENTINE M'CLUTCHY," "RODY THE ROVER," | "TALES AND STORIES OF THE IRISH PEASANTRY," ETC., ETC. | [engraving as [36c]] | " 'Doctor Sombre," said his lordship, "do NOT proceed with the ceremony until I shall | have spoken to Miss Gourlay's father. If it be necessary that I should speak more plainly, | I say I forbid the banns." | BOSTON: | PATRICK DONAHOE, 23 FRANKLIN STREET. | 1869.

Contents as [36c].

[36e]   Another edition, Dublin and London, Duffy, 1875 (1 vol., pp. viii + 9-480)

THE | BLACK BARONET; | OR, | THE CHRONICLES OF BALLYTRAIN. | BY WILLIAM CARLETON, | AUTHOR OF "WILLY REILLY," "VALENTINE M'CLUTCHY," "RODY THE ROVER, | "TALES AND STORIES OF THE IRISH PEASANTRY," ETC., ETC. | [engraving as [36c]] | " 'Doctor Sombre,' said his lordship, 'do NOT proceed with the ceremony until I shall | have spoken to Miss Gourlay's father. If it be necessary that I should speak more plainly, I | say I forbid the banns.' ' | DUBLIN: | JAMES DUFFY & SONS, 15, WELLINGTON-QUAY; | AND | 1A, PATERNOSTER-ROW, LONDON. | 1875.

Contents as [36c].

[36f]   American edition, New York and Montreal, Sadlier, n.d. [1875] (1 vol., pp. x + [11-490])

THE BLACK BARONET; | OR, | THE CHRONICLES OF BALLYTRAIN. | BY | WILLIAM CARLETON. | AUTHOR OF "JANE SINCLAIR," "VALENTINE M'CLUTCHY," "THE TITHE | PROCTOR," "THE BLACK PROPHET," "ART MAGUIRE," ETC., ETC. | [short decorative rule] | NEW YORK; | D. & J. SADLIER & Co., No. 31 BARCLAY ST. | MONTREAL: | 275 NOTRE DAME STREET.

Contents as [36c]. Verso of title page has 'Copyright 1886.'
This is a volume of Sadlier's 10-volume 'set' of Carleton's *Works*, 1875.

[36g]   American edition, New York and Montreal, Sadlier, n.d. (1 vol., pp. 5-580)

Title page as [36f].

Contains novel only. Like [36f], has 'Copyright 1886.' on verso of title page.

†[36h]   American edition, Boston and New York, Sadlier, Noonan, 1880.

The New York *Publishers' Weekly* lists *The Black Baronet: or, the Chronicles of Ballytrain* from Sadlier, New York, and Thomas B. Noonan, 23 & 25 Boylston Street, Boston, 1880, which I have not seen.

[36i]   Another edition, Dublin, Duffy, n.d. (1 vol., pp. [2] + viii + 476)

Title page as [36c] except no date.

Contents as [36c].

Routledge's *Traits and Stories of the Irish Peasantry*

In 1853/4, Routledge brought out 5 uniform but separate volumes of *Traits and Stories of the Irish Peasantry*, corresponding with the two original volumes of the *First Series* and the three of the *Second Series*. They were published separately from September 1853 to February 1854, so are classified as individual books. All cost 1s. 6d except [38a] which cost 2s. 0d. They were in board covers, but after February 1854 the five volumes could be bought together, bound in cloth, for 10s 0d.

[37a]   *Traits and Stories* – comprising 'Ned M'Keown', etc., London, Routledge, 1853 (1 vol., pp. [4] + viii + [340])

TRAITS AND STORIES | OF THE | IRISH PEASANTRY, | BY WILLIAM CARLETON. | COMPRISING | NED M'KEOWN. |

THE THREE TASKS. | SHANE FADH'S WEDDING. | LARRY
M'FARLAND'S WAKE. | BATTLE OF THE FACTIONS. |
[Gothic:] **With Two Illustrations by Phiz.** | LONDON: | GEORGE
ROUTLEDGE AND CO., | FARRINGDON STREET. | 1853.

Contains 'Publisher's Preface'; author's 'Preface'; 'Ned M'Keown';
'The Three Tasks'; 'Shane Fadh's Wedding'; 'Larry M'Farland's
Wake'; 'The Battle of the Factions'.

This is Vol. I of the *First Series*, Fourth Edition [2e], with a new title
page, publisher's preface, title plate and frontispiece. The signatures
and furniture are identical with [2e], including the uncounted,
unnumbered pages. The text concludes 'END OF VOL. I.' The
publisher's preface refers to recent critical 'encomiums'; they
introduce 'a New Edition of Carleton's "Traits and Stories" at a
popular price to the public at large'.

[37b]   'Fifth Edition', London, Routledge, 1856.

As [37a] but title page as [15f] except ' | GEORGE ROUTLEDGE
AND CO. | FARRINGDON STREET. | 1856.' for 'WILLIAM
TEGG. | 1864.'

[38a]   *Traits and Stories* – comprising 'The Party Fight and Funeral'
etc., London, Routledge, 1853 (1 vol., pp. [2] + 372)

TRAITS AND STORIES | OF THE | IRISH PEASANTRY. | BY |
WILLIAM CARLETON. | COMPRISING | THE PARTY
FIGHT AND FUNERAL. | THE HEDGE SCHOOL. | THE
STATION. | [Gothic:] **With Two Illustrations by Phiz.** | LONDON:
| GEORGE ROUTLEDGE AND CO., | FARRINGDON
STREET. | 1853.

Contains 'Publisher's Preface' as [37a]; 'The Party Fight and
Funeral'; 'The Hedge School'; 'The Station'.

This is Volume II of the *First Series*, Fourth edition [2e] with the
same publisher's preface as [37a] and a new title plate and frontispiece.

[39a]   *Traits and Stories* – comprising 'The Midnight Mass', etc.,
London, Routledge, 1853 (1 vol., pp. [xii] + 364)

TRAITS AND STORIES | OF THE | IRISH PEASANTRY. | BY | WILLIAM CARLETON. | COMPRISING | THE MIDNIGHT MASS. | THE DONAGH. | PHIL PURCEL, THE PIG-DRIVER. | THE GEOGRAPHY OF AN IRISH OATH. | AN ESSAY ON IRISH SWEARING. | [Gothic:] **With Two Illustrations by Phiz.** | LONDON: | GEORGE ROUTLEDGE AND CO., | FARRINGDON STREET. | 1853.

Contains 'Preface', and stories as title page.

[40a]   *Traits and Stories* – comprising 'The Lianhan Shee', etc., London, Routledge, 1854 (1 vol., pp. [2] + 376)

TRAITS AND STORIES | OF THE | IRISH PEASANTRY. | BY | WILLIAM CARLETON. | COMPRISING | THE LIANHAN SHEE. | THE POOR SCHOLAR. | WILDGOOSE LODGE. | TUBBER DERG, OR THE RED WELL. | [Gothic:] **With Two Illustrations by Phiz.** | LONDON: | GEORGE ROUTLEDGE AND CO., | FARRINGDON STREET. | 1854.

Contains stories as title page.

[41a]   *Traits and Stories* – comprising 'Denis O'Shaughnessy' etc., London, Routledge, 1854 (1 vol., pp. [2] + 342)

TRAITS AND STORIES | OF THE | IRISH PEASANTRY. | BY | WILLIAM CARLETON. | COMPRISING | DENIS O'SHAUGHNESSY GOING TO MAYNOOTH. | PHELIM O'TOOLE'S COURTSHIP. | [Gothic:] **With Two Illustrations by Phiz.** | LONDON: | GEORGE ROUTLEDGE AND CO., | FARRINGDON STREET. | 1854.

Contains stories as title page.

In 1854, D. & J. Sadlier brought out two Carleton collections in their Fireside Library series – No. VI, 'The Poor Scholar' etc., and No. VIII, 'Tubber Derg' etc. – with illustrated title plates and printed title pages [42a] and [43a]. In 1860 Sadlier combined the two as *Tales and Stories of the Irish Peasantry, Two Volumes in One* [46a]. The title pages of [42a] and [43a] are sometimes omitted, so I give the title plates as well.

The Poor Scholar and Other Tales of Irish Life

[42a]   American edition, New York, Boston, Montreal, Sadlier, 1854 (1 vol., pp. [2] + vii + [8-322]) (Fireside Library)

THE | POOR SCHOLAR, | AND | OTHER TALES OF IRISH LIFE. | BY | WILLIAM CARLETON, | AUTHOR OF "VALENTINE M'CLUTCHY," "ART MAGUIRE," | "TUBBER DERG," ETC. | [short decorative rule] | NEW YORK: | D. & J. SADLIER & CO., 164 WILLIAM STREET. | BOSTON: 128 FEDERAL STREET. | MONTREAL: COR. OF NOTRE DAME AND ST. FRANCIS XAVIER STS. | [short rule] | 1854.

Title plate:
THE | [Gothic:] **Poor Scholar.** | [Phiz illustration of scholar with stick and bag on road] | THE DEPARTURE. | NEW YORK: | D. & J. SADLIER & CO., 164 WILLIAM STREET. | BOSTON: 128 FEDERAL STREET. | MONTREAL: COR. OF NOTRE DAME AND ST. FRANCIS XAVIER STS. | [short rule] | 1854.

Contains publisher's 'Introduction'; 'The Poor Scholar'; 'A Peasant Girl's Love'; 'Talbot and Gaynor, the Irish Pipers'; 'Frank Finnegan, the Foster Brother'. Fireside Library No. VI. 'A Peasant Girl's Love' is by John Banim, not by Carleton.

[42b]   American edition, New York, Boston, Montreal, Sadlier, 1860 (1 vol., pp. [2] + vii+[8-322]) (Fireside Library)

[Within rule frame:] THE | POOR SCHOLAR, | AND | OTHER TALES OF IRISH LIFE. | BY | WILLIAM CARLETON, | AUTHOR OF "VALENTINE M'CLUTCHY," "ART MAGUIRE," | [short decorative rule] | NEW YORK: | D. & J. SADLIER & CO., 164 WILLIAM STREET. | BOSTON: 128 FEDERAL STREET. | MONTREAL: COR. OF NOTRE DAME AND ST. FRANCIS XAVIER STS. | [short rule] | 1860.

Title plate as [42a] except '1860.' for '1854.'

Contents as [42a].

[*The Poor Scholar, and Other Tales of Irish Life*, Sadlier 1860, 1880 and n.d., is not the same collection, but a combination of the two

'Fireside Library' collections. [42a] and [43a]. The combination was first entitled *Tales and Stories of the Irish Peasantry*, then *The Poor Scholar and Other Tales of Irish Life*. See below, [46a-f].]

Tubber Derg; or, the Red Well, and other Tales of Irish Life

[43a]   American edition, New York, Boston and Montreal, Sadlier, 1854 (1 vol., pp. viii + 9-322) (Fireside Library)

TUBBER DERG; | OR, | THE RED WELL, | AND | OTHER TALES OF IRISH LIFE. | BY | WILLIAM CARLETON, | AUTHOR OF "VALENTINE M'CLUTCHY," "ART MAGUIRE," | "THE POOR SCHOLAR", ETC. | [short decorative rule] | NEW YORK: | D. & J. SADLIER & CO., 164 WILLIAM STREET. | BOSTON: 128 FEDERAL STREET. | MONTREAL: COR. OF NOTRE DAME AND ST. FRANCIS XAVIER STS. | [short rule] | 1854.

Title plate:
TUBBER DERG; | OR, | THE RED WELL. | [engraving of man seated on bench, surrounded by family] | "HE HAD RAISED HIS EYES TO HEAVEN." | NEW YORK: | D. & J. SADLIER & CO., 164 WILLIAM STREET. | BOSTON: 128 FEDERAL STREET. | MONTREAL: COR. OF NOTRE DAME AND ST. FRANCIS XAVIER STS. | [short rule] | 1854.

Contains publisher's 'Introduction' as [42a]; 'Tubber Derg; or, the Red Well'; 'Barney Brady's Goose; or, Dark Doings at Slathbeg'; 'Tom Gressiey, the Irish Senachie'; 'The Castle of Aughentain; or, a Legend of the Brown Goat'; 'The White Horse of the Peppers'; 'Mickey M'Rorey, the Irish Fiddler'. Fireside Library No. VIII. 'The White Horse of the Peppers' is not by Carleton but by Samuel Lover.

[43b]   American edition. New York, Boston, Montreal, Sadlier, 1860 (1 vol., pp. [viii] + [9-322]) (Fireside Library)

TUBBER DERG; | OR, | THE RED WELL, | AND | OTHER TALES OF IRISH LIFE. | BY | WILLIAM CARLETON, | AUTHOR OF "VALENTINE M'CLUTCHY," "ART MAGUIRE," | "THE POOR SCHOLAR," ETC. | [short decorative rule] | NEW YORK: | D. & J. SADLIER & CO., 164 WILLIAM STREET. | BOSTON: 128 FEDERAL STREET. | MONTREAL: COR. OF NOTRE DAME AND ST. FRANCIS XAVIER STS. | [short rule] | 1860.

Title plate as [43a] except '1860.' for '1854.'

Contents as [43a]. This collection forms the second part of Sadlier's *Tales and Stories of the Irish Peasantry*, 1860 and n.d. ([46a-b] below) and their *Poor Scholar and Other Tales of Irish Life*, 1880 and n.d. ([44e] and [44f] below.)

†[43c]   American edition, New York, Worthington, 1875

Another American edition of *Tubber Derg* was published in 1875 by R. Worthington & Co, 750 Broadway, New York, according to the *Trade List Annual* for 1875, but I have not been able to trace it.

Willy Reilly and his Dear Coleen Bawn

An odd feature of the publishing history of *Willy Reilly* is the enormous number of late American editions of the novel. Of the following thirty editions, only three were published in the British Isles, and only three are dated before 1875, twenty years after its first publication. In that year, Robert De Witt, the New York publisher, announces a new edition in terms that explain its popularity and also make me fear that I must have missed many intervening editions: 'Unquestionably the best Irish story ever written. It had an enormous sale when first published, and sells even better now. Probably because, among its other merits, it is entirely free from sectarianism.' (*Publishers' Trade-List Annual*, 1875).

In identifying editions of the novel, the variations in the title are worth noticing: the *Coleen, Cooleen* or *Colleen* may be *dear, fair* or merely *bawn*. There may be one, two or no quotations on the title page; 'aught' and 'ought', 'Shakspeare' and 'Shakespeare' appear, and the punctuation varies.

[44a]   First edition, London, Hope, 1855 (3 vols., pp. xvi + 300; [iv] + 296; [iv] + 284)

WILLY REILLY | AND | HIS DEAR COLEEN BAWN: | A TALE, FOUNDED UPON FACT. | BY | WILLIAM CARLETON,

| AUTHOR OF "THE BLACK PROPHET;" "THE MISER;" "REDHALL, OR THE | BARONET'S DAUGHTER;" "TRAITS AND STORIES OF THE IRISH | PEASANTRY;" "VALENTINE M'CLUTCHY;" ETC. | IN THREE VOLUMES. | VOL. [I.] | " 'Oh, rise up, Willy Reilly, and come alongst with me! | I mean for to go with you, and leave this counterie; | To leave my father's dwelling, his houses and free lands;' — | And away goes Willy Reilly and his dear Coleen Bawn." | BALLAD OF "WILLY REILLY." | "Ah me! for aught that ever I could read, | Could ever hear by tale or history, | The course of true love never did run smooth." | SHAKSPEARE. | LONDON: | HOPE AND CO., 16, GREAT MARLBOROUGH-STREET. | 1855.

Contains author's 'Preface'; novel.
Sadleir No. [522], Brown No. 334, O'Donoghue p. lxii.

[44b]   American edition, Boston, Moore, 1856 (1 vol., pp. [iv] + [508])

WILLY REILLY | AND | HIS DEAR COLEEN BAWN: | A TALE, FOUNDED UPON FACT. | BY | WILLIAM CARLETON, | AUTHOR OF "THE BLACK PROPHET;" "THE MISER;" "REDHALL, OR THE | BARONET'S DAUGHTER;" "TRAITS AND STORIES OF THE IRISH | PEASANTRY;" "VALENTINE M'CLUTCHY;" ETC. | "Ah me! for aught that ever I could read, | Could ever hear by tale or history, | The course of true love never did run smooth." | SHAKSPEARE. | [short rule] | BOSTON: | A. MOORE & BROS., 2 CITY HALL AVENUE. | 1856:

Contents as [44a].

[44c]   'Second edition', Dublin, Duffy, 1857 (1 vol., pp. [5] 6-454)

WILLY REILLY, | AND | HIS DEAR COOLEEN BAWN. | [Gothic:] **A Tale Founded upon Fact.** | BY WILLIAM CARLETON, | AUTHOR OF "THE POOR SCHOLAR," "PADDY GO EASY," "VALENTINE | M'CLUTCHY," "RODY THE ROVER," ETC., ETC., ETC. | " 'Oh, rise up, Willy Reilly, and come alongst with me! | I mean for to go with you, and leave this counterie; | To leave my father's dwelling, his houses, and free

lands;' — | And away goes Willy Reilly and his fair Cooleen Bawn!"
— BALLAD. | "Ah me! for aught that ever I could read, | Could ever
hear by tale or history, | The course of true love never did run
smooth." — SHAKSPEARE. | [Gothic:] **Second Edition.** | [engraving of
men loading cart, house on fire] | DUBLIN: | JAMES DUFFY, 7,
WELLINGTON-QUAY. | 1857.

Contains new author's 'Preface'; novel.
Sadleir No. [522a]. O'Donoghue p. lxii gives WILLY REILLY
AND HIS DEAR COL[L]EEN BAWN (2nd revised edition, 1
vol., Dublin and Enniskillen), and mentions 'Another edition 1 vol.
Dublin 8vo, 1857.

[44d] Author's copyright edition, London, Routledge, n.d. (1
vol., pp. xiv + 422)

WILLY REILLY, | AND | HIS DEAR COOLEEN BAWN. |
[Gothic:] **A Tale founded upon fact.** | BY | WILLIAM CARLETON.
| [short rule] | *AUTHOR'S COPYRIGHT EDITION.* | [short rule]
| [Gothic:] **London:** | GEORGE ROUTLEDGE & SONS, LTD., |
BROADWAY, LUDGATE HILL.

Contains 'Preface', novel.
Sadleir No. [3465].

[44e] American edition, New York and Montreal, Sadlier, n.d.
[1875] (1 vol., pp. [488])

WILLY REILLY, | AND | HIS DEAR COLEEN BAWN. | *A
TALE, FOUNDED UPON FACT.* | BY | WILLIAM CARLETON,
| AUTHOR OF "THE BLACK PROPHET," "THE MISER,"
"REDHALL, OR THE BARONET'S | DAUGHTER," "TRAITS
AND STORIES OF THE IRISH PEASANTRY," | "VALENTINE
M'CLUTCHY," ETC. | [verses as [44a] except 'SHAKESPEARE.'] |
NEW YORK: | D. & J. SADLIER & CO., 31 BARCLAY
STREET. | MONTREAL: – COR. NOTRE DAME AND ST.
FRANCIS XAVIER STS. | [short rule]

Contains 'Preface', novel.
This is one of Sadlier's set of 10 volumes of Carleton's *Works*, 1875.

†[44f]   American edition, New York, De Witt, 1875

The *Publishers' Trade-List Annual* lists a paperback edition of *Willy Reilly and his Dear Coleen Bawn* in 1875 from Robert M. De Witt, 33 Rose Street, New York. I have not seen it.

[44g]   American edition, New York, Routledge, n.d. [1879] (1 vol., pp. [vi] + [422])

WILLY REILLY | AND HIS DEAR COOLEEN BAWN. | BY | WILLIAM CARLETON. | "Oh, rise up, Willy Reilly, and come alongst with me, | I mean for to go with you, and leave this counterie, | To leave my father's dwelling, his houses and free lands: — | And away goes Willy Reilly and his fair Cooleen Bawn." – BALLAD. | "Ah me! for aught that ever I could read, | Could ever hear in tale or history, | The course of true love never did run smooth." — SHAKSPEARE. | WITH EIGHT ILLUSTRATIONS | BY T. C. HEATH AND THOMAS GOODMAN. | [short rule] | NEW YORK | GEORGE ROUTLEDGE AND SONS | 9 LAFAYETTE PLACE

Contains Prefaces to first and second editions.
Listed in *American Catalogue* for 1879.

[44h]   American edition, Boston and New York, Noonan, Sadlier n.d. [1880] (1 vol., pp. [488])

Title page as [44e] except publishers' names and addresses: 'BOSTON: | THOMAS B. NOONAN & CO., | 23 & 25 BOYLSTON STREET. | NEW YORK: | D. & J. SADLIER & CO, | 31 BARCLAY STREET.'

Contains 'Preface', novel.
Listed in *American Catalogue* for 1880.

†[44i]   American edition, New York, Kenedy, 1880

The *American Catalogue* for 1880 also lists an illustrated paperback *Willy Reilly and his dear Coleen Bawn* from P. J. Kenedy, 5 Barclay Street, New York. I have not seen it.

[44j]   American edition, New York, George Munro (1 issue of the Seaside Library, Vol. XXVI No. 731) 1880

[Ornamental masthead:] THE | SEASIDE LIBRARY | Willy Reilly and His Dear Coleen Bawn. | By WILLIAM CARLETON. | This Number contains a Complete Story, Unchanged and Unabridged. | Vol. XXXVI. DOUBLE NUMBER. GEORGE MUNRO, PUBLISHER, NOS. 17 to 27 VANDEWATER STREET, NEW YORK. PRICE 20 CENTS. NO. 731 | Copyrighted 1880, by GEORGE MUNRO. — Entered at the Post Office at New York at Second Class Rates. — April 27, 1880. | [beneath this masthead:] WILLY REILLY | AND HIS | DEAR COLEEN BAWN. | *A TALE FOUNDED UPON FACT.* | By WILLIAM CARLETON. | [short rule] | The Works of the Following Eminent Writers | ARE CONTAINED IN THE SEASIDE LIBRARY: | [list of 80 American and European authors] | [short rule] | NEW YORK: | GEORGE MUNRO, PUBLISHER. | 17 TO 27 VANDEWATER STREET.

Contains *Willy Reilly* and 2 pages of advertisements for Munro's publications.

[44k]   American edition, New York, Lovell, 1880 (1 vol., pp. 394)

WILLY REILLY | AND | HIS DEAR COOLEEN BAWN. | BY | WILLIAM CARLETON. | "Oh, rise up, Willy Reilly, and come alongst with me, | I mean for to go with you, and leave this counterie, | To leave my father's dwelling, his houses and free lands: — | And away goes Willy Reilly and his fair Cooleen Bawn." – BALLAD. | "Ah me! for aught that ever I could read, | Could ever hear in tale or history, | The course of true love never did run smooth." – SHAKSPEARE. | [short rule] | *ILLUSTRATED* | [short rule] | [short decorative rule] | NEW YORK: | JOHN WURTELE LOVELL, PUBLISHER, | 14 & 16 ASTOR PLACE. | 1880.

Contains 'Prefaces'; novel.

[44l]   American edition, Chicago and St. Louis, Belford, Clarke, 1881 (1 vol., pp. 394)

WILLY REILLY | AND | HIS DEAR COOLEEN BAWN. | BY | WILLIAM CARLETON. | "Oh, rise up, Willy Reilly, and come alongst with me, | I mean for to go with you, and leave this counterie, | To leave my father's dwelling, his houses and free lands:

— | And away goes Willy Reilly and his fair Cooleen Bawn." — BALLAD. | "Ah me! for aught that ever I could read, | Could ever hear in tale or history, | The course of true love never did run smooth." — SHAKSPEARE. | [short rule] | *ILLUSTRATED.* | [short rule] | [short decorative rule] | CHICAGO AND ST. LOUIS: | BELFORD, CLARKE & CO. | 1881.

Contains 'Preface to the first edition'; 'Preface to the second edition'; novel.

[44m]   American edition, New York, Lovell, n.d. [1883] (1 vol,. pp. 394)

WILLY REILLY | AND | HIS DEAR COLLEEN BAWN | BY | WILLIAM CARLETON | [short rule] | "Oh, rise up, Willy Reilly, and come alongst with me, | I mean for to go with you, and leave this counterie, | To leave my father's dwelling, his houses and free lands: — | And away goes Willy Reilly and his fair Colleen Bawn." – BALLAD | "Ah me! for aught that ever I could read, | Could ever hear in tale or history, | The course of true love never did run smooth." – SHAKSPEARE | [short rule] | NEW YORK | JOHN W. LOVELL COMPANY | 150 WORTH STREET, CORNER MISSION PLACE

Contains 'Prefaces', novel.
Listed in the *American Catalogue* for 1883.

[44n]   American edition, Chicago and New York, Belford, Clarke, 1885 (1 vol., pp. 394)

Title page as [44l] except publisher's address and date: 'CHICAGO AND NEW YORK: | BELFORD, CLARKE & CO | 1885.'

Contains 'Prefaces', novel.

[44o]   American edition, New York, Mercantile Publishing Co., 1888 (1 vol., pp. 394)

WILLY REILLY | AND | HIS DEAR COOLEEN | BAWN. | BY | WILLIAM CARLETON. | "Oh, rise up, Willy Reilly, and come alongst with me, | I mean for to go with you, and leave this counterie, | To leave my father's dwelling, his houses and free lands: — | And away goes Willy Reilly and his fair Cooleen Bawn." — BALLAD. | "Ah me! for aught that ever I could read, | Could ever hear in tale or history, | The course of true love never did run smooth." — SHAKSPEARE. | [short decorative rule] | MERCANTILE PUBLISHING CO. | 1888.

Contains 'Prefaces', novel.

[44p]   American edition, New York, Allison, 1889 (1 vol., pp. [2] + [458]) (Allison's Standard Library)

WILLY REILLY, | AND | HIS DEAR COLEEN BAWN. | *A TALE, FOUNDED UPON FACT.* | BY | WILLIAM CARLETON, | AUTHOR OF "THE BLACK PROPHET," "THE MISER," "REDHALL, OR THE BARONET'S | DAUGHTER," "TRAITS AND STORIES OF THE IRISH PEASANTRY," | "VALENTINE M'CLUTCHY," ETC. | " 'O, rise up, Willy Reilly, and come alongst with me; | I mean for to go with you, and leave this counterie; | To leave my father's dwelling, his houses and free lands'; — | And away goes Willy Reilly and his dear Coleen Bawn." | BALLAD OF "WILLY REILLY." | "Ah me! for ought that ever I could read, | Could ever hear by tale or history, | The course of true love never did run smooth." | SHAKESPEARE. | NEW YORK: | WM. L. ALLISON, | 93, CHAMBERS ST. | [short rule] | 1889.

†[44q]   American edition, New York, Worthington, Banner Library, 1889.

The *American Catalogue* for 1889 lists a paperback edition of *Willy Reilly and his Dear Colleen Bawn*, Banner Library No. 5, from P. W. Worthington Co., 747 Broadway, New York, which I have not seen.

[44r]   American edition, New York, New York Publishing Co., 1895 (1 vol., pp. 394)

WILLY REILLY | AND | HIS DEAR COOLEEN BAWN. | BY | WILLIAM CARLETON. | "Oh, rise up, Willy Reilly, and come alongst with me, | I mean for to go with you, and leave this counterie, | To leave my father's dwelling, his houses and free lands: — | And away goes Willy Reilly and his fair Cooleen Bawn." – BALLAD. | "Ah me! for aught that ever I could read, | Could ever hear in tale or history, | The course of true love never did run smooth." – SHAKSPEARE | [short decorative rule] | NEW YORK | NEW YORK PUBLISHING COMPANY, | 26 CITY HALL PLACE, | 1895.

Contains 'Prefaces', novel.

†[44s]   American edition, New York, Routledge, n.d. [1896]

A paperback edition of *Willy Reilly and his Dear Coleen Bawn* is listed in the *American Catalogue* for 1896, from George Routledge & Sons Ltd., 119-121 West 23rd Street, New York. I have not seen it; it is likely to be a new issue of either their 'Author's copyright edition' [44d] or their 'Illustrated edition' [44g].

[44t]   American edition, New York, Boston, Caldwell, n.d. [1898] (1 vol., pp. 394). (Berkeley Library)

[Between stylised poppy plants left and right:] *Berkeley Library* | [short rule] | Willy Reilly | [fleuron] | WILLIAM CARLETON | ['sapere aude' device] | H. M. CALDWELL CO. | PUBLISHERS | NEW YORK – BOSTON

Contains two 'Prefaces', novel.
Frontispiece 'William Carleton' is *not* a portrait of William Carleton.
Listed in *American Catalogue* for 1898.

[44u]   American edition, New York, Burt, n.d. [1904] (1 vol., pp. [*2*] + 408) (Burt's Home Library)

WILLY REILLY | [double rule] | AND HIS DEAR COLLEEN BAWN | [rule] | By WILLIAM CARLETON | [Burt's Library of the World's Best Books device] | "Oh, rise up, Willy Reilly, and come alongst with me, | I mean for to go with you, and leave this counterie, | To leave my father's dwelling, his houses and free lands: — | And away goes Willy Reilly and his fair Colleen Bawn." — | BALLAD. | [double rule] | A. L. BURT COMPANY, [4 fleurons] | [3 fleurons] | PUBLISHERS, NEW YORK

Contains novel.
Listed in *American Catalogue* 1904.

[44v]   American edition, New York, Burt, n.d. (1 vol., pp. [4] + 408)

WILLY REILLY | AND | HIS DEAR COLLEEN BAWN | By WILLIAM CARLETON | A. L. BURT COMPANY, PUBLISHERS | NEW YORK

Contains novel.

[44w]   American edition, 'Seventh Thousand', Boston, Donahoe, n.d. (1 vol., pp. [508])

Title page as [44a] except, for publisher's name, address and date: 'SEVENTH THOUSAND. | BOSTON: | PATRICK DONAHOE, 23 FRANKLIN STREET.'

Contains 'Prefaces', novel.

[44x]   American edition, New York, Sheehy, Sadlier, n.d. (1 vol., pp. [488])

Title page as [44e] except publishers' names and addresses: 'NEW YORK: | JAMES SHEEHY, | 33 BARCLAY STREET. | D. & J. SADLIER & CO, | 31 BARCLAY STREET.'

[44y]   American edition, Chicago, Belford, Clarke, n.d. (1 vol., pp. 394)

Title page as [44l] except publisher's address, no date: 'CHICAGO: | BELFORD, CLARKE & CO., | 192 & 194 STATE STREET.'

Contents as [44l].

[44z]   American edition, Philadelphia, Potter, n.d. (1 vol., pp. 394)

Title page as [44l] except publisher's address, no date: 'PHILADELPHIA: JOHN E. POTTER AND COMPANY, | 6, 7 SANSOM STREET.'

Contents as [44l].

[44aa]   American edition, New York, American News Company, n.d. (1 vol., pp. 394)

Title page as [44o] except publisher's name, no date: 'NEW YORK: | THE AMERICAN NEWS COMPANY, | 39 AND 41 CHAMBERS STREET.'

Contents as [44o].

[44bb]   American edition, New York, Crowell, n.d. (1 vol., pp. [15-394])

Title page as [44o] except publisher's name, no date: 'NEW YORK | THOMAS Y. CROWELL & CO | No. 13 Astor Place'

Contains novel, no prefaces.

[44cc]   American edition, New York, Fenno, n.d. (1 vol., pp. [15-394])

Title page as [44m] except publisher's name and address: 'New York | R. F. FENNO & COMPANY | 9 & 11 East 16th Street'

Contains novel, no prefaces.

[44dd]   American edition, New York, International Book Co (1 vol., pp. [15-394]), Columbus Series.

Title page as [44m] except publisher's name and address: 'NEW YORK | INTERNATIONAL BOOK COMPANY | 5 and 7 East Sixteenth Street'

Contains novel, no prefaces.

[44ee]   American edition, New York, Lovell, n.d. (1 vol., pp. 394).

Title page as [44k] except publisher's lines: 'JOHN WURTELE LOVELL, | No. 24 Bond Street.'

D. J. O'Donoghue mentions a Fortieth Edition, Dublin, 1878 (p. lxiii) and S. J. Brown mentions a 1908 edition [No. 334].

[44ff]   *Willie Reilly*, Dublin, Dawson, n.d. [ca 1950]

Title page missing in only copy I have seen. The edition is advertised in *The Poor Scholar*, Dawson, n.d. [about 1950] as '*Willie Reilly* in an edition uniform with this'.

Alley Sheridan and Other Stories

[45a]   First edition, Dublin, Dixon Hardy, 1857 (1 vol., pp. [vi] +
[7-260].)

ALLEY SHERIDAN, | AND | OTHER STORIES, | BY |
WILLIAM CARLETON, Esq., | AUTHOR OF "WILLY
REILLY," "TRAITS AND STORIES | OF THE IRISH
PEASANTRY," &C., &C. | [short rule] | DUBLIN: | P. DIXON
HARDY AND SONS, | 23, UPPER SACKVILLE-STREET. | 1857.

Contains 'Publisher's Preface'; 'Alley Sheridan, or the Irish Runaway
Marriage'; 'Laying a Ghost'; 'Owen M'Carthy, or the Landlord and
Tenant'; 'Condy Cullen and the Gauger'; 'The Donagh, or the
Horse-stealers'; 'Sir Turlough, or the Church-yard Bride'.
Sadleir No. [491]; Brown No. 335A; O'Donoghue p. lxii.

[Title plate:] [ornamental caps set in curve:] ALLEY SHERIDAN
| AND | [Gothic:] **Other Stories,** | [engraving of man, young woman,
old woman with broom] | The resolute old dame came across his
shins with an activity and a degree | of science really surprising. Page
43. | [short rule] | [Gothic:] **Dublin: P. Dixon Hardy & Sons.**

[45b]   Another edition, Dublin, Dixon Hardy, n.d. (1 vol., pp. [*4*]
+ [vi] + [7-260])

ALLEY SHERIDAN, | AND | OTHER STORIES, | BY |
WILLIAM CARLETON, Esq., | AUTHOR OF "WILLY
REILLY," "TRAITS AND STORIES | OF THE IRISH
PEASANTRY," &c., &C. | [short wavy rule] | DUBLIN: | P.
DIXON HARDY AND SONS, | 23, UPPER SACKVILLE-
STREET. | SOLD BY ALL BOOKSELLERS.

Contents and title plate as [45a].

In 1860, D. & J. Sadlier combined their two Carleton 'Fireside
Library' collections, *The Poor Scholar and Other Tales of Irish Life*
[42a-b] and *Tubber Derg or the Red Well and Other Tales of Irish
Life* [43a-b]. At first the new collection was entitled *Tales and
Stories of the Irish Peasantry* (not to be confused with a different
collection from Duffy, 1845, with the same title [18a]). The collection
went into at least three editions in 16° with this title – 1860, 1864,
and n.d. [46a-c]. Sadlier then published the collection in 12° with the
same title, undated [46d]. This 12° edition was republished in 1875
(no date on title page) as one of the ten volumes of Sadlier's *Works*

of William Carleton, this time under the title of one of its parts – *The Poor Scholar and Other Tales of Irish Life* [46e] and this was reissued in 1880 [46f].

In addition to the possible confusion caused by the change of title, Sadlier used the title plates, contents pages and sometimes the title pages of the two parts, *The Poor Scholar etc* and *Tubber Derg etc* as well as the general title page and contents page of the double collection. The two parts are separately paginated, and sometimes one part is placed first, sometimes the other. The title plate of whichever part is placed first is generally used.

Tales and Stories of the Irish Peasantry/The Poor Scholar and Other Tales of Irish Life

[46a]   American edition, as *Tales and Stories of the Irish Peasantry, Two Volumes in One*, New York, Boston, Montreal, Sadlier, 1860 (1 vol., pp. vi + [7-324] + [viii] + [9-322]

[Within rule frame:] TALES AND STORIES │ OF THE │ IRISH PEASANTRY. │ BY │ WILLIAM CARLTON, [sic] │ AUTHOR OF "VALENTINE McCLUTCHY," "ART. MAGUIRE," │ ETC., ETC. │ *TWO VOLUMES IN ONE.* │ [Gothic:] **New York:** │ D. & J SADLIER & CO., 164 WILLIAM ST. │ BOSTON: – 128 FEDERAL STREET. │ MONTREAL: – COR. OF NOTRE DAME & FRANCIS XAVIER STS. │ 1860.

Title plate: the title plate of *Tubber Derg* etc., Sadlier 1854 [43a].

Contains: 'Introduction' (to 'Tubber Derg' etc.); 'Tubber Derg; or, the Red Well'; 'Barney Brady's Goose'; 'Tom Gressiey, the Irish Senachie'; 'A Legend of the Brown Goat'; 'The White Horse of the Peppers'; 'Mickey M'Rory, the Irish Fiddler'; 'Introduction' (to 'The Poor Scholar' etc.); 'The Poor Scholar'; 'A Peasant Girl's Love'; 'Talbot and Gaynor, the Irish Pipers'; 'Frank Finnegan, the Foster Brother'. The contents of 'Vol. I' and 'Vol. II' are displayed on the same page: 'Gressiey' is misspelt 'Gressley', 'M'Rorey' misspelt 'McRory', and 'Finnegan' misspelt 'Finegan'. 'Carleton' is misspelt 'Carlton' on the title page. 'The White Horse of the Peppers' is by Samuel Lover; 'A Peasant Girl's Love' is by John Banim.

[46b]   American edition, New York, Boston, Montreal, Sadlier, 1864 (1 vol., pp. vi + [7-324] + [viii] + [9-322])

TALES AND STORIES | OF THE | IRISH PEASANTRY. | BY | WILLIAM CARLTON, | AUTHOR OF "VALENTINE McCLUTCHY," "ART. MAGUIRE," | ETC., ETC. | *TWO VOLUMES IN ONE.* | [Gothic:] **New York:** | D. & J. SADLIER & Co., 31 BARCLAY ST. | BOSTON: – 128 FEDERAL STREET. | MONTREAL: – COR. OF NOTRE DAME & FRANCIS XAVIER STS. | 1864.

Title plate as [46a] except '1864.' for '1860.'

Contents as [46a].

[46c]   American edition, New York and Montreal, Sadlier, n.d. [1878] (1 vol., pp. vi + [7-324] + [viii] + [9-322] *or* [viii] + [9-322] + vi + [7-324])

Title page as [46b] except publisher's address, no date: 'NEW YORK: | PUBLISHED BY D. & J. SADLIER & CO., | 31 BARCLAY STREET, | MONTREAL:– COR. NOTRE DAME AND ST. FRANCIS XAVIER STS.'

Title plate as [46b] except publisher's address, no date: 'NEW YORK: | D. & J. SADLIER & CO. 31 BARCLAY STREET. | MONTREAL: COR. OF NOTRE DAME AND ST. FRANCIS XAVIER STR'

Contents as [46b] except preliminaries to each part rearranged to include separate 'Fireside Library' contents pages as well as joint contents page. I have seen examples with *The Poor Scholar* collection placed first, and others with *Tubber Derg* etc. placed first.

This was published as part of the *Household Library* series in 1878.

[46d]   American edition, New York, Boston, Montreal, Sadlier, n.d. [1 vol., pp. viii + [9-322] + vi + [7-324])

Title page as [46a] except publisher's address, no date: 'NEW YORK: | D. & J. SADLIER & CO., 31 BARCLAY STREET. | BOSTON:– 128 FEDERAL STREET. | MONTREAL. C. E. :– COR. OF NOTRE DAME & ST. FRANCIS XAVIER STS.

Title plate as [46a] except no date.

Contents as [46a] except *Poor Scholar* collection precedes *Tubber Derg* collection.

[46e]   American edition, New York, Sadlier, n.d. (1 vol., pp. vi + [7-198] + vi + [7-140])

TALES AND STORIES | OF THE | IRISH PEASANTRY. | BY | WILLIAM CARLETON, | Author of "Valentine McClutchy," "The Poor Scholar," "Redmond Count | O'Hanlon, the Irish Rapparee," "The Tithe Proctor," "Art Maguire," | "Willy Reilly," "Fardorougha, the Miser," "The Black Pro- | phet," "The Black Baronet," "Jane Sinclair," "The | Emigrants of Ahadarra," "The Evil Eye," &c. | [short rule] | NEW YORK: | D. & J. SADLIER & CO. | 33 BARCLAY STREET AND 38 PARK PLACE.

Contents as [46b] and although completely reset, still separately paginated and with separate title pages for each part.

[46f]   As *The Poor Scholar, and other Tales of Irish Life*, American edition, New York, Sadlier, n.d. [1875] (1 vol., pp. vi + [7-198] + vi + [7-140])

THE | POOR SCHOLAR, | AND | *Other Tales of Irish Life.* | BY | WILLIAM CARLETON, | Author of "Valentine McClutchy," "Tales and Stories of the Irish Peasantry" | "The Tithe Proctor," "Art Maguire," "Willy Reilly," "Fardo- | rougha, the Miser," "The Black Prophet," "The Black | Baronet," "Jane Sinclair," "The Emi- | grants of Ahadarra," "The | Evil Eye," &c. | [short rule] | NEW YORK: | D. & J. SADLIER & CO. | 33 BARCLAY STREET AND 38 PARK PLACE |

Contains the *Poor Scholar* and *Tubber Derg* collections, separately paginated and with their own introductions and title pages.
One of the ten volumes of Sadlier's *Works* of William Carleton, 1875.

[46g]   American edition, New York and Montreal, Sadlier, 1880 (1 vol., pp. vi + [7-198] + + vi + [7-140])

Title page as [46f] except publisher's name, address and date: 'NEW

YORK: | D. & J. SADLIER & CO., 31 BARCLAY STREET. |
MONTREAL: | No. 275 NOTRE-DAME STREET. | [short rule] | 1880.

Contents as [46e]. This 1880 title page has on its verso 'Copyright
1886.'

The Evil Eye, or the Black Spectre

This is *not* the same story as *The Evil Eye* contributed by Carleton
to *The Irish Tribune* in 1848; they have nothing in common apart
from one character's name.

[47a] First edition, Dublin, Duffy, 1860 (1 vol., pp. viii + 518)

THE EVIL EYE; | OR, | THE BLACK SPECTRE. | A
ROMANCE. | BY WILLIAM CARLETON, | AUTHOR OF
"TRAITS AND STORIES OF THE IRISH PEASANTRY;"
"VALENTINE M'CLUTCHY," | "WILLY REILLY;" "THE
BLACK BARONET;" "RODY THE ROVER;" | "PADDY GO
EASY;" "THE BROKEN PLEDGE;" &C. | [Gothic:] **Illustrated
with Thirteen Engravings on Wood,** | FROM DRAWINGS | BY
EDMUND FITZPATRICK, ESQ. | DUBLIN: | JAMES DUFFY
7, WELLINGTON-QUAY. | MDCCCLX.

This edition also has an engraved title plate, Dublin and London:

THE EVIL EYE; | OR, | THE BLACK SPECTRE. | [Gothic:] **A
Romance.** | BY WILLIAM CARLETON. | [in line circle, cloaked
man facing shadowy figure holding dagger] | DUBLIN: | JAMES
DUFFY, 7, WELLINGTON QUAY, | AND | LONDON: 22,
PATERNOSTER ROW. | 1860.

Contains 'Dedication to Edward and Anthony Fox'; 'Preface'; novel.
Sadleir No. [500]; Brown No. 336; O'Donoghue p. lxii.

[47b] Another edition, Dublin and London, Duffy, 1864 (1 vol.,
pp. viii + 518)

Title page as [47a] except date '1864'.

Contents as [47a].

[47c]   Another edition, Dublin and London, Duffy, 1869 (1 vol., pp. viii + 518)

[Title plate of [47a] adapted as title page:] THE EVIL EYE; | OR, | THE BLACK SPECTRE. | [within line circle, man facing shadow] | DUBLIN: | JAMES DUFFY, 15 WELLINGTON QUAY, | AND | LONDON: 22 PATERNOSTER ROW | 1869.

[47d]   American edition, New York and Montreal, Sadlier, 1875 (1 vol., pp. viii + 518)

THE EVIL EYE; | OR, | THE BLACK SPECTRE. | A ROMANCE. | BY WILLIAM CARLETON, | AUTHOR OF "TRAITS AND STORIES OF THE IRISH PEASANTRY," "VALENTINE | M'CLUTCHY," "WILLY REILLY," "THE BLACK BARONET," "RODY | THE ROVER," "PADDY GO EASY," THE BROKEN PLEDGE," &C. | [short decorative rule] | NEW YORK: | D. & J. SADLIER & Co., No. 31 BARCLAY ST. | MONTREAL: | COR. NOTRE DAME AND ST. FRANCIS XAVIER STS. | [short rule] | 1875.

Contents as [45a].

[47e]   American edition, New York and Montreal, Sadlier, n.d. [1875] (1 vol., pp. [2] + x + [11-490])

THE EVIL EYE; | OR, | THE BLACK SPECTRE. | A ROMANCE. | BY WILLIAM CARLETON, | AUTHOR OF "TALES AND STORIES OF THE IRISH PEASANTRY," "VALENTINE | M'CLUTCHY," "WILLY REILLY," "THE BLACK BARONET," "JANE, [sic] | SINCLAIR," "THE TITHE PROCTOR," "THE BROKEN PLEDGE, &c. | [short decorative rule] | NEW YORK: | D. & J. SADLIER & Co., No. 31 BARCLAY ST | MONTREAL: | COR. NOTRE DAME AND ST. FRANCIS XAVIER STS.

Contents as [47a].
This is another 1875 edition, one of the ten uniform volumes of Sadlier's *Works* of Carleton.

[47f]   Another edition, Dublin and London, Duffy, 1880 (1 vol., pp. [viii] + 330)

THE EVIL EYE; | OR, | THE BLACK SPECTRE. | BY WILLIAM CARLETON. | [in rule circle, cloaked man facing shadow as title plate of [47a] | [Gothic:] **Dublin:** | JAMES DUFFY AND SONS, 15 WELLINGTON QUAY, | AND | LONDON: 1A PATERNOSTER ROW. | 1880.

Contains 'Preface'; novel.

†[47g]   American edition, Boston, Noonan, 1880

The *American Catalogue* lists *The Evil Eye; or, the Black Spectre* published in 1880 by Thomas B. Noonan, 23 and 25 Boylston Street, Boston – I have not seen this.

[47h]   American edition, New York, Kenedy, 1896 (1 vol., pp. viii + 518 + [519-528] advertisements)

THE EVIL EYE; | OR, | THE BLACK SPECTRE. | A ROMANCE. | BY WILLIAM CARLETON, | AUTHOR OF "TALES AND STORIES OF THE IRISH PEASANTRY," "VALENTINE | M'CLUTCHY," "WILLY REILLY," "THE BLACK BARONET," "JANE, [sic] | SINCLAIR," "THE TITHE PROCTOR," "THE BROKEN PLEDGE," &c. | [short decorative rule] | NEW YORK: P.J. KENEDY, | EXCELSIOR PUBLISHING HOUSE, | 5 BARCLAY STREET. | 1896.

Contains 'Preface', novel. Verso of title page has 'Copyright, D. & J. Sadlier & Co., 1885.'

The Double Prophecy, or, Trials of the Heart

[48a]   First edition, London and Dublin, Duffy, 1862 (2 vols., pp. [x] + [232]; viii + 222)

THE | DOUBLE PROPHECY; | OR, | TRIALS OF THE HEART. | BY WILLIAM CARLETON | AUTHOR OF "TRAITS AND STORIES OF THE IRISH PEASANTRY" – | "WILLY REILLY" – "VALENTINE M'CLUTCHY" – | "THE EVIL EYE" – ETC., ETC. | IN TWO VOLUMES. | VOL [I.] |

LONDON: | JAMES DUFFY, 22, PATERNOSTER-ROW; | DUBLIN: 7, WELLINGTON-QUAY. | 1862.

Contains 'Dedication'; novel; 'Postliminous Preface'.
Sadleir No. [498]; Brown No. 337A; O'Donoghue p. lxiii.

Variant: Vol. I, pp. [*1*] + ii-viii + [*3*] + viii + [*2*] + [232]
This has the preliminaries to Vol. I extended and rearranged, with two p. viiis. On p. iv, notice 'reprinted from Duffy's "Hibernian Magazine." '; p. [v] dedication; p. [ix] a paragraph 'for the guidance of my Readers, (about the Northern dialect and a mistake about a character's death) which corrects the (misspelt) 'postliminious' preface; with errata at end of story. Brown says the story appeared in the *Irish American* of New York before it appeared in *Duffy's Hibernian Magazine*.

Redmond Count O'Hanlon, the Irish Rapparee

[49a]   First edition, Dublin and London, Duffy, 1862 (1 vol., pp. 174)

REDMOND | COUNT O'HANLON, | THE IRISH RAPPAREE, | AN HISTORICAL TALE. | BY WILLIAM CARLETON, | AUTHOR OF "TRAITS AND STORIES OF THE IRISH PEASANTRY," | "VALENTINE M'CLUTCHY, THE IRISH AGENT," "WILLY | REILLY," "THE EVIL EYE," "RODY THE ROVER," ETC. | DUBLIN: | JAMES DUFFY, 7, WELLINGTON-QUAY, | AND | 22, PATERNOSTER-ROW, LONDON. | 1862.

Contains novel, originally in *Duffy's Hibernian Magazine*, August – December 1860.
Sadleir No. [511]; Brown No. 337; O'Donoghue p. lxiii.

[49b]   American edition, New York and Montreal, Sadlier, 1875 (1 vol., pp. [2] + 138)

REDMOND | COUNT O'HANLON, | *The Irish Rapparee.* | AN HISTORICAL TALE. | BY | WILLIAM CARLETON, | Author of "Valentine McClutchy," "Tales and Stories of the Irish Peasantry,"

| "The Tithe Proctor," "Art Maguire," "Willy Reilly," "Fardo- | rougha, the Miser," "The Black Prophet," "The Black | Baronet," "Jane Sinclair," "The Emi- | grants of Ahadarra," "The Evil Eye," &c. | [short rule] | NEW YORK: | D. & J. SADLIER & CO., 31 BARCLAY STREET. | MONTREAL: | No. 275 NOTRE-DAME STREET. | [short rule] | 1875.

†[49c]   American edition, New York, Worthington, 1875

The *American Catalogue* for 1875 lists an edition of the novel from R. Worthington & Co., 750 Broadway, New York, which I have not seen.

[49d]   'A new edition', Dublin, Duffy, 1886 (1 vol., pp. 200)

REDMOND | COUNT O'HANLON, | THE IRISH RAPPAREE, | [Gothic:] **An Historical Tale,** | BY WILLIAM CARLETON, | AUTHOR OF "TRAITS AND STORIES OF THE IRISH PEASANTRY," | "VALENTINE M'CLUTCHY, THE IRISH AGENT," "WILLY | REILLY, "THE EVIL EYE," "RODY THE ROVER," ETC. | WITH AN | [Gothic:] **Appendix** | BY | THOMAS CLARKE LUBY, A.B., T.C.D. | A NEW EDITION. | [short double rule] | [Gothic:] **Dublin:** | JAMES DUFFY AND CO., LTD., | 15 WELLINGTON QUAY. | 1886.

Contains novel and appendix.

[49e]   Another edition, Dublin, Duffy, n.d. (1 vol., pp. 200)

Title page as [49d] except no date.

Contents as [49d].

[49f]   American edition, New York, Kenedy, 1896 (1 vol., pp. [2] + 138)

Title page as [49b] except publisher's name and address, date: 'NEW YORK: | P.J.KENEDY, | EXCELSIOR PUBLISHING HOUSE, | 5 BARCLAY STREET. | 1896.'

Verso of title page has 'Copyright, D. & J. Sadlier & Co., 1885.'

Contains novel.

[49g]   American edition, New York, Sadlier (1 vol., pp. [2] + 138)

Title page as [49b] except publisher's address, no date: 'NEW YORK: | D. & J. SADLIER & CO. | 33 BARCLAY STREET AND 38 PARK PLACE.'

Contains novel.

Verso of title page has 'Copyright 1885.'

The Silver Acre and other Tales

[50a]   First edition, London, Ward, Lock, 1862 (1 vol., pp. [2] + 238) (Shilling Volume Library)

[Within rule frame:] THE | SILVER ACRE | [Gothic:] **And other Tales** | BY | WILLIAM CARLETON | AUTHOR OF "TRAITS AND STORIES OF THE IRISH PEASANTRY," ETC. | [short rule] | LONDON | WARD AND LOCK 158 FLEET STREET | MDCCCLXII | [*The right of translation and reproduction is reserved*]

No. 15 of Ward & Lock's Shilling Volume Library.

Contains: 'The Silver Acre'; 'The Fair of Emyvale'; 'Master and Scholar'.

Sadleir No. [513]; Brown No. 338; O'Donoghue p. lxiii. Sadleir states (p. 162) that the collection also appeared as No. 20 in Simms & M'Intyre's Parlour Library.

In 1869, the year of Carleton's death, two publishers reissued his early short stories. Tegg brought out two 'editions' of the complete *Traits and Stories* ('Ninth Complete Edition' and 'Tenth Complete Edition', [15j] and [15k]). Duffy compiled three collections from other collections for his 'Sixpenny Library': *The Poor Scholar, Frank Martin and the Fairies, The Country Dancing Master, and Other Irish Tales* [51a], *Barney Brady's Goose, The Hedge School, The Three Tasks, and Other Irish Tales* [52a], and *Tubber Derg; or, The Red Well, Party Fight and Funeral, Dandy Kehoe's Christening, and Other Irish Tales* [53a]. All went into several 'editions':

The Poor Scholar, Frank Martin and the Fairies, The Country Dancing Master, and Other Irish Tales

[51a]   Dublin and London, Duffy, 1869 (1 vol., pp. [4] + 252) (Sixpenny Library)

THE | POOR SCHOLAR, | FRANK MARTIN AND THE FAIRIES, | THE COUNTRY DANCING MASTER, | AND | OTHER IRISH TALES. | BY WILLIAM CARLETON, | AUTHOR OF "WILLY REILLY," "VALENTINE M'CLUTCHY," "THE BLACK | BARONET," "THE EVIL EYE," ETC., ETC. | DUBLIN: | JAMES DUFFY, 15, WELLINGTON-QUAY: | LONDON: 22, PATERNOSTER-ROW. | 1869

Contains 'The Poor Scholar'; 'Mickey M'Rorey, the Irish Fiddler'; 'Buckram Back, the Country Dancing Master'; 'Mary Murray, the Irish Match Maker'; 'Bob Pentland, or the Guager [sic] Outwitted'; 'The Fate of Frank M'Kenna'; 'The Rival Kempers'; 'Frank Martin and the Fairies'; 'A Legend of Knockmany'.

Sadleir No. [507].

[51b]   Another edition, Dublin and London, Duffy, 1874 (1 vol., pp. [4] + 252)

Title page as [51a] except '1874' for '1869'.

[51c]   Another edition, Dublin and London, Duffy, n.d. (1 vol., pp. [4] + 252)

Title page as [51a] except no date.

Barney Brady's Goose, The Hedge School, The Three Tasks, and Other Irish Tales

[52a]   Dublin and London, Duffy, 1869 (1 vol., pp. [256]) (Sixpenny Library)

BARNEY BRADY'S GOOSE; | THE HEDGE SCHOOL; | THE THREE TASKS, | AND | OTHER IRISH TALES. | BY WILLIAM CARLETON, | AUTHOR OF "WILLY REILLY," VALENTINE M'CLUTCHY," "THE BLACK | BARONET," "THE EVIL

EYE," ETC., ETC. | DUBLIN: | JAMES DUFFY, 15,
WELLINGTON-QUAY; | LONDON: 22, PATERNOSTER-
ROW. | 1869.

Contains 'Barney Brady's Goose; or, Dark Doings at Slathbeg';
'The Three Tasks'; 'Second Sight and Apparition'; 'Neal Malone';
'The Hedge School'; 'Condy Cullen; or, the Exciseman Defeated';
'Moll Roe's Marriage; or, the Pudding Bewitched'.

[52b]   Another edition, Dublin and London, 1874 (1 vol., pp.
[256])

Title page as [52a] except publishers' name and address, date:
'DUBLIN: | JAMES DUFFY & SONS, | 15 Wellington Quay, |
And 1a Paternoster Row, London, | 1874.'

[52c]   Another edition, Dublin and London, Duffy, n.d. (1 vol.,
pp. [256])

Title page as [52b] except no date.

[52d]   Another edition, Dublin, Duffy, n.d. (1 vol., pp. [256])

Title page as [52c] except publisher's name and address: 'DUBLIN:
| JAMES DUFFY AND CO., Limited, | 14 & 15 Wellington
Quay.'

[52e]   Another edition, Dublin, Duffy, n.d. (1 vol., pp. [256])

Title page as [52c] except publisher's name and address: '[Gothic:]
Dublin: | JAMES DUFFY AND CO., Ltd., | 15 Wellington
Quay.'

**Tubber Derg; or, the Red Well, The Party Fight and Funeral, Dandy
Kehoe's Christening, and Other Irish Tales**

[53a]   Dublin and London, Duffy, 1869 (1 vol., pp. 256) (Sixpenny
Library)

TUBBER DERG; | OR, | THE RED WELL. | PARTY FIGHT
AND FUNERAL, | DANDY KEHOE'S CHRISTENING, | AND
| OTHER IRISH TALES. | BY WILLIAM CARLETON, |

AUTHOR OF "WILLY REILLY," "VALENTINE M'CLUTCHY" "THE BLACK | BARONET," "THE EVIL EYE," ETC., ETC. | DUBLIN: | JAMES DUFFY, 15, WELLINGTON-QUAY: | LONDON: 22 PATERNOSTER-ROW. | 1869

Contains 'Tubber Derg; or the Red Well'; 'Party Fight and Funeral'; 'Dandy Kehoe's Christening'; 'Talbot and Gaynor, the Irish Pipers'; 'Frank Finnegan, the Foster Brother'; 'The Three Wishes'.

[53b]   Another edition, Dublin and London, Duffy 1874 (1 vol., pp. 256)

Title page as [53a] except publisher's name and addresses, and date: 'DUBLIN: | JAMES DUFFY AND SONS, | 15 WELLINGTON-QUAY, | AND 22 PATERNOSTER-ROW, LONDON. | 1874

[53c]   Another edition, Dublin and London, Duffy, 1874 (1 vol., pp. 256)

Title page as [53a] except publishers' names and addresses, date: 'DUBLIN: | JAMES DUFFY & SONS, 15 WELLINGTON QUAY, | AND 1 PATERNOSTER ROW, LONDON, | 1874

[53d]   Another edition, Dublin and London, Duffy, n.d. (1 vol., pp. 256)

Title page as [53c] except no date.

[53e]   Another edition, Dublin, Duffy, n.d. (1 vol., pp. 256)

Title page as [53a] except publisher's name and address: 'DUBLIN: | JAMES DUFFY AND CO., LIMITED, | 14 & 15 WELLINGTON QUAY.'

[53f]   Another edition, Dublin, Duffy, n.d. (1 vol., pp. 256)

Title page as [53a] except publisher's name and address: '[Gothic:] **Dublin:** | JAMES DUFFY AND CO., LTD., | 38 WESTMORELAND STREET.'

The Fair of Emyvale

†[54a]　London, Ward, Lock & Tyler, 1870

Sadleir No. [501]; Brown No. 338A; O'Donoghue p. lxiii. Sadleir says 'I am unable to describe the first edition of this story which was, presumably, no. 10 of the Parlour Library Sixpenny Series, published by Ward, Lock & Tyler in 1869-70' ([3755 bii] in Section III); he also mentions a Parlour Library edition when that series was published by Simms & M'Intyre. I have been unable to find any edition.

Traits and Stories of the Irish Peasantry, (3 stories only)

[55a]　Toronto, Adam, Stevenson, 1871 (1 vol., pp. 112)

TRAITS AND STORIES | OF | *The Irish Peasantry* | BY | WILLIAM CARLETON. | [vignette of jaunting car as [15h]] | From the Tenth English Edition, with the Author's Corrections | and Explanatory Notes, &c. | [short decorative rule] | AUTHORIZED AND COPYRIGHT EDITION. | [short decorative rule] | TORONTO: | ADAM, STEVENSON & CO. | 1871.

Contains 'Geography of an Irish Oath'; 'Going to Maynooth'; 'The Midnight Mass'. The list of contents, which is on the back cover, is followed by the announcement that 'The 3rd Series, in completion of the Work, is now in press, and will be issued immediately.' I have not seen either the first or the third 'series', nor any other reference to them.

Jane Sinclair; or, the Fawn of Springvale (with other stories)

In 1872, D. & J. Sadlier, New York and Montreal, brought out a collection of Carleton's stories in a curious format: three of the stories had their own title pages, although they were consecutively paginated. The title page of the first story, 'Jane Sinclair, or, the Fawn of Springvale', was duplicated, the first one standing as the title page to the whole collection, though without any indication that there was more than one story in the book. (It is possible that this edition originated as a part-work.) I give the title pages to each story. The sequence is: p. [1] 'Jane Sinclair' title page; p. [2] blank; p. [3] 'Jane Sinclair' title page as p. [3]; p. [4] blank; p. [5] text of

'Jane Sinclair' to p. 225; p. [226] blank; p. [227] 'Lha Dhu' title page; p. [228] blank; p. [229] text of 'Lha Dhu' to p. 274; p. [275] 'The Dead Boxer' title page; p. [276] blank; p. [277] text of 'The Dead Boxer' to p. 390; p. [391] 'Ellen Duncan' half title; p. [392] blank; p. [393] text of 'Ellen Duncan' to p. 415; p. [416] text of 'The Proctor's Daughter' to p. 432. 'Ellen Duncan' and 'The Proctor's Daughter' are by 'Denis O'Donoho', not Carleton.

[56a]   New York and Montreal, Sadlier, 1872 (1 vol., pp. 432)

JANE SINCLAIR; | OR, | THE FAWN OF SPRINGVALE. | BY | WILLIAM CARLETON, | Author of "Valentine McClutchy," "Traits and Stories of the Irish | Peasantry," "Rody the Rover," "Art Maguire," "Willy Reilly," | "Fardorougha, the Miser." "Paddy Go Easy," | "The Black Prophet," "Black Baronet," &c. | NEW YORK: | D. & J. SADLIER & CO., 31 BARCLAY STREET. | MONTREAL:- COR. NOTRE DAME AND ST. FRANCIS XAVIER STS. | [short rule] | 1872.

[p. [227]:] LHA DHU; | OR, | THE DARK DAY. | BY | WILLIAM CARLETON, | Author of "Valentine McClutchy," "Traits and Stories of the Irish | Peasantry," "Rody the Rover," "Art Maguire," "Willy Reilly," | "Fardorougha, the Miser," "Paddy Go Easy," | "The Black Prophet," "Black Baronet," &c. | NEW YORK: | D. & J. SADLIER & CO., 31 BARCLAY STREET. | MONTREAL:- COR. NOTRE DAME AND ST. FRANCIS XAVIER STS. | [short rule] | 1872.

[p. [275]:] THE DEAD BOXER. | BY | WILLIAM CARLETON, | Author of "Valentine McClutchy," "Traits and Stories of the Irish | Peasantry," "Rody the Rover," "Art Maguire," "Willy Reilly," | "Fardorougha, the Miser," "Paddy Go Easy," | "The Black Prophet," "Black Baronet," &c. | [short decorative rule] | NEW YORK: | D. & J. SADLIER & CO., 31 BARCLAY STREET. | MONTREAL:- COR. NOTRE DAME AND ST. FRANCIS XAVIER STS. | [short rule] | 1872.

[56b]   American edition, New York and Montreal, Sadlier, n.d. [1875] (1 vol., pp. 432)

Title page as [56a] except no short rule or date.

Other title pages as [56a] except no short rule or date.

This is one of the ten uniform volumes of Carleton's *Works* published by Sadlier in 1875.

The Clarionet, The Dead Boxer, and Barney Branagan (with 'Wildgoose Lodge')

[57a]   London and New York, Routledge, n.d. [1875] (1 vol., pp. [414])

THE CLARIONET; | THE DEAD BOXER, | AND | BARNEY BRANAGAN. | BY | WILLIAM CARLETON, | AUTHOR OF "JANE SINCLAIR," "FARDOROUGHA," ETC. | LONDON: | GEORGE ROUTLEDGE & SONS, | THE BROADWAY, LUDGATE; | NEW YORK: 416, BROOME STREET.

Contains 'Preface'; 'The Clarionet'; 'The Dead Boxer'; 'Barney Branagan'; 'Wildgoose Lodge'.

One of the five volumes of Routledge's *Carleton's Novels and Tales*.

Traits and Stories of the Irish Peasantry in One Volume.

From 1875 to about 1880 there was renewed publishing interest, on both sides of the Atlantic, in the 'complete' *Traits and Stories of the Irish Peasantry*. Whereas previous editions had kept to the two-volume format of 1843/44, these new editions were in one volume. At first, these were simply Volumes I and II of 1843/44 bound together [58a-d] then rearranged [59a] or reset [60a-b]. From 1877, however, Routledge completely reorganised the collection, into two '*series*' [61a-c] not related to Carleton's original two series, and then into four 'series' [62a-e]. Maxwell added three further stories to the collection [63a]. There were also, at about this time, numerous collections of three or four stories with the title *Traits and Stories of the Irish Peasantry*, which are entered after this group of complete *Traits and Stories*.)

[58a]   'New edition', London and New York, Tegg, Scribner, Welford & Armstrong, 1875 (1 vol., pp. [2] + [704])

[top and left-hand side, Phiz engraving of peasants from [15a] title-head of 'Ned M'Keown'] [ornamental caps:] TRAITS AND STORIES | OF | [Gothic:] **The Irish Peasantry,** | BY | [ornamental caps:] WILLIAM CARLETON. | [short wavy rule] | NEW EDITION. | [short wavy rule] | With the Author's Latest Corrections. | LONDON: WILLIAM TEGG & CO. | NEW YORK: | SCRIBNER, WELFORD, & ARMSTRONG. | [short rule] | 1875.

Contains 'Introduction' and stories as [15a]: 'Ned M'Keown'; 'The Three Tasks'; 'Shane Fadh's Wedding'; 'Larry M'Farland's Wake'; 'The Battle of the Factions'; 'The Station'; 'The Party Fight and Funeral'; 'The Lough Derg Pilgrim'; 'The Hedge School'; 'The Midnight Mass'; 'The Donagh; or the Horse-stealers'; 'Geography of an Irish Oath'; 'The Lianhan Shee'; 'Going to Maynooth'; 'Phelim O'Toole's Courtship'; 'The Poor Scholar'; 'Wildgoose Lodge'; 'Tubber Derg; or, the Red Well'; 'Neal Malone'.

†[58b]   American edition, New York, Worthington, 1875

The *Publishers' Trade-List Annual* for 1875 lists another edition in this format, at $2·50, from R. Worthington & Co., 750 Broadway, New York. I have not seen it.

†[58c]   American edition, New York, Worthington, 1888 (Library of Selected Romances)

The American Catalogue for 1888 lists this edition from Worthington, 747 Broadway, in its Library of Selected Romances at $1·50. I have not seen it.

[58d]   Another edition, London, Tegg, n.d. (1 vol., pp. [2] + [704])

[top and left hand side, peasants as [58a]]. [ornamental caps:] TRAITS AND STORIES | OF | [Gothic:] **The Irish Peasantry,** | BY | [ornamental caps:] WILLIAM CARLETON. | [short wavy rule] | NEW EDITION. | [short wavy rule] | With the Author's Latest Corrections, | an Introduction, | AND | [ornamental italic caps:] *EXPLANATORY NOTES.* | [short rule] | LONDON: WILLIAM TEGG.

Contents as [58a].

[58e]   Another edition, London, Tegg, n.d. (1 vol., pp. [2] + 704])

[top and left hand side, peasants as [58a].] [ornamental caps:] TRAITS AND STORIES | OF | [Gothic:] **The Irish Peasantry.** | BY | [ornamental caps:] WILLIAM CARLETON. | [short rule] | With the Author's Latest Corrections. | [short rule] | ILLUSTRATED BY | DANIEL MACLISE, R.A. | LONDON: | WILLIAM TEGG & CO., PANCRAS LANE, | CHEAPSIDE.

Contents as [58a] but plates by Maclise.

[59a]   'Two Volumes in One', London, Ward, Lock, n.d. (1 vol., pp. [6] + xxiv + 424 + [2] + 432)

TRAITS AND STORIES | OF | THE IRISH PEASANTRY. | BY | WILLIAM CARLETON. | [vignette of jaunting car as [15h]] | WITH THE AUTHOR'S LAST CORRECTIONS, AN INTRODUCTION, | EXPLANATORY NOTES, | AND | NUMEROUS ILLUSTRATIONS, | BY HARVEY, GILBERT, PHIZ, FRANKLIN, MACMANUS, &c. | TWO VOLUMES IN ONE. | LONDON: | WARD, LOCK, AND CO., WARWICK HOUSE, | SALISBURY SQUARE, E.C.

This is a rearrangement, by a new publisher, of Tegg's 'Eleventh Edition' [15l], the two volumes rearranged internally but keeping their own stories, and kept distinct by separate pagination. Though the order of the tales is altered, the text is as [15l], with more signs of wear. In several places the stories are run on after each other without the tailpiece and title illustrations. The plates are a selection from earlier 'editions' of [15a-l].]

Contains: ('Volume I':) 'Introduction' ('Autobiographical Intro-duction' of 1842 [15a]); 'The Three Tasks'; 'Shane Fadh's Wedding'; 'The Lough Derg Pilgrim'; 'Larry M'Farland's Wake'; 'The Hedge School'; 'The Party Fight and Funeral'; 'The Battle of the Factions'; 'The Midnight Mass'; 'The Station'; 'Ned M'Keown'; 'Phil Purcel, the Pig Driver'; 'The Donagh, or the Horse-Stealers'; ('Volume II':) 'Geography of an Irish Oath'; 'The Lianhan Shee'; 'Going to Maynooth'; 'Phelim O'Toole's Courtship'; 'Wildgoose Lodge'; 'The Poor Scholar'; 'Neal Malone'; 'Tubber Derg, or, the Red Well'.

[59b]   American edition, 'Various complete stories in one volume', New York, Lovell, n.d. (1 vol., pp. [980])

Traits and Stories | OF THE | IRISH PEASANTRY; | CONSISTING OF | VARIOUS COMPLETE STORIES IN ONE VOLUME. | BY | WILLIAM CARLETON, | AUTHOR OF "WILLY REILLY," ETC. | [short decorative rule] | NEW·YORK: | FRANK F. LOVELL & CO., | No. 83 ELM STREET.

Contains: 'The Three Tasks'; 'Shane Fadh's Wedding'; 'The Lough Derg Pilgrim'; 'The Party Fight and Funeral'; 'Battle of the Factions'; 'Larry M'Farland's Wake'; 'The Hedge School'; 'The Midnight Mass'; 'The Station'; 'Ned M'Keown'; 'Phil Purcel, the Pig-driver'; 'The Donah; or, the Horse Stealers'; 'The Geography of an Irish Oath'; 'The Lianhan Shee'; 'Going to Maynooth'; 'Phelim O'Toole's Courtship'; 'Wildgoose Lodge'; 'The Poor Scholar'; 'Neal Malone'; 'Tubber Derg; or, the Red Well'.

These are the stories of [59b], in the same order, but without the 'General Introduction', and consecutively paginated.

[60a]   *Traits and Stories of the Irish Peasantry*, 'New edition' in one volume, London, Tegg, n.d. (1 vol., pp. [ii] + [704])

[top and left hand side of title page have Phiz illustration of many peasants, originally used with title heading of 'Ned M'Keown' in [14a].] [Ornamental caps:] Traits and Stories | OF | [Gothic:] **The Irish Peasantry,** | BY | [ornamental caps:] William Carleton. | [short wavy rule] | NEW EDITION. | [short wavy rule] | With the Author's Latest Corrections, | an Introduction, | AND | [ornamental caps:] EXPLANATORY NOTES. | [short rule] | London: WILLIAM TEGG.

Contains the introduction and stories of [15a] 'New Edition' reset in small type, cramped settings, stories following on without tailpieces or title heads.

†[60b]   American edition, New York, Worthington, 1875

The *Publishers' Trade-List Annual* for 1875 lists an edition in this format from R. Worthington & Co, 750 Broadway, New York, at 50 cents, which I have not seen.

[61a] 'Complete edition', London and New York, Routledge, 1877 (1 vol., pp. [*8*] + [414] + [*4*] + [406]) (Two 'series')

[in rule frame:] TRAITS AND STORIES | OF THE | IRISH PEASANTRY | BY | WILLIAM CARLETON | COMPLETE EDITION | *LONDON* | GEORGE ROUTLEDGE AND SONS | Broadway, Ludgate Hill | NEW YORK: 416 BROOME STREET | 1877

This edition is composed of the 'First Series' and 'Second Series' of *Traits and Stories* also published by Routledge in 1877 [64a] and [65a]. The stories are divided into a 'First Series' and a 'Second Series' which are separately paginated. The division does not correspond to Carleton's own *First* and *Second Series*; four of his *Second Series* stories are here placed in the 'First Series'. The 'Dedication' to John Birney from [2e] and 'Preface to the First Edition' as [2b] precede the 'First Series'.

Contains: ('First Series':) 'Ned M'Keown'; 'The Three Tasks, or, The Little House under the Hill'; 'Shane Fadh's Wedding'; 'Larry M'Farland's Wake'; 'The Battle of the Factions'; 'The Party Fight and Funeral'; 'The Hedge School'; 'The Station'; 'The Midnight Mass'; 'The Donagh; or, the Horse Stealers'; 'Phil Purcell, the Pig-Driver'; 'The Lianhan Shee'; ('Second Series':) 'The Geography of an Irish Oath'; 'An Essay on Irish Swearing'; 'The Poor Scholar'; 'Wildgoose Lodge'; 'Tubber Derg; or, The Red Well'; 'Denis O'Shaughnessy Going to Maynooth'; 'Phelim O'Toole's Courtship'.

The collection is related to the 1836 conjoint edition of *Traits and Stories* – it excludes 'Neal Malone', which was added in the 1842/4 'New Edition' [15a/b] and has 'The Geography of an Irish Oath' and 'An Essay on Irish Swearing' separate.
The type is set throughout within a rule frame.

[61b]   Another edition, London and New York, Routledge n.d.

Title page as [61a] except no date.

Contents as [61a].

[61c]   Another edition, London, Glasgow, Manchester and New York, Routledge, n.d. (1 vol., pp. [*12*] + [822])

Title page as [61a] except publisher's name and addresses: 'LONDON | GEORGE ROUTLEDGE AND SONS, LIMITED | BROADWAY, LUDGATE HILL | GLASGOW, MANCHESTER, AND NEW YORK'

Variant title page has publisher's name and addresses: 'LONDON | GEORGE ROUTLEDGE AND SONS | BROADWAY, LUDGATE HILL | GLASGOW, MANCHESTER, AND NEW YORK.

The title page to the 1877 Routledge 'First Series' [64a] and a first series half-title occur in the preliminaries before the 'Dedication', and the title page to the 1877 Routledge 'Second Series' and a second series half-title occur before 'The Geography of an Irish Oath'.
The text throughout is set within rule frames.

Traits and Stories of the Irish Peasantry, 'Complete Edition', (4 'Series')

[62a]   'Complete Edition', (4 'Series'), London, Routledge, n.d. (1 vol., pp. [viii] + [194] + [4] + 220 + [4] + 184 + [4] + 222)

TRAITS AND STORIES | OF THE | IRISH PEASANTRY | BY | WILLIAM CARLETON | COMPLETE EDITION | [Routledge 'R' device] | LONDON | GEORGE ROUTLEDGE AND SONS, LTD. | BROADWAY HOUSE, LUDGATE HILL.

The stories are divided into 4 'series' which are separately paginated. There seems to be no special reason for dividing the stories into 4 groups, except perhaps the spacing and symmetry of the book and its 'Contents' page. The stories are those of Routledge's other 'Complete Edition' [61a-c] in two 'series', with those series subdivided. Like [61a-c], the collection contains the stories from Carleton's *First* and *Second Series* of 1836 [10a], ignoring the changes that Carleton had made for the 'New Edition' of 1842: 'Denis O'Shaughnessy going to Maynooth', for example, has its longer title; 'The Geography of an Irish Oath' and 'An Essay on Irish Swearing' are separate, not joined as in [15a]. 'Neal Malone' is not included.

Contains: 'Dedication' to John Birney and 'Preface to the First Edition' as [2e]; ('First Series':) 'Ned M'Keown'; 'The Three Tasks; or, The Little House under the Hill'; 'Shane Fadh's Wedding'; 'Larry M'Farland's Wake'; 'The Battle of the Factions'; 'The Party Fight and Funeral'; ('Second Series':) 'The Hedge School'; 'The Station'; 'The Midnight Mass'; 'The Donagh, or, The Horse Stealers'; 'Phil Purcel, the Pig-Driver'; 'The Lianhan Shee'; ('Third Series':) 'The Geography of an Irish Oath'; 'An Essay on Irish Swearing'; 'The Poor Scholar'; 'Wildgoose Lodge'; ('Fourth Series':) 'Tubber Derg; or, The Red Well'; 'Denis O'Shaughnessy Going to Maynooth'; 'Phelim O'Toole's Courtship'.

The pagination of this edition is separate for each of the four 'series'; each is preceded by its own series half-title and series 'Contents' page.

[62b]   'Complete Edition', London, Manchester, New York, Routledge, n.d. [1896] (1 vol., pp. [viii] + [194] + [4] + 220 + [4] + 184 + [4] + 222) (Four 'series')

Title page as [62a] except publisher's name and addresses: 'LONDON | GEORGE ROUTLEDGE AND SONS, LIMITED | BROADWAY, LUDGATE HILL | MANCHESTER AND NEW YORK' and no 'R' device.

Listed in the *American Catalogue* for 1896.

[62c]   'Complete Edition' (4 'Series'), London, New York, Routledge, Dutton, n.d. 1907 (1 vol., pp. [viii] + [194] + [4] + 220 + [4] + 184 + [4] + 222)

Title page as [62a] except publishers' names and addresses: 'LONDON: | GEORGE ROUTLEDGE AND SONS, LTD. | NEW YORK: E. P. DUTTON AND CO.'

Listed in the *American Catalogue* for 1907.

[62d]   'Complete edition', London, Routledge, n.d. (1 vol., pp. [6] + [194] + [2] + 220 + [2] + 184 + [2] + 222 + [2]) (Four 'series')

TRAITS AND STORIES | OF THE | IRISH PEASANTRY | BY | WILLIAM CARLETON | COMPLETE EDITION | [Routledge

'R' device] | LONDON | GEORGE ROUTLEDGE AND SONS, LTD. | BROADWAY HOUSE, LUDGATE HILL.

As [62a] except no separate series half-titles before each series; separate 'Contents' pages still present.

[62e] 'Complete edition', London, Manchester and New York, Routledge, n.d. (1 vol., pp. [4] + [194] + [2] + 220 + [2] + 184 + [2] + 222) (Four 'series')

TRAITS AND STORIES | OF THE | IRISH PEASANTRY | BY | WILLIAM CARLETON | COMPLETE EDITION | LONDON | GEORGE ROUTLEDGE AND SONS, LIMITED | BROADWAY, LUDGATE HILL | MANCHESTER AND NEW YORK

As [62d] except preliminaries condensed.

[63a] *Traits and Stories of the Irish Peasantry* [plus the 'Silver Acre' etc.], London, Maxwell, Vickers, n.d. (1 vol., pp. [4] + 780)

[top and left hand side of title page, title illustrations to 'Ned M'Keown', 'New Edition', 1842 [15a]] [Gothic:] **Traits and Stories** | OF | THE IRISH PEASANTRY. | BY | WILLIAM CARLETON. | [short rule] | *WITH THE AUTHOR'S LATEST CORRECTIONS.* | [short rule] | ILLUSTRATED BY | DANIEL MACLISE, R.A. | [short decorative rule] | LONDON: | J. & R. MAXWELL, 4 SHOE LANE; | AND GEORGE VICKERS, ANGEL COURT, STRAND.

Contains: 'Introduction'; 'Ned M'Keown'; 'The Three Tasks'; 'Shane Fadh's Wedding'; 'Larry M'Farland's Wake'; 'The Battle of the Factions'; 'The Station'; 'The Party Fight and Funeral'; 'The Lough Derg Pilgrim'; 'The Hedge School'; 'The Midnight Mass'; 'The Donagh; or, the Horse-Stealers'; 'Phil Purcell, the Pig-Driver'; 'The Geography of an Irish Oath'; 'The Lianhan Shee'; 'Going to Maynooth'; 'Phelim O'Toole's Courtship'; 'The Poor Scholar'; 'Wildgoose Lodge'; 'Tubber Derg; or, the Red Well'; 'Neal Malone'; 'The Silver Acre'; 'The Fair of Emyvale'; 'Master and Scholar'.

This collection includes the introduction and stories from the New Edition of 1842/44 [15a], with the addition of three much later stories: 'The Silver Acre'; 'The Fair of Emyvale'; 'Master and Scholar'.

[64a]   *Traits and Stories of the Irish Peasantry*, 'First Series', London and New York, Routledge, 1877 (1 vol., pp. [x] + [414])

[In rule frame:] TRAITS AND STORIES | OF THE | IRISH PEASANTRY | BY | WILLIAM CARLETON | FIRST SERIES | *LONDON & NEW YORK* | GEORGE ROUTLEDGE & SONS | 1877

Contains 'Dedication to John Birney'; 1830 'Preface' as [2a]; 'Ned M'Keown'; 'The Three Tasks, or the Little House under the Hill'; 'Shane Fadh's Wedding'; 'Larry M'Farland's Wake'; 'The Battle of the Factions'; 'The Party Fight and Funeral'; 'The Hedge School'; 'The Station'; 'The Midnight Mass'; 'The Donagh; or, the Horse Stealers'; 'Phil Purcel, the Pig-Driver'; 'The Lianhan Shee'. This does not correspond with Carleton's own *First Series* [2a]: the last four stories are from his *Second Series* [4a]. The stories correspond with the first 'Series' of Routledge's 'complete' 'two-series' edition [61a], also published in 1877. This edition is uniform with their 'second series' below [65a].

[65a]   *Traits and Stories of the Irish Peasantry*, 'Second Series', London and New York, Routledge, 1877 (1 vol., pp. [x] + [406])

[in rule frame:] TRAITS AND STORIES | OF THE | IRISH PEASANTRY | BY | WILLIAM CARLETON | SECOND SERIES | *LONDON & NEW YORK* | GEORGE ROUTLEDGE & SONS | 1877

Contains 'The Geography of an Irish Oath'; 'An Essay on Irish Swearing'; 'The Poor Scholar'; 'Wildgoose Lodge'; 'Tubber Derg; or, the Red Well'; 'Denis O'Shaughnessy Going to Maynooth'; 'Phelim O'Toole's Courtship'. This lacks four of Carleton's own *Second Series* [4a]; in the companion Routledge 'First Series' [64a], these four stories are added to Carleton's *First Series*. The type is set within a rule frame throughout, and the collection corresponds to the second part or 'Second Series' of Routledge's 'Two-Series' 'Complete Edition', 1877 [61a].

Traits and Stories of the Irish Peasantry – cheap series from Ward, Lock; Munro; Lovell.

The later editions of *Traits and Stories* 'Complete in One Volume' were split up into cheap editions by three publishers, Lovell, George Munro and Ward, Lock. Ward, Lock divided their late 'Two Volumes in One' [59a] into ten for their Sixpenny library; Lovell divided their 'Various Complete Stories in One Volume' into ten for the 'Lovell's Library' series (10 cents, paperback), and Munro also divided the collection into ten for the 'Seaside Library Pocket Edition'. All three publishers divided the collection into the same groups of stories, and all used the general heading *Traits and Stories of the Irish Peasantry* as well as the titles of the stories in that part. The pagination of the full collections was used.

The Ward, Lock series and the Munro series were published around 1880; the Lovell series is listed in the *American Catalogue* for 1886.

[66a] *Traits and Stories of the Irish Peasantry – Shane Fadh's Wedding and Other Stories*, London, Ward, Lock, n.d. (1 vol., pp. [2] + [29-96] + 399-424) (Sixpenny Library)

TRAITS AND STORIES OF THE IRISH PEASANTRY. | [rule] | SHANE FADH'S WEDDING | AND | OTHER STORIES. | BY | WILLIAM CARLETON | *WITH ILLUSTRATIONS.* | [Ward, Lock device] | LONDON: | WARD, LOCK, AND CO., | WARWICK HOUSE, SALISBURY SQUARE, E.C.

Contains 'Shane Fadh's Wedding', 'The Lough Derg Pilgrim' and 'The Donagh, or The Horse-Stealers' from [59a].

[66b] Another edition, London and New York, Ward, Lock.

Title page as [66a] except publisher's name and address: 'WARD, LOCK AND CO., | LONDON: WARWICK HOUSE, SALISBURY SQUARE, E.C. | NEW YORK: BOND STREET.'

Contents as [66a].

[66c] American edition, New York, Munro, n.d. (Seaside Library Pocket Edition).

TRAITS AND STORIES OF THE IRISH PEASANTRY. | [rule] | SHANE FADH'S WEDDING | AND | OTHER STORIES. | BY |

WILLIAM CARLETON. | [short rule] | NEW YORK: | GEORGE MUNRO'S SONS, PUBLISHERS, | 17 to 27 VANDEWATER STREET.

Contains 'Shane Fadh's Wedding', 'The Lough Derg Pilgrim' and 'The Donagh, or the Horse-Stealers'.

[66d]   American edition, New York, Lovell, n.d. [1886] (Lovell's Library No. 820)

TRAITS AND STORIES OF THE IRISH PEASANTRY. | [rule] | SHANE FADH'S WEDDING, AND | OTHER STORIES. | BY | WILLIAM CARLETON, | [short rule] | NEW YORK: | JOHN W. LOVELL, CO., | 150 WORTH STREET.

Contains 'Shane Fadh's Wedding', 'The Lough Derg Pilgrim' and 'The Donagh, or the Horse-Stealers'.

[67a]   *Traits and Stories of the Irish Peasantry – Larry M'Farland's Wake and The Hedge School*, London, Ward, Lock, n.d. (1 vol., pp. [2] + [97-180]) (Sixpenny Library)

TRAITS AND STORIES OF THE IRISH PEASANTRY. | [rule] | LARRY M'FARLAND'S WAKE | AND | THE HEDGE SCHOOL. | BY | WILLIAM CARLETON. | *WITH ILLUSTRATIONS.* | [Ward, Lock device] | LONDON: | WARD, LOCK, AND CO., | WARWICK HOUSE, SALISBURY SQUARE, E.C.

Contains 'Larry M'Farland's Wake'; 'The Hedge School'.

[67b]   Another edition, London and New York, Ward, Lock

Title page as [67a] except publisher's name and address: 'WARD, LOCK AND CO., | LONDON: WARWICK HOUSE, SALISBURY SQUARE, E.C. | NEW YORK: BOND STREET.'

Contents as [66a].

[67c]   American edition, New York, Munro, n.d. (Seaside Library Pocket Edition)

TRAITS AND STORIES OF THE IRISH PEASANTRY. | [rule] | LARRY McFARLAND'S WAKE | AND | THE HEDGE

SCHOOL. | BY | WILLIAM CARLETON. | [short rule] | NEW
YORK: | GEORGE MUNRO'S SONS, PUBLISHERS, | 17 to 27
VANDEWATER STREET.

Contains 'Larry McFarland's Wake'; 'The Hedge School'.

[67d]   American edition, New York, Lovell, n.d. [1886] (Lovell's
Library No. 821)

TRAITS AND STORIES OF THE IRISH PEASANTRY. | [rule] |
LARRY M'FARLAND'S WAKE | AND | THE HEDGE
SCHOOL. | BY | WILLIAM CARLETON. | [short rule] | NEW
YORK: | JOHN W. LOVELL, CO., | 150 WORTH STREET.

Contains 'Larry M'Farland's Wake'; 'The Hedge School'.

[68a]   *Traits and Stories of the Irish Peasantry – The Party Fight and
Funeral and The Battle of the Factions*, London, Ward, Lock, n.d.
(1 vol., pp. [2] + [181-264]) (Sixpenny Library)

TRAITS AND STORIES OF THE IRISH PEASANTRY. | [rule] |
THE PARTY FIGHT AND FUNERAL | AND | THE BATTLE
OF THE FACTIONS. | BY | WILLIAM CARLETON. | *WITH
ILLUSTRATIONS.* | [Ward, Lock device] | LONDON: | WARD,
LOCK, AND CO., | WARWICK HOUSE, SALISBURY
SQUARE, E.C.

Contains 'The Party Fight and Funeral'; 'The Battle of the Factions'.

[68b]   Another edition, London and New York, Ward, Lock

Title page as [68a] except publisher's name and address: 'WARD,
LOCK AND CO., | LONDON: WARWICK HOUSE,
SALISBURY SQUARE, E.C. | NEW YORK: BOND STREET.'

Contents as [68a].

[68c]   American edition, New York, Munro, n.d. (Seaside Library
Pocket Edition)

TRAITS AND STORIES OF THE IRISH PEASANTRY. | [rule] |
THE PARTY FIGHT AND FUNERAL | AND | THE BATTLE

OF THE FACTIONS. | BY | WILLIAM CARLETON. | [short rule] | NEW YORK: | GEORGE MUNRO'S SONS, PUBLISHERS, | 17 to 27 VANDEWATER STREET.

Contains 'The Party Fight and Funeral'; 'The Battle of the Factions'.

[68d]   American edition, New York, Lovell, n.d. [1886] (Lovell's Library No. 822)

TRAITS AND STORIES OF THE IRISH PEASANTRY. | [rule] | THE PARTY FIGHT AND FUNERAL | AND | THE BATTLE OF THE FACTIONS. | BY | WILLIAM CARLETON. | [short rule] | NEW YORK: | JOHN W. LOVELL, CO., | 150 WORTH STREET.

Contains 'The Party Fight and Funeral'; 'The Battle of the Factions'.

[69a]   *Traits and Stories of the Irish Peasantry – The Midnight Mass and The Station*, London, Ward, Lock, n.d. (1 vol., pp. [2] + [265-356]) (Sixpenny Library)

TRAITS AND STORIES OF THE IRISH PEASANTRY. | [rule] | THE MIDNIGHT MASS | AND | THE STATION. | BY | WILLIAM CARLETON. | WITH ILLUSTRATIONS. | [Ward, Lock device] | LONDON: | WARD, LOCK, AND CO., | WARWICK HOUSE, SALISBURY SQUARE, E.C.

Contains 'The Midnight Mass'; 'The Station'.

[69b]   Another edition, London and New York, Ward, Lock

Title page as [69a] except publisher's name and address: 'WARD, LOCK AND CO., | LONDON: WARWICK HOUSE, SALISBURY SQUARE, E.C. | NEW YORK: BOND STREET.'

Contents as [69a].

[69c]   American edition, New York, Munro, n.d. (Seaside Library Pocket Edition)

TRAITS AND STORIES OF THE IRISH PEASANTRY. | [rule] | THE MIDNIGHT MASS | AND | THE STATION. | BY |

WILLIAM CARLETON. | [short rule] | NEW YORK: | GEORGE MUNRO'S SONS, PUBLISHERS, | 17 to 27 VANDEWATER STREET.

Contains 'The Midnight Mass'; 'The Station'.

[69d]   American edition, New York, Lovell, n.d. [1886] (Lovell's Library No. 823)

TRAITS AND STORIES OF THE IRISH PEASANTRY. | [rule] | THE MIDNIGHT MASS | AND | THE STATION. | BY | WILLIAM CARLETON. | [short rule] | NEW YORK: | JOHN W. LOVELL, CO., | 150 WORTH STREET.

Contains 'The Midnight Mass'; 'The Station'.

[70a]   *Traits and Stories of the Irish Peasantry – Phil Purcel the Pig Driver and Other Stories*, London, Ward, Lock, n.d. (1 vol., pp. [2 + [1-28] + 357-398]) (Sixpenny Library)

TRAITS AND STORIES OF THE IRISH PEASANTRY. | [rule] | PHIL PURCEL THE PIG-DRIVER | AND | OTHER STORIES. | BY | WILLIAM CARLETON. | *WITH ILLUSTRATIONS.* | [Ward, Lock device] | LONDON: | WARD, LOCK, AND CO., | WARWICK HOUSE, SALISBURY SQUARE, E.C.

Contains 'Phil Purcel, the Pig-driver'; 'Ned M'Keown'; 'The Three Tasks'.

[70b]   Another edition, London and New York, Ward, Lock

Title page as [70a] except publisher's name and address: 'WARD, LOCK AND CO., | LONDON: WARWICK HOUSE, SALISBURY SQUARE, E.C. | NEW YORK: BOND STREET.'

Contents as [69a].

[70c]   American edition, New York, Munro, n.d. (Seaside Library Pocket Edition)

TRAITS AND STORIES OF THE IRISH PEASANTRY. | [rule] | PHIL PURCEL THE PIG-DRIVER | AND | OTHER STORIES. | BY | WILLIAM CARLETON. | [short rule] | NEW

YORK: | GEORGE MUNRO'S SONS, PUBLISHERS, | 17 to 27 VANDEWATER STREET.

Contains 'Phil Purcel the Pig-Driver'; 'Ned M'Keown'; 'The Three Tasks'.

[70d]   American edition, New York, Lovell, n.d. [1886] (Lovell's Library No. 824)

TRAITS AND STORIES OF THE IRISH PEASANTRY. | [rule] | PHIL PURCEL THE PIG-DRIVER | AND | OTHER STORIES. | BY | WILLIAM CARLETON. | [short rule] | NEW YORK: | JOHN W. LOVELL, CO., | 150 WORTH STREET.

Contains 'Phil Purcel the Pig-driver'; 'Ned M'Keown'; 'The Three Tasks'.

[71a]   *Traits and Stories of the Irish Peasantry – An Irish Oath and Lianhan Shee*, London, Ward, Lock, n.d. (1 vol., pp. [2] + [1-96]) (Sixpenny Library)

TRAITS AND STORIES OF THE IRISH PEASANTRY. | [rule] | AN IRISH OATH | AND | LIANHAN SHEE. | BY | WILLIAM CARLETON. | *WITH ILLUSTRATIONS.* | [Ward, Lock device] | LONDON: | WARD, LOCK, AND CO., | WARWICK HOUSE, SALISBURY SQUARE, E.C.

Contains 'The Geography of an Irish Oath'; 'The Lianhan Shee'.

[71b]   Another edition, London and New York, Ward, Lock

Title page as [70a] except publisher's name and address: 'WARD, LOCK AND CO., | LONDON: WARWICK HOUSE, SALISBURY SQUARE, E.C. | NEW YORK: BOND STREET.'

Contents as [71a].

[71c]   American edition, New York, Munro, n.d. (Seaside Library Pocket Edition)

TRAITS AND STORIES OF THE IRISH PEASANTRY. | [rule] | AN IRISH OATH | AND | LIANHAN SHEE. | BY | WILLIAM CARLETON. | [short rule] | NEW YORK: | GEORGE MUNRO'S SONS, PUBLISHERS, | 17 to 27 VANDEWATER STREET.

Contains 'The Geography of an Irish Oath'; 'The Lianhan Shee'.

[71d] American edition, New York, Lovell, n.d. [1886] (Lovell's Library No. 825)

TRAITS AND STORIES OF THE IRISH PEASANTRY. | [rule] | AN IRISH OATH | AND | LIANHAN SHEE. | BY | WILLIAM CARLETON. | [short rule] | NEW YORK: | JOHN W. LOVELL, CO., | 150 WORTH STREET.

Contains 'The Geography of an Irish Oath'; 'The Lianhan Shee'.

[72a] *Traits and Stories of the Irish Peasantry – Going to Maynooth*, London, Ward, Lock, n.d. (1 vol., pp. [2] + [97-188]) (Sixpenny Library)

TRAITS AND STORIES OF THE IRISH PEASANTRY. | [rule] | GOING TO MAYNOOTH. | BY | WILLIAM CARLETON. | *WITH ILLUSTRATIONS.* | [Ward, Lock device] | LONDON: | WARD, LOCK, AND CO., | WARWICK HOUSE, SALISBURY SQUARE, E.C.

Contains 'Going to Maynooth'.

[72b] Another edition, London and New York, Ward, Lock

Title page as [72a] except publisher's name and address: 'WARD, LOCK AND CO., | LONDON: WARWICK HOUSE, SALISBURY SQUARE, E.C. | NEW YORK: BOND STREET.

Contents as [72a].

[72c] American edition, New York, Munro, n.d. (Seaside Library Pocket Edition)

TRAITS AND STORIES OF THE IRISH PEASANTRY. | [rule] | GOING TO MAYNOOTH. | BY | WILLIAM CARLETON. | [short rule] | NEW YORK: | GEORGE MUNRO'S SONS, PUBLISHERS, | 17 to 27 VANDEWATER STREET.

Contains 'Going to Maynooth'.

[72d]   American edition, New York, Lovell, n.d. [1886] (Lovell's Library No. 826)

TRAITS AND STORIES OF THE IRISH PEASANTRY. | [rule] | GOING TO MAYNOOTH. | BY | WILLIAM CARLETON. | [short rule] | NEW YORK: | JOHN W. LOVELL, CO., | 150 WORTH STREET.

Contains 'Going to Maynooth'.

[73a]   *Traits and Stories of the Irish Peasantry – Phelim O'Toole's Courtship and Wildgoose Lodge*, London, Ward, Lock, n.d. (1 vol., pp. [2] + [189-272])

TRAITS AND STORIES OF THE IRISH PEASANTRY. | [rule] | PHELIM O'TOOLE'S COURTSHIP | AND | WILDGOOSE LODGE. | BY | WILLIAM CARLETON. | *WITH ILLUSTRATIONS.* | [Ward, Lock device] | LONDON: | WARD, LOCK, AND CO., | WARWICK HOUSE, SALISBURY SQUARE, E.C.

Contains 'Phelim O'Toole's Courtship'; 'Wildgoose Lodge'.

[73b]   Another edition, London and New York, Ward, Lock

Title page as [73a] except publisher's name and address: 'WARD, LOCK AND CO., | LONDON: WARWICK HOUSE, SALISBURY SQUARE, E.C. | NEW YORK: | BOND STREET.'

Contents as [73a].

[73c]   American edition, New York, Munro, n.d. (Seaside Library Pocket Edition)

TRAITS AND STORIES OF THE IRISH PEASANTRY. | [rule] | PHELIM O'TOOLE'S COURTSHIP | AND | WILDGOOSE LODGE. | BY | WILLIAM CARLETON. | [short rule] | NEW YORK: | GEORGE MUNRO'S SONS, PUBLISHERS, | 17 to 27 VANDEWATER STREET.

Contains 'Phelim O'Toole's Courtship'; 'Wildgoose Lodge'.

[73d]   American edition, New York, Lovell, n.d. [1886] (Lovell's Library No. 827)

TRAITS AND STORIES OF THE IRISH PEASANTRY. | [rule] | PHELIM O'TOOLE'S COURTSHIP | AND | WILDGOOSE LODGE. | BY | WILLIAM CARLETON. | [short rule] | NEW YORK: | JOHN W. LOVELL, CO., | 150 WORTH STREET.

Contains 'Phelim O'Toole's Courtship'; 'Wildgoose Lodge'.

[74a]   *Traits and Stories of the Irish Peasantry – Dominick the Poor Scholar*, London, Ward, Lock, n.d. (1 vol., pp. [2] + [273-364]) (Sixpenny Library)

TRAITS AND STORIES OF THE IRISH PEASANTRY. | DOMINICK, THE POOR SCHOLAR. | BY | WILLIAM CARLETON. | *WITH ILLUSTRATIONS.* | [Ward, Lock device] | LONDON: | WARD, LOCK, AND CO., | WARWICK HOUSE, SALISBURY SQUARE, E.C.

Contains 'The Poor Scholar'.

[74b]   Another edition, London and New York, Ward, Lock

Title page as [74a] except publisher's name and address: 'WARD, LOCK AND CO., | LONDON: WARWICK HOUSE, SALISBURY SQUARE, E.C. | NEW YORK: BOND STREET.'

Contents as [74a].

[74c]   American edition, New York, Munro, n.d. (Seaside Library Pocket Edition)

TRAITS AND STORIES OF THE IRISH PEASANTRY. | [rule] | DOMINICK, THE POOR SCHOLAR. | BY | WILLIAM CARLETON. | [short rule] | NEW YORK: | GEORGE MUNRO'S SONS, PUBLISHERS, | 17 to 27 VANDEWATER STREET.

Contains 'The Poor Scholar'.

[74d]   American edition, New York, Lovell, n.d. [1886] (Lovell's Library No. 828)

TRAITS AND STORIES OF THE IRISH PEASANTRY. | [rule] | DOMINICK, THE POOR SCHOLAR. | BY | WILLIAM

CARLETON. | [short rule] | NEW YORK: | JOHN W. LOVELL, CO., | 150 WORTH STREET.

Contains 'The Poor Scholar'.

[75a]   *Traits and Stories of the Irish Peasantry – Neal Malone and Tubber Derg*, London, Ward, Lock, n.d. (1 vol., pp. [2] + [365-432]) (Sixpenny Library)

TRAITS AND STORIES OF THE IRISH PEASANTRY. | NEAL MALONE | AND | TUBBER DERG. | BY | WILLIAM CARLETON. | *WITH ILLUSTRATIONS.* | [Ward, Lock device] | LONDON: | WARD, LOCK, AND CO., | WARWICK HOUSE | SALISBURY SQUARE, E.C.

Contains 'Neal Malone'; 'Tubber Derg'.

[75b]   Another edition, London and New York, Ward, Lock

Title page as [75a] except publisher's name and address: 'WARD, LOCK AND CO., | LONDON: WARWICK HOUSE, SALISBURY SQUARE, E.C. | NEW YORK: BOND STREET.'

Contents as [75a].

[75c]   American edition, New York, Munro, n.d. (Seaside Library Pocket Edition)

TRAITS AND STORIES OF THE IRISH PEASANTRY. | NEAL MALONE | AND | TUBBER DERG. | BY | WILLIAM CARLETON. | [short rule] | NEW YORK: | GEORGE MUNRO'S SONS, PUBLISHERS, | 17 to 27 VANDEWATER STREET.

Contains 'Neal Malone'; 'Tubber Derg'.

[75d]   American edition, New York, Lovell, n.d. [1886] (Lovell's Library No. 829)

TRAITS AND STORIES OF THE IRISH PEASANTRY. | [rule] | NEAL MALONE | AND | TUBBER DERG. | BY | WILLIAM CARLETON. | [short rule] | NEW YORK: | JOHN W. LOVELL, CO., | 150 WORTH STREET.

Contains 'Neal Malone'; 'Tubber Derg'.

Collier's *Works of William Carleton*

The Works of William Carleton, published by Collier in New York in 1881, is the fullest collection of Carleton's work ever put together by any publisher (Sadlier's 10-volume *Works of William Carleton* of 1875 has nine novels but only a few short stories). The Collier collection contains thirty Carleton pieces, though it is not a *Complete Works*, as it excludes many familiar tales such as 'Father Butler', 'The Misfortunes of Barney Branagan', 'Barney Brady's Goose', and all the *Tales and Sketches of the Irish Peasantry*. It does include two stories not by Carleton – 'Ellen Duncan' and 'The Proctor's Daughter', both by 'Denis O'Donoho'.

The Works of William Carleton is also interesting in its bibliographical history, which needed some detective work. Most examples of the collection have very erratic pagination, or 'End of Vol. I' in the middle of Volume II or at the end of Volume III. The title pages and contents pages do not always agree with each other, or with the contents of the volumes. To put it briefly, this confusion is caused by the fact that three different editions appeared in 1881 – all with the same setting but differently arranged and with different title and contents pages. The first [76a] was an illustrated two-volume *Works*. All subsequent pagination is based on this. But the stories were immediately redistributed into two different three-volume works [76b] and [76c], both illustrated, both dated 1881. [76c] became the standard format, and was reissued in 1882 (illustrated), in 1892 (not illustrated) and in three undated 'editions', one illustrated and two not illustrated [76d-76h].

This may seem clearer if I tabulate it before giving the bibliographical details:

[76a] 1881. Illustrated two-volume *Works* ('P.F. Collier, Publisher'):

Vol. I: 'Willy Reilly'; 'Fardorougha the Miser'; 'The Black Baronet'; 'The Evil Eye'; 'The Black Prophet'; 'Wildgoose Lodge'; 'Tubber Derg'; 'Neal Malone'; 'Art Maguire'.

Vol. II: 'Jane Sinclair'; 'Lha Dhu'; 'The Dead Boxer'; 'Ellen Duncan'; 'The Proctor's

Daughter'; 'Valentine M'Clutchy'; 'The Tithe Proctor'; 'Emigrants of Ahadarra'; '*Traits and Stories of the Irish Peasantry*' [i.e. a 'block' of 17 stories, 'Ned M'Keown' to 'The Poor Scholar'.]

[76b] 1881. Illustrated three-volume *Works*, ('P.F. Collier, Publisher'), the contents of the 2 volumes of [76a] redistributed as follows:

Vol. I: 'Willy Reilly'; 'Fardorougha the Miser'; 'The Black Baronet'; 'The Evil Eye' [i.e. the first part of [76a] Vol. I.]

Vol. II: 'Jane Sinclair'; 'Lha Dhu'; 'The Dead Boxer'; 'Valentine M'Clutchy'; 'The Tithe Proctor'; 'The Black Prophet'; 'Wildgoose Lodge'; 'Tubber Derg'; 'Neal Malone'; 'Art Maguire' (these ten stories on the title page) plus 'Ellen Duncan' and 'The Proctor's Daughter' (which do not appear on the title page but are included in the list of contents). [These 12 stories are drawn from Vols. I and II of [76a].]

Vol. III: 'The Emigrants of Ahadarra' and the 17-story 'block' of *Traits and Stories of the Irish Peasantry* [i.e. the last part of [76a] Vol. II.]

[76c] 1881. Illustrated three-volume *Works*, the contents of the two volumes of [76a] redistributed as follows:

Vol. I: 'Willy Reilly'; 'Fardorougha the Miser'; 'The Black Baronet'; 'The Evil Eye' (as [76b] Vol. I).

Vol. II: 'Jane Sinclair'; 'Lha Dhu'; 'The Dead Boxer'; 'Ellen Duncan'; 'The Proctor's Daughter'; 'Valentine M'Clutchy'; 'The Tithe Proctor'; 'The Emigrants of Ahadarra' (i.e. the first part of [76a] Vol. II.)

Vol. III: *Traits and Stories of the Irish Peasantry* (the 17-story 'block' from [76a] Vol. II); 'The Black Prophet'; 'Wildgoose Lodge'; 'Tubber Derg'; 'Neal Malone'; 'Art Maguire' (i.e. the last parts of [76a] Vols. II and I.)

[76d] 1882. 3-volume *Works*, illustrated ('P.F. Collier')
Contents as [76c]

[76e] 1882. 3-volume *Works*, not illustrated ('Peter Fenelon Collier')
Contents as [76c]

[76f] n.d. 3-volume *Works*, illustrated ('P.F. Collier')
Contents as [76c]

[76g] n.d. 3-volume *Works*, not illustrated ('P.F. Collier')
Contents as [76c]

[76h] n.d. 3-volume *Works*, not illustrated ('Peter Fenelon Collier')
Contents as [76c]

Because these reissues were all reimpositions from the stereotypes of [76a], the pagination is not sequential in [76b-h]. And where, for example, 'Art Maguire' has 'End of Vol. I' after the text in [76a], these words reappear in the middle of Vol. II of [76b] and at the end of Vol. III of [76c-h]. It is worth noting here that whereas on the title pages *Traits and Stories of the Irish Peasantry* is used as the heading for the 17-story 'block' ['Ned M'Keown' to 'The Poor Scholar'], in the lists of contents it is also used as the heading for the four stories 'Wildgoose Lodge', 'Tubber Derg', 'Neal Malone' and 'Art Maguire'.

These, then, are the eight standard presentations of Collier's *Works*. In late examples, so many volumes have title pages, contents lists and text at variance that it seems probable that they were bound at random. Colliers were pre-eminent in 'subscription' selling which usually meant door-to-door sales. It is possible that the variations in format of Carleton's *Works* reflected local or other variations in doorstep demand.

[76a]   American edition, Collier's Unabridged two-volume *Works of William Carleton*, New York, Collier, 1881 (2 vols., pp. [vi] + [1046]; [vi] + [1132]). Illustrated.

[Vol. I:] COLLIER'S UNABRIDGED EDITION. | [rule] | THE WORKS | OF | WILLIAM CARLETON. | [short rule] | VOLUME I. | [short rule] | [the next 6 lines ranged diagonally left to right:] WILLY REILLY. | FARDOROUGHA THE MISER. | THE BLACK BARONET; | OR, THE CHRONICLES OF BALLYTRAIN. | THE EVIL EYE; | OR, THE BLACK SPECTRE. | THE BLACK PROPHET. | [the next 4 lines ranged diagonally left to right:] WILD GOOSE LODGE. | TUBBER DERG. | NEAL MALONE. | ART MAGUIRE. | [short rule] | ILLUSTRATED. | [short rule] | NEW YORK: | P.F. COLLIER, PUBLISHER. | 1881.

[Vol. II:] COLLIER'S UNABRIDGED EDITION. | [rule] | THE WORKS | OF | WILLIAM CARLETON. | [short rule] | VOLUME II. | [short rule] | JANE SINCLAIR. | LHA DHU; | OR, THE DARK DAY. | THE DEAD BOXER. | VALENTINE McCLUTCHY, | THE IRISH AGENT. | THE TITHE-PROCTOR. | THE EMIGRANTS OF AHADARRA. | TRAITS AND STORIES OF THE IRISH PEASANTRY: | [the next 8 lines arranged in 2 columns ranged left and centre. Ranged left:] NED M'KEOWN. | THE THREE TASKS. | SHANE FADH'S WEDDING. | LARRY M'FARLAND'S WAKE. | THE BATTLE OF THE FACTIONS. | THE STATION. | THE PARTY FIGHT AND FUNERAL. | THE LOUGH DERG PILGRIM. | [ranged centre:] THE HEDGE SCHOOL. | THE MIDNIGHT MASS. | THE DONAGH; OR, THE HORSE STEALERS. | PHIL PURCEL, THE PIG-DRIVER. | THE GEOGRAPHY OF AN IRISH OATH. | THE LIANHAN SHEE. | GOING TO MAYNOOTH. | PHELIM O'TOOLE'S COURTSHIP. | THE POOR SCHOLAR. | [short rule] | ILLUSTRATED. | NEW YORK · | P.F. COLLIER, PUBLISHER. | 1881.

Contains: [Vol. I:] *Willy Reilly*; *Fardorougha*; *The Black Baronet*; *The Evil Eye*; *The Black Prophet*; and (listed under the heading TRAITS AND STORIES OF THE IRISH PEASANTRY:) 'Wildgoose Lodge'; 'Tubber Derg'; 'Neal Malone'; 'Art Maguire'. [Vol. II:] 'Jane Sinclair'; 'Lha Dhu'; 'Ellen Duncan' (not on title page); 'The Proctor's Daughter'; *Valentine M'Clutchy*; *The Tithe*

Proctor; and (under the heading TRAITS AND STORIES OF THE IRISH PEASANTRY:) the 'Introduction' to *Traits and Stories* 1842 [15a]; 'Ned M'Keown'; 'The Three Tasks'; 'Shane Fadh's Wedding'; 'Larry M'Farland's Wake'; 'The Battle of the Factions'; 'The Station'; 'The Party Fight and Funeral'; 'The Lough Derg Pilgrim'; 'The Hedge School'; 'The Midnight Mass'; 'The Donagh; or, the Horse Stealers'; 'Phil Purcel, the Pig-driver'; 'The Geography of an Irish Oath'; 'The Lianhan Shee'; 'Going to Maynooth'; 'Phelim O'Toole's Courtship'; 'The Poor Scholar'.

[76b]   American edition, three-volume *Works*, Unabridged, New York, Collier, 1881 (3 vols., pp. [vi] + [776]; [vi] + [492] + [777-1046]; [6] + [493-1132]. Illustrated.

[Vol. I:] COLLIER'S UNABRIDGED EDITION. | [rule] | THE WORKS | OF | WILLIAM CARLETON. | [short rule] | VOLUME I. | [next 6 lines range diagonally left to right:] WILLY REILLY. | FARDOROUGHA THE MISER. | THE BLACK BARONET; | OR, THE CHRONICLES OF BALLYTRAIN. | THE EVIL EYE; | OR, THE BLACK SPECTRE. | [short rule] | ILLUSTRATED. | [short rule] | NEW YORK: | P.F. COLLIER, PUBLISHER. | 1881.

[Vol. II:] COLLIER'S UNABRIDGED EDITION. | [rule] | THE WORKS | OF | WILLIAM CARLETON. | [short rule] | VOLUME II. | [to left of vertical rule:] JANE SINCLAIR. | LHA DHU; | OR, THE DARK DAY. | THE DEAD BOXER. | VALENTINE McCLUTCHY, | THE IRISH AGENT. | THE TITHE-PROCTOR. | [to right of the vertical rule:] THE BLACK PROPHET: | A TALE OF IRISH FAMINE. | WILDGOOSE LODGE. | TUBBER DERG; | OR, THE RED WELL. | [short rule] | NEAL MALONE. | ART MAGUIRE; | OR, THE BROKEN PLEDGE. | [short rule] | ILLUSTRATED. | [short rule] | NEW YORK: | P.F. COLLIER, PUBLISHER. | 1881.

[Vol. III:] COLLIER'S UNABRIDGED EDITION. | [rule] | THE WORKS | OF | WILLIAM CARLETON. | [short rule] | VOLUME III. | [short rule] | THE EMIGRANTS OF AHADARRA. | TRAITS AND STORIES OF THE IRISH PEASANTRY: | [the next 8 lines in two columns, ranged left and ranged centre. Ranged left:] NED M'KEOWN. | THE THREE TASKS. | SHANE FADH'S WEDDING. | LARRY M'FARLAND'S WAKE. | THE

BATTLE OF THE FACTIONS. | THE STATION. | THE PARTY
FIGHT AND FUNERAL. | THE LOUGH DERG PILGRIM. |
[ranged centre:] THE HEDGE SCHOOL. | THE MIDNIGHT
MASS. | THE DONAGH; OR, THE HORSE STEALERS. |
PHIL PURCEL, THE PIG-DRIVER. | THE GEOGRAPHY OF
AN IRISH OATH. | THE LIANHAN SHEE. | GOING TO
MAYNOOTH. | PHELIM O'TOOLE'S COURTSHIP. |
[centred:] THE POOR SCHOLAR. | [short rule] | ILLUSTRATED.
| [short rule] | NEW YORK · | P.F. COLLIER, PUBLISHER. |
1881.

Contents as title pages except Vol. II. Text of stories is reimposed
from the stereotypes of [76a], resulting in a non-sequential pagination
in Vols. II and III. Vol. I corresponds to the first pages of [76a] Vol.
I, paginated [6-776]. Its table of contents is that of [76a] Vol. I,
truncated. Vol. II contains 'Ellen Duncan' and 'The Proctor's
Daughter' in addition to the stories listed on its title page. It
contains 'Jane Sinclair', 'Lha Dhu', 'Ellen Duncan', 'The Proctor's
Daughter' and *The Tithe Proctor* as [76a] Vol. II pp. [5-492], and
The Black Prophet, 'Wildgoose Lodge', 'Tubber Derg', 'Neal
Malone' and 'Art Maguire' as [76a] Vol. I pp. [777-1046]. The list of
contents is taken in part from the lists in [76a] Vols. I and II, with
'Wildgoose Lodge', 'Tubber Derg', 'Neal Malone' and 'Art
Maguire' listed under the heading *Traits and Stories of the Irish
Peasantry*. Vol. III has *The Emigrants of Ahadarra* and the 17-story
'block' from [76a] Vol. II pp. [493-1132]. Its table of contents is
taken from the last part of that of [76a] Vol. II.

[76c]   American edition, 3-volume *Works*, Unabridged, New
York, Collier, 1881 (3 vols., pp. [vi] + [776]; [vi] + [640]; [4] + [641-
1132] + [777-1046]). Illustrated.

Vol. I as [76b] Vol. I.

[Vol. II:] COLLIER'S UNABRIDGED EDITION. | [rule] | THE
WORKS | OF | WILLIAM CARLETON. | [short rule] | VOLUME
II. | [short rule] | [to left of central vertical rule:] JANE SINCLAIR.
| LHA DHU; | OR, THE DARK DAY. | THE DEAD BOXER. |
ELLEN DUNCAN. | [to the right of central vertical rule:] THE
PROCTOR'S DAUGHTER. | VATENTINE [*sic*] McCLUTCHY, |

THE IRISH AGENT. | THE TITHE PROCTOR. | THE EMIGRANTS OF AHA- | DARRA. | [short rule] | ILLUSTRATED. | [short rule] | NEW YORK: | P.F. COLLIER, PUBLISHER. | 1881.

[Vol. III:] COLLIER'S UNABRIDGED EDITION. | [rule] | THE WORKS | OF | WILLIAM CARLETON. | [short rule] | VOLUME III. | [short rule] | TRAITS AND STORIES OF THE IRISH PEASANTRY: | [the next 8 lines in two columns, ranged left and ranged centre. Ranged left:] NED M'KEOWN. | THE THREE TASKS. | SHANE FADH'S WEDDING. | LARRY M'FARLAND'S WAKE. | THE BATTLE OF THE FACTIONS. | THE STATION. | THE PARTY FIGHT AND FUNERAL. | THE LOUGH DERG PILGRIM. | [ranged centre:] THE HEDGE SCHOOL. | THE MIDNIGHT MASS. | THE DONAGH; OR, THE HORSE STEALERS. | PHIL PURCEL, THE PIG-DRIVER. | THE GEOGRAPHY OF AN IRISH OATH. | THE LIANHAN SHEE. | GOING TO MAYNOOTH. | PHELIM O'TOOLE'S COURTSHIP. | [centred:] THE POOR SCHOLAR. | THE BLACK PROPHET. | [the next 4 lines ranged diagonally left to right:] WILD GOOSE LODGE. | TUBBER DERG. | NEAL MALONE. | ART MAGUIRE. | [short rule] | ILLUSTRATED. | [short rule] | NEW YORK · | P.F. COLLIER, PUBLISHER. | 1881.

Contents: Vol. I as [76b] Vol. I; Vol. II has pages [5-640] as [76a] Vol. II, reimposed from the same stereotypes ('Jane Sinclair', 'Lha Dhu', 'Ellen Duncan', 'The Proctor's Daughter', *Valentine M'Clutchy*, *The Tithe Proctor*, *The Emigrants of Ahadarra*), with its list of contents as the first part of [76a] Vol. II. Volume III has the 17-story 'block' of *Traits and Stories of the Irish Peasantry* as [76a] Vol. II, pp. [641-1132], and *The Black Prophet* and 'Wildgoose Lodge', 'Tubber Derg', 'Neal Malone' and 'Art Maguire' as [76a] Vol. I, pp. [777-1046]. The list of contents has the heading *Traits and Stories of the Irish Peasantry* over the Introduction and 17 stories 'Ned M'Keown' to 'The Poor Scholar'; then *The Black Prophet; a Tale of Irish Famine* with list of chapters; then another heading *Traits and Stories of the Irish Peasantry* over the 4 stories 'Wildgoose Lodge', 'Tubber Derg', 'Neal Malone' and 'Art Maguire'.

[76d] American edition, 3-volume *Works*, unabridged, New York, Collier, 1882 (3 vols., pp. [vi] + [776]; [vi] + [640]; [4] + [641-1132]; [777-1046]) Illustrated.

[Vol. I:] as [76b] Vol. I except '1882.' for '1881.'

[Vol. II:] as [76c] Vol. II except '1882.' for '1881.' (Still 'Vatentine McClutchy').

[Vol. III:] as [76c] Vol. III except '1882.' for '1881.'

Contents as [76c].

[76e] American edition, 3-volume *Works*, unabridged, New York, Collier, 1892 (3 vols., pp. [vi] + [776]; [vi] + [640]; [4] + [641-1132] + [777-1046]. Not illustrated.

[Vol. I:] as [76b] Vol. I except omits '[short rule] | ILLUSTRATED. | [short rule]' and changes publisher's name-style and date: 'NEW YORK: | PETER FENELON COLLIER, PUBLISHER. | 1892.'

Vols. II and III are as [76c] Vols. II and III, with the omission of 'ILLUSTRATED' and alteration of publisher's name and date as Vol. I here.

[76f] American edition, 3-volume *Works*, unabridged, New York, Collier, n.d. (3 vols., pp. [vi] + [776]; [vi] + [640]; [4] + [641-1132] + [777-1046]). Illustrated.

Title pages as [76c] except date omitted.

Contents as [76c].

[76g] American edition, 3-volume *Works*, unabridged, New York, Collier, n.d. (3 vols., pp. [vi] + [776]; [vi] + [640]; [4] + [641-1132] + [777-1046]). Not illustrated.

Title pages as [76c] except '[short rule] | ILLUSTRATED. | [short rule]' omitted and date omitted.

Contents as [76c].

[76h] American edition, 3-volume *Works*, unabridged, New York, Collier, n.d. (3 vols., pp. [vi] + [776]; [vi] + [640]; [4] +

[641-1132] + [777-1046]). Not illustrated.

Title pages as [76e] except date omitted.

Contents as [76c].

[76i] [Reprint], New York, Books for Libraries Press, 1970 (2 vols., pp. [vi] + [1046]; [vi] + [1132]).

THE WORKS | OF | WILLIAM CARLETON. | [short rule] | VOLUME I. | [short rule] | ILLUSTRATED | *Short Story Index Reprint Series* | [device] | BOOKS FOR LIBRARIES PRESS | FREEPORT, NEW YORK.

Reprint of [76a].

Amusing Irish Tales

[77a] *Amusing Irish Tales*, London, Glasgow, Hamilton Adams, Morison, 1889 (1 vol., pp. [2] + 256)

AMUSING | IRISH TALES | BY | William Carleton | *Author of "The Colleen Bawn," "Traits and Stories of the | Irish Peasantry," "The Fawn of Springvale," "The Squanders | of Castle Squander," "Fardarougha the Miser,"* | *&c., &c.* | LONDON: HAMILTON, ADAMS & CO | GLASGOW: THOMAS D. MORISON | 1889

Contains 'Editorial Note'; 'Buckram-back, The Country Dancing Master'; 'Mary Murray, The Irish Match-Maker'; 'Bob Pentland, The Irish Smuggler; or, The Gauger Outwitted'; 'Tom Gressiey, The Irish Senachie; or, The Origin of the name of Gordon'; 'Barney M'Haigney, The Irish Prophecy Man'; 'Fin M'Coul, The Knockmany Giant'; 'Around Ned's Fireside; or, The Story of the Squire'; 'The Irish Student; or, How the Protestant Church was Invented by Luther and the Devil'; 'Mickey M'Rorey, The Country Fiddler'; 'Rose Moan, The Country Mid-Wife'; 'Corney Keho's Baby; or, The Irish Christening'; 'Barney Brady's Goose; or, Mysterious Doings at Slathbeg'; 'Condy Cullen; And how he defeated the Exciseman'; 'Phil Purcel, The Connaught Pig-Driver'; 'Father Philemy; or, The Holding of the Station'.

S.J. Brown in a note to *Tales and Sketches of the Irish Peasantry* (his No.331) describes it as the original one shilling edition of *Tales and Stories* and *Amusing Irish Tales*, but the collections have only certain stories in common. Others are extracts from longer pieces –

'Around Ned's Fireside; or, the Story of the Squire' from 'Ned M'Keown'; 'The Irish Student' from an early version of 'Denis O'Shaughnessy going to Maynooth'.

[77b]   'New edition', London, Glasgow, Hamilton Adams, Morison, 1892 (1 vol., pp. [2] + 256)

AMUSING | IRISH TALES | BY | William Carleton | *Author of* *"The Colleen Bawn," "Traits and Stories of the | Irish Peasantry," "The Fawn of Springvale," "The Squanders | of Castle Squander," "Fardarougha the Miser," | &c., &c. | NEW EDITION | LONDON:* HAMILTON, ADAMS & CO | GLASGOW: THOMAS D. MORISON | 1892

Contents as [77a].

[77c]   'Fourth edition', London, Glasgow, Simpkin, Marshall, Hamilton, Kent, Morison, n.d. (1 vol., pp. 256)

AMUSING | IRISH TALES | BY | William Carleton | *Author of* *"The Colleen Bawn," "Traits and Stories of the | Irish Peasantry," "The Fawn of Springvale," "The Squanders | of Castle Squander," "Fardarougha the Miser," | &c., &c. | FOURTH EDITION |* LONDON | SIMPKIN, MARSHALL, HAMILTON, KENT & CO | GLASGOW: THOMAS D. MORISON

Contents as [77a].

The Red-Haired Man's Wife

[78a]   First edition, Dublin and London, Sealy, Bryers & Walker, Simpkin, Marshall, 1889 (1 vol., pp. viii + [274])

THE | RED-HAIRED MAN'S WIFE. | BY | WILLIAM CARLETON, | AUTHOR | "TRAITS AND STORIES OF THE IRISH PEASANTRY," "WILLY REILLY | AND HIS DEAR COLLEEN BAWN," "THE POOR SCHOLAR," | "PADDY-GO-EASY," "VALENTINE M'CLUTCHY," | "RODY THE ROVER," "THE BLACK | BARONET, "THE EVIL EYE," | ETC., ETC. | [short double rule] | DUBLIN: | SEALY, BRYERS & WALKER, | 94, 95 & 96 Middle Abbey Street. | LONDON: |

SIMPKIN, MARSHALL & CO., | 4 Stationers' Hall Court. | [short rule] | 1889.

Contains: 'Publisher's Preface' (explaining that the manuscript had been lost and found); story.

Sadleir No. [509]; Brown No. 340; O'Donoghue p. lxiv. O'Donoghue, quoted by Sadleir and Brown, claims that missing parts of a burnt manuscript were supplied after Carleton's death by one MacDermott, who then serialised the tale in 1870 in the *Carlow College Magazine*. I have not been able to find it in that magazine.

[79a] [Partwork:] *Irish Life and Character; or, Tales and Stories of the Irish Peasantry*, London, Henry Lea, n.d. (1 vol., pp. 364)

IRISH LIFE | AND | CHARACTER; | OR, | TALES and STORIES of the IRISH PEASANTRY. | [short rule] | BY WILLIAM CARLETON, ESQ. | AUTHOR OF "VALENTINE MC'CLUTCHY." | [short rule] | LONDON: HENRY LEA, 22, WARWICK LANE. | PATERNOSTER ROW.

A partwork first, then bound as a book. 35 parts – price one penny with 'steel engraving gratis'.

Contains 'Barney Brady's Goose'; 'The Three Tasks'; 'Neal Malone'; 'The Hedge School'; 'Condy Cullen; or, the Exciseman Defeated'; 'Moll Roe's Marriage; or, the Pudding Bewitched'.

This is part of *Tales and Sketches/Stories of the Irish Peasantry* [18a], omitting the last story, 'Second Sight and Apparition'. It has the *Tales and Stories of the Irish Peasantry* title plate, with '*LONDON*. | HENRY LEA, 22 WARWICK LANE.'

[80a] *Stories from Carleton*, edited by W.B. Yeats, London, New York, Toronto, Walter Scott, Gage n.d. [1889] (1 vol., pp. [xx] + 302) (Camelot Series)

Stories from carleton: | WITH AN INTRODUCTION | BY W.B. YEATS. | LONDON: | WALTER SCOTT, 24 WARWICK LANE. | NEW YORK AND TORONTO: | W.J. GAGE & CO.

Contains: Dedication 'To my friend the Author of "Shamrocks" '

(Katharine Tynan) and 'Introduction' by Yeats; 'The Poor Scholar'; 'Tubber Derg; or, the Red Well'; 'Wildgoose Lodge'; 'Shane Fadh's Wedding'; 'The Hedge School'.

Wade No. 214.

[80b]   Another edition, London, Felling-on-Tyne, New York, Walter Scott (The Scott Library) n.d. (1 vol., pp. [xviii] +302)

STORIES FROM CARLETON. | WITH AN INTRODUCTION | BY W. B. YEATS. | THE WALTER SCOTT PUBLISHING CO., LTD. | LONDON AND FELLING-ON-TYNE. | NEW YORK: 3 EAST 14TH STREET.

Contents as [80a].

[80c]   Another edition (reprint), New York, Lemma Publishing Corporation, 1973 (1 vol., pp. [2] + [xx] + 302)

STORIES FROM | CARLETON | WITH AN INTRODUCTION | BY | [bold:] **W. B. YEATS** | LEMMA PUBLISHING CORPORATION | NEW YORK | 1973

Facsimile reprint of [80a].

[81a]   *Phil Purcell the Pig-driver and other stories*, London, Manchester, New York, Routledge, 1895 (1 vol., pp. [4] + 220) (The Caxton Novels)

PHIL PURCELL | THE PIG-DRIVER | *AND OTHER STORIES* | BY WILLIAM CARLETON | [short rule] | LONDON | GEORGE ROUTLEDGE AND SONS, LIMITED | BROADWAY, LUDGATE HILL | MANCHESTER AND NEW YORK | 1895

Contains: 'The Hedge School'; 'The Station'; 'The Midnight Mass'; 'The Donagh; or, the Horse Stealers'; 'Phil Purcell, the Pig-Driver'; 'The Lianhan Shee'.

This is the second 'series' of Routledge's 'Four-series' *Traits and Stories*, n.d. [62a], in paper covers.

The Dead Boxer

[82a]   American edition, *The Dead Boxer, or, the Secret Blow and Counter Secret*, Boston, Jones, n.d. (1 vol., pp. 52)

[Ornamental caps:] THE DEAD BOXER: | — OR, THE — | SECRET BLOW AND COUNTER SECRET. | [engraving of woman and gloomy man] | ELLEN EXTORTING LAMH LAUDHER'S PROMISE. | [short rule] | BY WILLIAM CARLETON. | [short rule] | BOSTON: | J. JONES, 2 WATER STREET.

Contains 'The Dead Boxer'.

[83a] *Traits and Stories of the Irish Peasantry*, edited by D.J. O'Donoghue, London, Dent, 1896 (4 vols., pp. lvi + [220]; [viii] + 304; viii + [328]; [viii] + [336]).

TRAITS AND STORIES OF | [red:] THE IRISH PEASANTRY | BY | WILLIAM CARLETON | [sundial motif] | EDITED BY | D.J. O'DONOGHUE | LONDON | [red:] J. M. DENT AND CO. | MDCCCXCVI

Contains (Vol. I:) 'Introduction'; 1830 'Preface'; 'Author's Introduction' [part of Carleton's 'General Introduction' [15a], 1842]; 'Ned M'Keown'; 'The Three Tasks'; 'Shane Fadh's Wedding'; 'Larry M'Farland's Wake'; 'The Station'; 'An Essay on Irish Swearing'; (Vol. II:) 'The Battle of the Factions'; 'The Midnight Mass'; 'The Party Fight and Funeral'; 'The Hedge School'; 'The Lough Derg Pilgrim'; (Vol. III:) 'Preface to the Second Series' [1833]; 'The Donagh; or, the Horse Stealers'; ' Phil Purcel, the Pigdriver'; 'The Lianhan Shee'; 'The Geography of an Irish Oath'; 'The Poor Scholar'; 'Wildgoose Lodge'; (Vol. IV:) 'Tubber Derg; or, the Red Well'; 'Denis O'Shaughnessy going to Maynooth'; 'Phelim O'Toole's Courtship'; 'Neal Malone'; 'Glossary of Irish phrases'.

[83b]   London and New York, Dent, Macmillan, 1896 (4 vols., pp. lvi + [220]; [viii] + 304; viii + [328]; [viii] + [336])

Title page as [75a] except publishers' names and addresses: 'LONDON | J.M. DENT AND CO. | NEW YORK: MACMILLAN AND CO. | MDCCCXCVI

Variant 'MACMILLAN AND CO. LTD.' for 'MACMILLAN AND CO.'

[84a]   [partly by Carleton] *The Life of William Carleton/Auto-biography* London, Downey, 1896 (2 vols., pp. lxiv + 292; viii + 364)

THE LIFE OF WILLIAM | CARLETON: *BEING* | HIS AUTOBIOGRAPHY AND LET-|TERS; AND AN ACCOUNT OF HIS | LIFE AND WRITINGS, FROM THE | POINT AT WHICH THE AUTOBIO-|GRAPHY BREAKS OFF, BY DAVID J. | O'DONOGHUE. *With an Introduction by* | MRS. CASHEL HOEY | IN TWO VOLUMES. WITH TWO PORTRAITS | VOL. [I.] | DOWNEY & CO., 12, YORK STREET, COVENT | GARDEN, LONDON. 1896

Contains: (Vol. I:) 'Preface' by D.J. O'Donoghue; 'Introduction' by Frances Cashel Hoey; 'Bibliography' of Carleton's writings; Carleton's unfinished 'Autobiography'; (Vol. II:) 'Life of William Carleton' by O'Donoghue.

The 'Autobiography' was later published by Macgibbon & Kee, with a 'Preface' by Patrick Kavanagh. See [91a] below.

[84b]   Another edition (reprint), New York and London, Garland, 1979 (2 vols., pp. *6* + xiv + [296]; *6* + viii + 362 + *8*)

The Life of | William Carleton | *William Carleton* | completed by | *David O'Donoghue* | *in two volumes* | Volume [I] | *Garland Publishing, Inc., New York & London* | 1979

With Garland Series title page and reprint title pages of [76b].

Reprint of [76a] (Garland Reprint No. 44)

[85a]   *Irish Tales*, edited by W.B. Yeats, New York and London, Putnam, n.d. [1904] (1 vol., pp. *[2]* + [iv] + [150] (Ariel Booklets No. 77)

[The whole page in Gothic:] **Irish Tales** | **By** | [red:] **William Carleton** | **Wildgoose Lodge. Condy Cullen** | **The Curse** | **Battle of the Factions** | **With a Biographical Introduction by** | [red:] **W. B. Yeats** | [Putnam device] | **New York and London** | [red:] **G.P. Putnam's Sons** | **The Knickerbocker Press**

Contains: 'Introduction' by W.B. Yeats; 'Wildgoose Lodge'; 'Condy Cullen'; 'The Curse' (from 'The Party Fight and Funeral'); 'The Battle of the Factions'. These are the Carleton stories from

Yeats's anthology of *Representative Irish Tales* (see 'Subsequent Printings' section). The 'Introduction' is the introductory article to the Carleton section of that collection.

Wade does not mention this Yeats selection of *Irish Tales* by Carleton, but he does note that the stories by and articles about Maria Edgeworth and the Banims were separately published as *Irish Tales* by those authors (Wade No. 215a).

[86a] *Stories by William Carleton*, introduced by Tighe Hopkins, London, Blackie, n.d. [1905] (1 vol., pp. xxiv + [404]) (Red Letter Library)

[Title plate instead of title page:]
[Within rose-decorated frame:] STORIES | BY | WILLIAM CARLETON [6 roses] WITH AN INTRODUCTION BY | [rose] TIGHE HOPKINS [rose] | [device] | BLACKIE & SON Lᴛᴅ LONDON

Contains 'Introduction' by Tighe Hopkins; 'The Party Fight and Funeral'; 'The Hedge School'; 'Phelim O'Toole's Courtship'; 'Neal Malone'.

[86b] American edition, New York, Boston, Caldwell, n.d. [1905] (1 vol., pp. xxiv + [404]) (Red Letter Library)

As [86a] except publishers' name and address: 'H.M. CALDWELL CO. | PUBLISHERS | NEW YORK — BOSTON'

[87a] *Traits and Stories of the Irish Peasantry*, American Edition, Boston, Niccolls, 1911 (4 vols., pp. [8] + [xlx] + 404 + [2]; [8] + 428 + [2]; [8] + [500] + [2]; [8] + [494] + [2]) (Celtic Edition)

[green-gold 'Celtic' lettering:] TRAITS | AND | STORIES | OF | THE | IRISH | PEASANTRY | BY WILLIAM CARLETON | [decorative panel of shamrocks, with central Celtic cross; on left of cross, outside panel:] *In Four Volumes* | *Vol [I]* | [on right of cross, outside panel: *With etchings by* | *Phiz, Wrightson* | *Lee and others* | [on left of cross, within panel:] *Francis A Niccolls* | *& Company* | [on right of cross, within panel:] *Boston 1911*

This is the 'Celtic Edition. Of which one thousand numbered and registered copies have been printed', as declared on the verso of all title pages, with handwritten number. It contains (Vol. I:) 'Dedication to Butt'; 'Ned M'Keown'; 'The Three Tasks'; 'Shane Fadh's Wedding'; 'Larry M'Farland's Wake'; 'Battle of the Factions'; 'The Station'; 'Wildgoose Lodge'; (Vol. II:) 'The Party Fight and Funeral'; 'The Lough Derg Pilgrim'; 'The Hedge School'; 'The Midnight Mass'; (Vol. III:) 'The Donagh, or, the Horse-Stealers'; 'Phil Purcell the Pig Driver'; 'Geography of an Irish Oath'; 'The Lianhan Shee'; 'Going to Maynooth'; (Vol. IV:) 'Phelim O'Toole's Courtship'; 'The Poor Scholar'; 'Tubber Derg'; 'Neal Malone'.

These are the 20 stories of the 1842 'New Edition' [15a], but in a different order and without the 'Autobiographical Introduction'.

[88a]   *Carleton's Stories of Irish Life*, 'Every Irishman's Library', Dublin, Talbot Press, 1918 (1 vol., pp. xxxiv + 364)

[Within double rule frame:] [Green:] Every Irishman's Library | *General Editors:* ALFRED PERCEVAL GRAVES, M.A. | WILLIAM MAGENNIS, M.A. DOUGLAS HYDE, LL.D. | [double rule] | [Green:] CARLETON'S STORIES | OF IRISH LIFE | ['Fiat Lux' device] | [Green:] WITH AN INTRODUCTION | BY DARRELL FIGGIS | [double rule] | DUBLIN: | THE TALBOT PRESS LIMITED | 89 TALBOT STREET

Contains: 'Introduction' by Darrell Figgis; 'Neal Malone'; 'Phelim O'Toole's Courtship'; 'The Geography of an Irish Oath'; 'Bob Pentland, or the Gauger outwitted'; 'The Party Fight and Funeral'; 'The Midnight Mass'; 'The Hedge School'; 'Denis O'Shaughnessy going to Maynooth'.

Brown No. 343

[88b]   Another edition, Dublin and London, Talbot Press, Fisher Unwin, n.d. (1 vol., pp. xxiv + 364)

[Within double rule frame:] Every Irishman's Library | *General Editors:* ALFRED PERCEVAL GRAVES, M.A. | WILLIAM MAGENNIS, M.A. DOUGLAS HYDE, LL.D. | ['Fiat Lux' device] | WITH AN INTRODUCTION | BY DARRELL FIGGIS | [double rule] | [on l.h.s. of vertical rule:] DUBLIN: | THE TALBOT PRESS, LTD. | 89 TALBOT STREET | [on r.h.s. of vertical rule:] LONDON: | T. FISHER UNWIN, LTD. | 1 ADELPHI TERRACE

[88c]   American edition, New York, Stokes, n.d. (1 vol., pp. xxiv + 364)

CARLETON'S STORIES | OF IRISH LIFE | WITH AN INTRODUCTION | BY DARRELL FIGGIS | ['fiat lux' device] | NEW YORK: | FREDERICK A. STOKES COMPANY | PUBLISHERS

[88d]   Another edition, Dublin, Cork, Belfast, Phoenix, 1919 (1 vol., pp. xxiv + 364) (The Irish Library)

CARLETON'S | STORIES | OF IRISH LIFE | [Irish Library device] | *With an Introduction by* | *Darrell Figgis* | THE PHOENIX PUBLISHING COMPANY | LIMITED | DUBLIN CORK & BELFAST

[89a]   *The Poor Scholar*, Dublin, Dawson, n.d. [1950?] (1 vol., pp. [*4*] + [168] + [*4*])

CARLETON | THE | POOR SCHOLAR | [lyre and wreath device] | WM. DAWSON & SONS, LTD. | MOLESWORTH PLACE | DUBLIN

Contains 'The Poor Scholar'.

Paperback. The publisher's advertisements announce *Willie* [sic] *Reilly* 'in an edition uniform with this' which I have not seen.

[90a]   *Phelim O'Toole*, edited by Anthony Cronin, London, New English Library, 1962. (1 vol., pp. [xii] + 228) (Four Square Classics)

WILLIAM CARLETON | [short decorative rule] | THE COURTSHIP OF | PHELIM O'TOOLE | SELECTED, EDITED AND INTRODUCED BY | ANTHONY CRONIN | [Four Square Classics device] | THE NEW ENGLISH LIBRARY LTD.

Contains: 'Introduction' by Anthony Cronin; 'The Courtship of Phelim O'Toole'; 'The Party Fight and Funeral'; 'Denis O'Shaughnessy going to Maynooth'; 'The Hedge School'; 'Shane Fadh's Wedding'; 'The Battle of the Factions'.

[91a]   *Autobiography of William Carleton*, Preface by Patrick Kavanagh, London, MacGibbon & Kee, 1968 (1 vol., pp. 238)

The Autobiography of | WILLIAM CARLETON | With a Preface by | PATRICK KAVANAGH | [publisher's device] | MACGIBBON & KEE

Contains 'Preface' by Patrick Kavanagh; 'Publisher's note'; Carleton's unfinished 'Autobiography'.

[92a]   *Wildgoose Lodge and other stories*, edited by Maurice Harmon, Cork and Dublin, Mercier Press, 1973 (1 vol., pp. viii + 150)

MERCIER IRISH CLASSICS | *Traits and Stories of the Irish Peasantry, Volume I* | WILDGOOSE LODGE | and other stories | by | WILLIAM CARLETON | With an Introduction by | MAURICE HARMON | THE MERCIER PRESS | Cork and Dublin

Contains: 'General Introduction to the Series' and 'Introduction to Volume One' by Maurice Harmon; 'Wildgoose Lodge'; 'Ned M'Keown'; 'The Lianhan Shee'; 'The Lough Derg Pilgrim'.

[93a]   *Denis O'Shaughnessy going to Maynooth*, edited by Maurice Harmon, Cork and Dublin, Mercier Press, 1973 (1 vol., pp. x + 120)

MERCIER IRISH CLASSICS | *Traits and Stories of the Irish Peasantry, Volume II* | DENIS O'SHAUGHNESSY | GOING TO MAYNOOTH | by | WILLIAM CARLETON | With an Introduction by | MAURICE HARMON | THE MERCIER PRESS | Cork and Dublin

Contains: 'Introduction' by Maurice Harmon; 'Denis O'Shaughnessy Going to Maynooth'; 'Neil Malone'.

[94a]   *Phelim O'Toole's Courtship and other stories*, edited by Maurice Harmon, Cork and Dublin, Mercier Press, 1973 (1 vol., pp. viii + 150)

MERCIER IRISH CLASSICS | *Traits & Stories of the Irish Peasantry, Volume III* | PHELIM O'TOOLE'S | COURTSHIP | and other stories | by | WILLIAM CARLETON | With an Introduction by | MAURICE HARMON | THE MERCIER PRESS | Cork and Dublin

Contains: 'Introduction' by Maurice Harmon; 'Phelim O'Toole's Courtship'; 'The Three Tasks'; 'An Essay on Irish Swearing'.

[95a]   *The Party Fight and Funeral* etc., edited by Maurice Harmon, Cork and Dublin, Mercier Press, 1973 (1 vol., pp. viii + 156)

MERCIER IRISH CLASSICS | *Traits & Stories of the Irish Peasantry, Volume IV* | THE PARTY FIGHT | AND FUNERAL | by | WILLIAM CARLETON | With an Introduction by | MAURICE HARMON | THE MERCIER PRESS | Cork and Dublin

Contains 'Introduction' by Maurice Harmon; 'The Party Fight and Funeral'; 'The Midnight Mass'.

†[96a]   *Tubber Derg; Denis O'Shaughnessy; Phelim O'Toole's Courtship; and Neal Malone*, edited by Eileen Sullivan Ibarra, Gainesville, Florida, Renaissance Print and Publishing Co., 1974

[97a]   *King Richard McRoyal or The Dream of an Antiquarian*, edited by Liam Bradley, Armagh, Southern Education and Library Board Library Service, 1983 (1 vol., pp. [xvi] + [24])

King Richard McRoyal or | The Dream of an | Antiquarian | Showing brief glimpses of the writer's state of health | and the great advantages of an Absolute Monarchy | over a mixed government. | by | WILLIAM CARLETON | Edited with an Introduction by | LIAM BRADLEY | PUBLISHED BY | SOUTHERN EDUCATION AND LIBRARY BOARD | LIBRARY SERVICE | 1 Markethill Road, Armagh.

Contains 'Introduction'; 'Notes on the text'; story.

ORIGINAL PERIODICAL CONTRIBUTIONS

INTRODUCTION

Carleton's work was intimately linked with the Irish periodical press. Not only did the Rev. Caesar Otway, as is well known, start him on his literary career by asking him to write down his experiences at Lough Derg for the *Christian Examiner*, but until the very end of his life he went on contributing to magazines – his last series of articles for the *Shamrock* was actually published three weeks after his death. He wrote over seventy stories, articles and poems for a dozen Irish periodicals, and five of his novels first appeared as magazine serials. Some of his collections consisted entirely of stories originally written for periodicals, and all contained at least one such reprint. At several points in his career he was closely associated with certain periodicals: he was the principal fiction writer of the *Christian Examiner* for nearly four years, and he was a consistent contributor to the *Dublin University Magazine* from 1833 to 1842 and from 1846 to 1860. His connections with the *Nation*, the *Irish Tribune* and *The Shamrock* were apparently so strong that he found it necessary to disclaim them. (*Nation*, 26 November 1842; *Irish Tribune*, Vol. I, No. 5, 8 July 1848, p. 72; *Shamrock*, Vol. IV, No. 83, 2 May 1869, p. 516). The open adherence of an author to one periodical or another publicised any change of his religious or political position, so it was particularly noticeable when the former pillar of the rabidly anti-Catholic *Christian Examiner* became a regular contributor to Duffy's ultra-Catholic magazines in the 1850s, or when the stalwart of the conservative and unionist *Dublin University Magazine* wrote for the anti-Unionist *Nation* or *Tribune*, whatever his disclaimers.

Carleton's periodical allegiances indicate much less his own changing opinions than the prevailing moods of his time. His work for the *Christian Examiner* must be judged in the context of that intensely Protestant propagandist organ, but the *Christian Examiner* itself must be judged in its context too: it seemed a run-of-the-mill periodical in the 1820s, when religious publications were attacking each others' faiths with violent and outspoken abuse.

From April 1828 to December 1831, Carleton's stories were not incidental to the magazine, but major features of it, month by month. He used the stock-in-trade of the *Examiner*'s anti-Catholic armoury in a way that seems to us offensive but was standard periodical practice. To defend Otway against D.J. O'Donoghue and subsequent commentators, one should point out that he was one of the first Irish editors to see the literary possibility of good fiction in a religious journal; that he did *not* fall out with Carleton because he had put decent Catholic characters into 'Denis O'Shaughnessy going to Maynooth'; that the serial was curtailed not because of any dispute between the men but because Otway stopped editing the magazine at the end of 1831 and his successor included no fiction whatever; and that as editor of the *Dublin Penny Journal*, he continued to commission stories from Carleton for that magazine; and, above all, that Carleton did not diminish but augment his anti-Catholicism in his *Examiner* stories when they were first published in book form.

As the religious atmosphere cooled down after Catholic Emancipation, Carleton's periodical contributions became milder. In 1829, he wrote 'Dick Magrath, a sketch of living character', which was only mockingly anti-Catholic, for the gently Protestant *Dublin Family Magazine*; changing its name in 1830 to the *Dublin Monthly Magazine*, this became one of the first of the new non-sectarian literary journals. These publications, such as the *Dublin Penny Journal*, the *Dublin Literary Gazette*, the *Irish Penny Magazine*, did much for the revival of an Irish national identity, generating – or responding to – an interest in Irish literature, arts, archaeology, folklore, language, history and topography. One of the earliest of these, the *Dublin Literary Gazette, or Weekly Chronicle of Criticism, Belles Lettres, and Fine Arts*, published anonymously in 1830 Carleton's 'Confessions of a Reformed Ribbonman', a powerful tale which was later to become 'Wildgoose Lodge'. Within five months of its foundation, the *Gazette* changed its name and form to the *National Magazine*, a monthly whose editorial intention was to encourage the arts in Ireland. It commissioned much excellent original work, both fiction and non-fiction (such as studies of Irish ballads and ballad-singers). Carleton's five stories for the magazine suit its uncontentious pages: no single-minded vilification of the priesthood, but a range of subjects from Hellfire Clubs to runaway marriages, and a well-considered fictional account of the plight of the tenant farmer in 'The Landlord and Tenant' (later expanded into 'Tubber Derg; or, the Red Well') which appeared in April 1831, in the last number of the magazine. Carleton also contributed two suitably rancourless stories to the apolitical *[Dublin] University Review and Quarterly* in 1833.

Carleton was a major contributor to that most successful of Irish periodicals, the *Dublin University Magazine*, from its first year (1833). Modelled on *Fraser's* and *Blackwood's* magazines, with a strong editorial presence, conservative politics and a decisively Irish tone, the magazine commissioned serials and single stories from Carleton; in spite of its Protestant slant, his stories for it are not in his bigoted anti-priest style, but mostly in his good-humoured comic vein, with the serials 'Jane Sinclair' and 'Fardorougha the Miser' more ambitious 'literary' productions. After a lapse caused by a quarrel with Charles Lever who edited the magazine from 1842 to 1845, Carleton wrote for it again from 1846 to 1860, his work at this period including 'The Black Prophet', a well-timed famine novel based on the earlier crop failure of 1822.

In 1840 and 1841, he contributed fourteen sketches of Irish characters and customs to the *Irish Penny Journal*, one of those excellent penny journals, with a high standard of original and Irish material, which failed within a year. Thereafter, although the *Dublin University Magazine* continued, most of the energy which had fired the literary periodicals went into the much more political outlets of the *Citizen* (January to December 1842) and the *Nation* (October 1842 onwards). In their pages, the national intellectual spirit became less scholarly and more journalistic; less unifying and more propagandist. Carleton contributed one comic and one harrowing tale to the *Citizen* ('Moll Roe's Marriage, or, the Pudding Bewitched' and 'Records of the Heart: the Parents' Trial'). He did not contribute any fiction to the *Nation*, despite his close association with the editorial board, and their view of him as the great man of Irish literature and therefore a great patriot. Instead he contributed two poems, a long eulogy of John Banim and some anonymous ephemera in the heavily bantering style of 'The Tea-Kettle Correspondence' (1845). He also produced a scurrilous, sneering and unjust attack on Charles Lever, who had not only published but generously praised his work in the *Dublin University Magazine*. Carleton's writing for the *Nation* tallies with its equation of Irishness and excellence; the 'native' Banim is praised, the cosmopolitan Lever reviled. In the wake of the *Nation* came the *Irish Tribune*, militant and inflammatory; Carleton contributed 'The Evil Eye or the Black Spectre, a Tale of Mystery' to it in 1848 as a serial, abruptly discontinued when he got his civil list pension.

After the famine of 1845 and the abortive rising of 1848, the patterns of literary as of other life in Ireland broke up. In the fifties, a cosy family journalism with a strong Catholic content prevailed, mainly under the proprietorship of James Duffy. Carleton's contributions to *Duffy's Hibernian Magazine*, particularly 'The Rapparee' (1860) and 'The Double Prophecy' (1861), conform well to its romantic, pseudo-historical Irishness. He wrote a fresher, livelier story in four instalments, 'The Miller of Mohill', for Duffy's finer penny *Illustrated Dublin Journal* (1861). Another well-designed literary pennyworth, *The Shamrock*, published Carleton's 'Nostalgia, or Home Sickness' just after his death in 1869.

Carleton attempted unsuccessfully to become a contributor to English magazines. As early as 30 January 1829 he was proposing himself as a contributor to *Blackwood's Magazine*; he tried again on 10 February 1839, and again on 12 September 1848 without success (Letters to William Blackwood, National Library of Scotland). It is strange, in view of the considerable critical interest which his books aroused in English and Scottish periodicals, how little original work he published in them. His 'Black-and-all-black. A legend of the Padareen Mare, related on Christmas Eve by an old senachie' appeared in the *Illustrated London News* Supplement for 21 December 1850; chapters of 'The Squanders of Squander Castle' (sic) appeared irregularly in the same journal in 1851, just before book publication. In 1852 and 1853, the *Illustrated London Magazine* published 'The Fair of Emyvale', 'Master and Scholar' and 'The Silver Acre'. Carleton's original work found no other outlet in British periodicals. He seems uniquely involved with the movements in Irish periodicals, and particularly attuned to the needs and tastes of their editors and readers.

There were various practical reasons for Carleton's close association with the periodical world. He was always short of money and made very little from his books, so he needed what he earned by writing for magazines. He also relied on them to 'promote' his books by showing samples of his works, even in extracts, but particularly in long original pieces. His reputation and popularity were greatly enhanced by the appearance of his serials in the *Dublin University Magazine*, with its immense prestige and large circulation (four thousand copies a month in 1844, many sold in England).

It is also evident that Carleton was proud of his association with the magazines. His introduction to the New Edition of *Traits and Stories of the Irish Peasantry* (1842) shows how the revival of Irish literary life, his own work, and the new periodicals (however short lived) all acted upon each other:

About this time (1830) the literary taste of the metropolis began to feel the first symptoms of life. As yet, however, they were very faint. Two or three periodicals were attempted, and though of very considerable merit and conducted by able men, none of them, I believe, reached a year's growth. The "Dublin Monthly Magazine" and the "Dublin University Review," all perished in their infancy – not, however, because they were unworthy of success, but because Ireland was not then what she is fast becoming, a reading, and consequently a thinking, country. To every one of these the author contributed, and he has the satisfaction of being able to say that there has been no publication projected purely for the advancement of literature in his own country, to which he has not given the aid of his pen, such as it was, and this whether he received remuneration or not. Indeed, the consciousness that the success of his works had been the humble means of inciting others to similar exertion in their own country, and of thus giving the first impulse to our literature, is one which has on his part created an enthusiastic interest in it which will only die with him.
(General Introduction, *Traits and Stories of the Irish Peasantry*, Curry, Dublin, 1842 [15a] pp. vi-vii.)

It seems clear here that Carleton, speaking as an established and authoritative writer, is proud of his close relationship with the periodical press, and there is absolutely no hint, as he goes on to praise the longlived *Dublin University Magazine* for being 'a bond of union for literary men of every class', that he considered writing for magazines to be hack work: to Carleton, even at the height of his fame, periodicals were 'literature'.

A note on this section.
This section contains pieces originally published in magazines. They are listed in chronological order of their first publication, whether they are stories, poems or articles. Where a story is serialised, all instalments are in the same entry. Each entry contains a reference to the *first* book publication of the piece; later book publication will be found in the index.

I have omitted three pieces suggested by D.J. O'Donoghue. A poem in archaic language, 'The Death of Lewry' (*Dublin University Magazine*, Vol. XII, No. 67, July 1838, pp. 130-131) and the 'Autobiography of the Rev. Blackthorn M'Flail, Parish Priest of

Ballymacwhackem' (serialised in that magazine from March 1837, Vol. IX, No. 41) are put forward as Carleton's work in the *Life of William Carleton* (Vol. II, p. 37 and p. 34n) on grounds no more conclusive than 'style', and the poem's Tyrone connection. The style is debatable, and all Carleton's work for the magazine from 1834 on was attributed to him. As 'Fardorougha the Miser' overlapped with 'Blackthorn M'Flail', the two would make an excessively high Carleton content for those months. O'Donoghue (Life, Vol. II, p. 123, also suggests the 'The Life and Labours of a Catholic Curate', *Duffy's Irish Catholic Magazine*, (Vol. I, No. 10, November 1847) has 'a style very like Carleton's. But for its subject one might immediately assume it to be his'. The style is a syrupy and uplifting journalese not particularly attributable to Carleton.

ORIGINAL PERIODICAL CONTRIBUTIONS

CHRONOLOGICAL LIST

1828

1. A PILGRIMAGE TO PATRICK'S PURGATORY. [by] W. *Christian Examiner and Church of Ireland Gazette*, Vol. VI, No. XXXIV, April 1828, pp. 268-286; Vol. VI, No. XXXV, May 1828, pp. 323-362.

Republished (omitting opening paragraphs) in book form with *Father Butler* – see *Father Butler. The Lough Dearg Pilgrim*, Curry, 1829 [1a].

2. THE BROKEN OATH. [by] WILTON. *Christian Examiner*, Vol. VI, No. XXXVI, June 1828, pp. 425-439; Vol. VII, No. XXXVII, July 1828, pp. 27-39.

Republished as book by Duffy, 1845 [19a], retitled *Art Maguire; or, The Broken Pledge. A narrative*, much revised with a long continuation.

3. FATHER BUTLER. [by] WILTON. *Christian Examiner*, Vol. VII, No. XXXVIII, August 1828, pp. 109-119; Vol. VII, No. XXXIX, Sept. 1828, pp. 192-202; Vol. VII, No. XL, Oct. 1828, pp. 271-290; Vol. VII, No. XLI, Nov. 1828, pp. 355-365; Vol. VII, No. XLII, Dec. 1828, pp. 423-443.

Republished as book with 'The Lough Dearg Pilgrim' as *Father Butler. The Lough Dearg Pilgrim*, Curry, 1829 [1a].

4. [Poem] RETROSPECTIONS. By the Author of the Lough Derg Pilgrim. WILTON. *Christian Examiner*, Vol. VII, No. XXXIX, Sept. 1828, pp. 233-234.

5. [Poem] THE MIDNIGHT HOUR. [by] WILTON. *Christian Examiner*, Vol. VII, No. XLI, Nov. 1828, p. 390.

1829

6. THE STATION. [by] WILTON. *Christian Examiner*, Vol.
VIII, No. XLIII, Jan. 1829, pp. 45-60; Vol. VIII, No. XLIV, Feb.
1829, pp. 250-269; Vol. VIII, No. XLV, March 1829, pp. 422-438.

Included in *Traits and Stories of the Irish Peasantry*, First Series,
first edition, Curry, 1830 [2a].

7. DICK M'GRATH. A SKETCH OF LIVING CHARACTER.
[by] WILTON. *Dublin Family Magazine*, Vol. I, No. V, Aug. 1829,
pp. 336-343.

8. [Poem] THE RETROSPECT. [by] WILTON. *Dublin Family
Magazine*, Vol. I, No. V, Aug. 1829, pp. 293-294.

9. THE DEATH OF A DEVOTEE. [by] WILTON. *Christian
Examiner*, Vol. IX, No. LV, Oct. 1829, pp. 267-283.

Included in *Tales of Ireland*, Curry, 1834 [8a].

1830

10. CONFESSIONS OF A REFORMED RIBBONMAN. *Dublin
Literary Gazette, or Weekly Chronicle of Criticism, Belles Lettres,
and Fine Arts*, Vol. I, No. 4, 23 Jan. 1830, pp. 49-51; Vol. I, No. 5,
30 Jan. 1830, pp. 66-68.

Retitled WILDGOOSE LODGE for inclusion in *Traits and Stories
of the Irish Peasantry*, Second Series, first edition, Wakeman 1833
[4a].

11. THE PRIEST'S FUNERAL. [by] WILTON. *Christian
Examiner*, Vol. X, No. LVIII, Jan. 1830, pp. 41-51; Vol. X, No.
LIX, Feb. 1830, pp. 128-142.

Included in *Tales of Ireland*, Curry, 1834 [8a].

12. THE BROTHERS – A NARRATIVE. [by] WILTON. *Christian
Examiner*, Vol. X, No. LX, March 1830, pp. 205-213; Vol. X, No.
LXI, April 1830, pp. 287-296; Vol. X, No. LXII, May 1830, pp. 365-
377; Vol. X, No. LXIII, June 1830, pp. 440-452.

Included in *Tales of Ireland*, Curry, 1834 [8a].

13. LACHLIN MURRAY AND THE BLESSED CANDLE. [by] WILTON. *Christian Examiner*, Vol. X, No. LXV, Aug. 1830, pp. 598-610.

Included in *Tales of Ireland*, Curry, 1834 [8a].

14. THE LIANHAN SHEE – AN IRISH SUPERSTITION. [by] WILTON. *Christian Examiner*, Vol. X, No. LXVIII, Nov. 1830, pp. 845-861.

Included in *Traits and Stories of the Irish Peasantry*, Second Series, First Edition, Wakeman 1833 [4a].

15. ALLEY SHERIDAN – AN IRISH STORY. *National Magazine*, Vol. I, No. 5, Nov. 1830, pp. 544-570.

Included in *Popular Tales and Legends of the Irish Peasantry* [By Carleton, 'Denis O'Donoho' and Mrs. Hall], Wakeman 1834 [9a].

16. [Essay and poem] IRISH LEGENDS. SIR TURLOUGH; OR, THE CHURCH-YARD BRIDE. *National Magazine*, Vol. I, No. 5, Nov. 1830, pp. 599-603.

Included in *Characteristic Sketches of Ireland and the Irish* [by Carleton, Lover, Mrs. Hall], Hardy & Walker, 1840 [13a].

17. THE DONAGH – OR THE HORSE-STEALERS. *National Magazine*, Vol. I, No. 6, Dec. 1830, pp. 637-654.

Included in *Traits and Stories of the Irish Peasantry*, Second Series, first edition, Wakeman, 1833 [4a], with minor revisions.

18. THE ILLICIT DISTILLER OR THE FORCE OF CONSCIENCE. [by] WILTON. *Christian Examiner*, Vol. X, No. LXIX, Dec. 1830, pp. 929-939.

Included in *Tales of Ireland*, Curry, 1834 [8a].

1831

19. LAYING A GHOST. *National Magazine*, Vol. II, No. I, Jan. 1831, pp. 41-48. [Unsigned, but attributed in 'Contents' to 'the Author of "Traits and Stories of the Irish Peasantry" '.]

Included in *Popular Tales and Legends of the Irish Peasantry* [by Carleton, Lover, Mrs. Hall], Wakeman, 1834 [9a].

20. THE LANDLORD AND TENANT, AN AUTHENTIC STORY. BY THE AUTHOR OF "TRAITS AND STORIES OF THE IRISH PEASANTRY." *National Magazine*, Vol. II, No. 4, April 1831, pp. 383-401.

Retitled TUBBER DERG, OR THE RED WELL for inclusion in *Traits and Stories of the Irish Peasantry*, Second Series, first edition, Wakeman, 1833 [4a] with some revisions and a continuation that doubles its length.

21. THE HISTORY OF A CHIMNEY SWEEP. [by] WILTON. *Christian Examiner*, Vol. XI, No. LXX, April 1831, pp. 276-291.

Republished in book form by Curry, 1831 [3a] as THE LITTLE CHIMNEY SWEEP.

22. THE MATERIALIST. [by] WILTON. *Christian Examiner*, Vol. XI, No. LXXIII, July 1831, pp. 512-532.

23. DENNIS O'SHAUGHNESSY GOING TO MAYNOOTH. [by] S.M. *Christian Examiner*, Vol. XI, No. LXXV, Sept. 1831, pp. 686-696; Vol. XI, No. LXXVI, Oct. 1831, pp. 765-779; Vol. XI, No. LXXVII, Nov. 1831, pp. 842-854; Vol. XI, No. LXXVIII, Dec. 1831, pp. 930-945.

Included in *Traits and Stories of the Irish Peasantry*, Second Series, first edition, Wakeman, 1833 [4a], with numerous revisions, major omissions, and long sections interpolated; 'Denis' for 'Dennis' in title and text.

1833

24. NEAL MALONE. *University Review and Quarterly Magazine*, Vol. I, No. 1, Jan. 1833, pp. 151-170. [Unsigned, but attributed in contents list to 'the Author of "Traits and Stories of the Irish Peasantry." ']

Included in *Tales of Ireland*, Curry, 1834 [8a].

25. THE DREAM OF A BROKEN HEART. *Dublin University*

Review and Quarterly Magazine, Vol. I, No. 2, April 1833, pp. 341-362. [This is the same magazine as in **24** above; '*Dublin*' was added to the title from the second number onwards. The story is unsigned, but attributed in the contents list to 'the Author of Traits and Stories of the Irish Peasantry'.]

Included in *Tales of Ireland*, Curry, 1834 [8a], with minor revisions.

26. THE DEAD BOXER. – AN IRISH LEGEND. BY THE AUTHOR OF "TRAITS AND STORIES OF THE IRISH PEASANTRY". *Dublin University Magazine*, Vol. II, No. 12, Dec. 1833, pp. 617-654.

Included in *The Fawn of Spring-Vale, the Clarionet, and other Tales*, Curry, 1841 [14a].

1834

27. THE RESURRECTIONS OF BARNEY BRADLEY. BY THE AUTHOR OF "TRAITS AND STORIES OF THE IRISH PEASANTRY." *Dublin University Magazine*, Vol. III, No. 14, Feb. 1834, pp. 177-193.

Included in *The Fawn of Spring-Vale, the Clarionet, and other Tales*, Curry, 1841 [14a].

28. STORIES OF SECOND SIGHT AND APPARITION. *Dublin University Magazine*, Vol. III, No. 17, May 1834, pp. 546-559.

Included in *Tales and Sketches of the Irish Peasantry*, Dublin, Duffy, 1842 [18a].

29. SHA DHU; OR, THE DARK DAY. BY THE AUTHOR OF "TRAITS AND STORIES OF THE IRISH PEASANTRY." *Dublin University Magazine*, Vol. IV, No. 22, Oct. 1834, pp. 426-441.

Included in *The Fawn of Spring-Vale, the Clarionet, and other Tales*, Curry, 1841 [14a], as LHA DHU.

1836

30. JANE SINCLAIR; OR, THE FAWN OF SPRINGVALE. BY WILLIAM CARLETON. *Dublin University Magazine*, Vol. VIII,

No. 45, Sept. 1836, pp. 334-350; Vol. VIII, No. 46, Oct. 1836, pp. 474-492; Vol. VIII, No. 47, Nov. 1836, pp. 593-616; Vol. VIII, No. 48, Dec. 1836, pp. 702-721.

Included in *The Fawn Of Spring-Vale, the Clarionet, and other Tales*, Curry, 1841 [14a].

1837

31. FARDOROUGHA, THE MISER: OR, THE CONVICTS OF LISNAMONA. BY WILLIAM CARLETON. *Dublin University Magazine*, Vol. IX, No. 50, Feb. 1837, pp. 212-230; Vol. IX, No. 51, March 1837, pp. 251-271; Vol. IX, No. 52, April 1837, pp. 426-442; Vol. IX, No. 53, May 1837, pp. 521-546; Vol. X, No. 60, Dec. 1837, pp. 671-692; Vol. XI, No. 61, Jan. 1838, pp. 95-111; Vol. XI, No. 62, Feb. 1838, pp. 250-276.

Published as a book, Curry, 1839 [11a].

1838

32. RICKARD THE RAKE. – IN THREE SNATCHES. *Dublin University Magazine*, Vol. XI, No. 63, March 1838, pp. 364-383.

Introduction, cut, included in *Tales and Sketches of the Irish Peasantry*, Duffy, 1845 [18a], as THE IRISH RAKE.

33. BARNEY BRADY'S GOOSE; OR, DARK DOINGS AT SLATHBEG. BY WILLIAM CARLETON. *Dublin University Magazine*, Vol. XI, No. 65, May 1838, pp. 604-624.

Included in *Tales and Sketches of the Irish Peasantry*, Duffy, 1845 [18a].

1839

34. THE THREE WISHES – AN IRISH LEGEND. BY WILLIAM CARLETON. *Dublin University Magazine*, Vol. XIV, No. 83, Nov. 1839, pp. 600-613.

Included in *Tales and Sketches of the Irish Peasantry*, Duffy, 1845 [18a].

1840

35. RECORDS OF THE HEART. BY WILLIAM CARLETON. NO. I – THE PARENTS' TRIAL. *The Citizen*, Vol. II, No. 8, June 1840, pp. 21-37.

Included in *Tales and Sketches of the Irish Peasantry*, Duffy, 1845 [18a], as A RECORD OF THE HEART; OR, THE PARENTS' TRIAL.

36. THE IRISH FIDDLER, BY W. CARLETON. *Irish Penny Journal*, Vol. I, No. 7, 15 Aug. 1840, pp. 52-55.

Included in *Tales and Sketches of the Irish Peasantry*, Duffy, 1845 [18a] as MICKEY M'ROREY, THE IRISH FIDDLER.

37. THE COUNTRY DANCING-MASTER, AN IRISH SKETCH, BY WILLIAM CARLETON. *Irish Penny Journal*, Vol. I, No. 9, 29 Aug. 1840, pp. 69-72.

Included in *Tales and Sketches of the Irish Peasantry*, Duffy, 1845 [18a] as BUCKRAM-BACK, THE COUNTRY DANCING-MASTER.

38. THE IRISH MATCHMAKER. BY WILLIAM CARLETON. *Irish Penny Journal*, Vol. I, No. 14, 3 Oct. 1840, pp. 116-120.

Included in *Tales and Sketches of the Irish Peasantry*, Duffy, 1845 [18a] as MARY MURRAY, THE IRISH MATCH-MAKER.

39. BOB PENTLAND, OR THE GAUGER OUTWITTED. BY WILLIAM CARLETON. *Irish Penny Journal*, Vol. I, No. 16, 17 Oct. 1840, pp. 125-127.

Included in *Tales and Sketches of the Irish Peasantry*, Duffy, 1845 [18a].

40. IRISH SUPERSTITIONS – GHOSTS AND FAIRIES. BY WILLIAM CARLETON. *Irish Penny Journal*, Vol. I, No. 21, 21 Nov. 1840, pp. 164-166.

Included in *Tales and Sketches of the Irish Peasantry*, Duffy, 1845 [18a], as THE FATE OF FRANK M'KENNA.

41. IRISH SUPERSTITIONS – GHOSTS AND FAIRIES. THE RIVAL KEMPERS. BY WILLIAM CARLETON. *Irish Penny Journal*, Vol. I, No. 24, 12 Dec. 1840, pp. 188-191.

Included in *Tales and Sketches of the Irish Peasantry*, Duffy, 1845 [18a] as THE RIVAL KEMPERS.

42. THE IRISH MIDWIFE. BY WILLIAM CARLETON. *Irish Penny Journal*, Vol. I, No. 26, 26 Dec. 1840, pp. 202-204.

Included in *Tales and Sketches of the Irish Peasantry*, Duffy, 1845 [18a] with **44** and **47** below as ROSE MOAN, THE IRISH MIDWIFE.

1841

43. THE MISFORTUNES OF BARNEY BRANAGAN; SHOWING HOW HE BECAME A WEALTHY MAN BY THE SAME. BY WILLIAM CARLETON. *Dublin University Magazine*, Vol. XVII, No. 97, Jan. 1848, pp. 80-100; Vol. XVII, No. 98, Feb. 1841, pp. 233-244; Vol. XVII, No. 99, March 1841, pp. 319-327; Vol. XVII, No. 100, April 1841, pp. 445-455; Vol. XVII, No. 101, May 1841, pp. 585-598.

Included in *The Fawn of Spring-Vale, the Clarionet, and other Tales*, Curry, 1841 [14a].

44. THE IRISH MIDWIFE. – PART II. BY WILLIAM CARLETON. *Irish Penny Journal*, Vol. I, No. 27, 2 Jan. 1841, pp. 209-213.

Included in *Tales and Sketches of the Irish Peasantry*, Duffy, 1845 [18a] with **42** above and **47** below as ROSE MOAN, THE IRISH MIDWIFE.

45. IRISH SUPERSTITIONS. – NO. III. GHOSTS AND FAIRIES. BY W. CARLETON. *Irish Penny Journal*, Vol. I, No. 34, 20 Feb. 1841, pp. 269-271.

Included in *Tales and Sketches of the Irish Peasantry*, Duffy, 1845 [18a] as FRANK MARTIN AND THE FAIRIES.

46. MOLL ROE'S MARRIAGE; OR THE PUDDING BEWITCHED. A TALE FOR AN IRISH WAKE. BY WILLIAM

CARLETON. *The Citizen*, Vol. III, No. 17, March 1841, pp. 155-161.

Included in *Tales and Sketches of the Irish Peasantry*, Duffy, 1845 [18a].

47. THE IRISH MIDWIFE, PART III. – DANDY KEHO'S CHRISTENING. BY WILLIAM CARLETON. *Irish Penny Journal*, Vol. I, No. 40, 3 April 1841, pp. 313-316.

Included in *Tales and Sketches of the Irish Peasantry*, Duffy, 1845 [18a] with **42** and **44** above as ROSE MOAN, THE IRISH MIDWIFE.

48. THE FOSTER BROTHER. BY WILLIAM CARLETON. *Irish Penny Journal*, Vol. I, No. 43, 24 April 1841, pp. 338-340.

Included in *Tales and Sketches of the Irish Peasantry*, Duffy, 1845 [18a] as FRANK FINNEGAN, THE FOSTER BROTHER.

49. THE IRISH SHANAHUS, BY WILLIAM CARLETON. *Irish Penny Journal*, Vol. I, No. 48, 29 May 1841, pp. 378-380.

Included in *Tales and Sketches of the Irish Peasantry*, Duffy, 1845 [18a] as TOM GRESSIEY, THE IRISH SENACHIE.

50. THE CASTLE OF AUGHENTAIN, OR A LEGEND OF THE BROWN GOAT, A TALE OF TOM GRASSIEY [sic], THE SHANAHUS. BY WILLIAM CARLETON. *Irish Penny Journal*, Vol. I, No. 49, 5 June 1841, pp. 386-389.

Included in *Tales and Sketches of the Irish Peasantry*, Duffy, 1845 [18a].

51. THE IRISH PROPHECY MAN. BY WILLIAM CARLETON. *Irish Penny Journal*, Vol. I, No. 50, 12 June 1841, pp. 393-396.

Included in *Tales and Sketches of the Irish Peasantry*, Duffy, 1845 [18a] as BARNEY M'HAIGNEY, THE IRISH PROPHECY MAN.

1843

52. THE LATE JOHN BANIM. *The Nation*, 23 Sept. 1843, pp. 794-795.

53. THE DUBLIN UNIVERSITY MAGAZINE AND MR. LEVER. *The Nation*, 7 Oct. 1843, pp. 826-827.

1844

54. THE CASTLE CUMBER CORRESPONDENCE. *The Nation*, 30 March 1844, p. 392.

1845

55. THE TEA KETTLE CORRESPONDENCE. *The Nation*, 26 April 1845, p. 475.

This is given in 'Writers in the Nation' as 'A member of Mr. McJoulter's congregation and a postman' (Dy 26 Apr 45 475) and is also the item given there as 'The tea-kettle correspondence' (Dy 29 Apr 45, 475). The mistake is caused by the confusion of signature and title, and date '29' April for '26'.

1846

56. THE BLACK PROPHET: A TALE OF IRISH FAMINE. *Dublin University Magazine*, Vol. XXVII, No. 161, May 1846, pp. 600-623; Vol. XXVII, No. 162, June 1846, pp. 739-760; Vol. XXVIII, No. 163, July 1846, pp. 75-94; Vol. XXVIII, No. 164, August 1846, pp. 214-231; Vol. XXXVIII, No. 165, September 1846, pp. 334-359; Vol. XXVIII, No. 166, October 1846, pp. 466-490; Vol. XXVIII, No. 167, November 1846, pp. 578-600; Vol. XVIII, No. 168, December 1846, pp. 717-747.

Published in book form, Belfast, Simms & M'Intyre, 1847 [25a].

57. A LAMENT. (poem). *The Nation*, 28 Feb. 1846. p. 312 (Answers to Correspondents)

1847

58. O'SULLIVAN'S LOVE: A LEGEND OF EDENMORE. *Dublin University Magazine*, Vol. XXIX, No. 171, March 1847, pp. 277-295; Vol. XXIX, No. 172, April 1847, pp. 428-446.

Republished with *Parra Sastha* and Lever's *Knight of Gwynne*, Philadelphia, Carey & Hart, 1847 [28a].

59. AN IRISH ELECTION IN THE TIME OF THE FORTIES.
Dublin University Magazine, Vol. XXX, No. 176, August 1847, pp.
176-192; Vol. XXX, No. 177, Sept, 1847, pp. 287-297.

1848

60. THE EVIL EYE; A TALE OF MYSTERY BY WILLIAM
CARLETON. *The Irish Tribune*, Vol. I, No. 1, 10 June, 1841, pp.
13-14; Vol. I, No. 2, 17 June, 1841, pp. 28-29; Vol. I, No. 3, 24 June
1841, pp. 45-46.

Vol. I, No. 1, 10 June, p. 11 has a paragraph introducing the serial;
Vol. I, No. 4, 1st July, announces that 'the French news obliges us to
discontinue the Evil Eye'. It also reports (p. 56) under the heading
'Irish Genius' that a pension of £200 for William Carleton has been
approved. On July 8th the paper declares that 'the assertion is
totally unfounded' that William Carleton is one of its proprietors.
    This story is not to be confused with the novel of the same name
The Evil Eye or the Black Spectre (Dublin, Duffy, 1860 [47a]). They
have nothing in common except the name of one character.

1850

61. BLACK-AND-ALL-BLACK. A LEGEND OF THE PADE-
REEN MARE. Related on a Christmas Eve, by an old Senachie.
By W. Carleton. *Illustrated London News*, Vol. XVII, No. 461,
Christmas Supplement, Dec. 21 1850, pp. 494-495.

1852

62. THE SQUANDERS OF SQUANDER CASTLE [*sic*]. By
William Carleton. *Illustrated London News*, Vol. XX, No. 541,
Supplement, Jan 17 1852, pp. 60-63 (Chapters I and II); Vol. XX,
No. 543, Jan 31 1852, pp. 108-110 (Chapters III and IV). The title is
altered to THE SQUANDERS OF CASTLE SQUANDER for
Vol. XX, No. 557, May 1 1852, pp. 354-355. This is not a complete
serialisation, but a synopsis of the story, long extracts and a brief
critical assessment of the newly published book [35a], London,
London Illustrated Library, 1852.

1853

63. THE FAIR OF EMYVALE. By William Carleton. *Illustrated London Magazine*, Vol. I, Part 1, July 1853, pp. 17-21; Vol. I, Part 2, Aug. 1853, pp. 57-66; Vol. I, Part 3, Sept. 1853, pp. 101-107.

Included in *The Silver Acre and other Tales*, London, Ward, Lock, 1862 [50a].

64. THE SILVER ACRE. By William Carleton. *Illustrated London Magazine*, Vol. I, Part 5, Nov. 1853, pp. 221-228; Vol. I, Part 6, Dec. 1853, pp. 267-272; Vol. II, Part 7, Jan. 1854, pp. 12-16; Vol. II, Part 8, Feb. 1854, pp. 47-57.

Republished in *The Silver Acre and other Tales*, London, Ward, Lock, 1862 [50a].

1854

65. MASTER AND SCHOLAR: being the wonderful history of 'Sam' and Pat Frayne; or, a thirst after knowledge. By William Carleton. *Illustrated London Magazine*, Vol. II, Part 11, May 1854, pp. 198-206.

Included in *The Silver Acre and other Tales*, London, Ward, Lock, 1862 [50a].

66. TAEDET ME VITAE (Poem). *The Nation*, 30 December 1854, p. 249.

1855

67. THE KING'S THIEF. *The Commercial Journal and Family Herald*, Dublin, 22 September 1855, p.3, 29 September 1855, p. 3, 6 October 1855, p. 3, 13 October 1855, p. 3.

1856

68. FAIR GURTHA; OR, THE HUNGRY GRASS. A legend of the Dumb Hill. *Dublin University Magazine*, Vol. XLVII, No. 280, April 1856, pp. 415-435.

1858

69. 'William Carleton – the Farewell address delivered by Barney Williams at the Theatre Royal' ('the only correct version', from Carleton's play 'Irish Manufacture', 1842). *The Nation*, 18 December 1858, p. 245.

1860

70. UTROM HORUM? OR THE REVENGE OF SHANE ROE NA SOGGARTH; a legend of the Golden Fawn. *Dublin University Magazine*, Vol. LV, No. 329, May 1860, pp. 528-541; Vol. LV, No. 330, June 1860, pp. 653-674.

71. THE MAN WITH THE BLACK EYE. *Duffy's Hibernian Magazine*, Vol. I, No. 1, July 1860, pp. 9-21.

72. THE RAPPAREE. *Duffy's Hibernian Magazine*, Vol. I, No. 2, Aug. 1860, pp. 57-68; Vol. I, No. 3, Sept. 1860, pp. 101-106; Vol. I, No. 4, Oct. 1860, pp. 156-161; Vol. I, No. 5, Nov. 1860, pp. 197-207; Vol. I, No. 6, Dec. 1850, pp. 254-263.

Published as *Redmond Count O'Hanlon, the Irish Rapparee*, Dublin, Duffy, 1862 [49a].

1861

73. THE DOUBLE PROPHECY; OR, TRIALS OF THE HEART. *Duffy's Hibernian Magazine*, Vol. II, No. 7, Jan. 1861, pp. 1-11; Vol. II, No. 8, Feb. 1861, pp. 49-59; Vol. II, No. 9, March 1861, pp, 96-103; Vol. II, No. 10, April 1861, pp. 141-149; Vol. II, No. 11, May 1861, pp. 187-196; Vol. II, No. 12, June 1861, pp. 237-248; Vol. II, No. 13, July 1861, pp. 1-10; Vol. II, No. 14, Aug. 1861, pp. 49-56; Vol. II, No. 15, Sept. 1861, pp. 97-103.

Published in book form by Duffy, Dublin, 1862 [48a].

74. THE MILLER OF MOHILL. A tale in three chapters. [There are in fact 4 episodes]. *The Illustrated Dublin Journal*, Vol. I, No. 1, 7 Sept. 1861, pp. 1-4; Vol. I, No. 2, 14 Sept. 1861, pp. 17-20; Vol. I, No. 3, 21 Sept. 1861, pp. 33-36; Vol. I, No. 4, 28 Sept. 1861, pp. 60-62.

1862

75. NOSTALGIA; OR, HOME SICKNESS. *Duffy's Hibernian Sixpenny Magazine*, Vol. II, No. 9, Sept. 1862, pp. 202-215. [Includes poem 'Taedet Me Vitae'].

1868

76. THE WEIRD WOMAN OF TAVNIMORE; OR, MILKING THE TETHERS. A tale of witchcraft. *The Shamrock*, Vol. IV, No. 82, 25 April 1868, pp. 498-499; Vol. IV, No. 83, 2 May 1868, pp. 513-516; Vol. IV, No. 84, 9 May 1868, pp. 529-532; Vol. IV, No. 85, 16 May 1868, pp. 545-549.

1869

77. THE ROMANCE OF INSTINCT. *The Shamrock*, Vol. V, No. 72, 20 Feb. 1869, pp. 340-342; Vol. V, No. 73, 27 Feb. 1869, pp. 360-362; Vol. V, No. 74, 6 March 1869, pp. 376-377; Vol. V, No. 75, 13 March, 1869, pp. 392-393; Vol. V, No. 76, 20 March 1869, pp. 444-445.

1906

78. A NEW PYRAMUS AND THISBE. (THE BATTLE OF AUGHRIM). An unpublished sketch by William Carleton, Author of "Traits and Stories of the Irish Peasantry." *Blackwood's Magazine*, Vol. CLXXIX, No. MLXXXIV, February 1906, pp. 273-277.

This is the first publication of part of Carleton's unpublished novel *Anne Cosgrave*.

SUBSEQUENT APPEARANCES IN ANTHOLOGIES AND PERIODICALS

INTRODUCTION

In this section are listed pieces of Carleton's work reprinted in newspapers, magazines and anthologies after they had been published in book form, or copied from one periodical by another. Many such reprints were of extracts, not full stories. They were often cut or altered to suit the new editor, and were sometimes 'borrowed' without the permission of the author or the previous publisher. Philip Dixon Hardy, as editor of the *Dublin Penny Journal*, defended the practice of abridging:

Messrs. CURRY and Co of Sackville-street, in the most handsome manner, unsolicited and freely, have given us permission to make extracts from a well known volume, of which they are the proprietors and publishers, "TRAITS AND STORIES OF THE IRISH PEASANTRY". In availing ourselves of this privilege in the present number, we will be under the necessity of *abridging*, and, in some measure, *altering*: for the limits of our publication would not permit the insertion of an entire story. In so doing, we may run the risk of abridging unskilfully, and perhaps marring the effect – we will endeavour to avoid this, as far as we can, and assure such of our readers (*if any there be*) who are able to purchase the work itself, and admire the specimen we present, that if they do themselves and the publishers the injustice of supposing that we, by any possibility, *can* or *will* extract the best of the volume, and that they can get for a few pence what would otherwise cost them as many shillings, they completely mistake both the character of the work and our intentions. (*Dublin Penny Journal*, Vol. I, No. 4, 21 July 1832, p. 29)

As for 'borrowings', although many were legitimate, many were not, and the columns of the penny magazines are laden with accusations and apologies. Hardy is often accused of piracy by other editors, authors and publishers, but as frequently accuses others: 'In inserting the foregoing story ['Kate Connor'], we deem it only fair to observe, that it was copied into Chambers' Journal without permission, or even acknowledgement, from the National Magazine, conducted by us, and to which it was sent by Mrs. S. C. Hall.' (*Dublin Penny Journal*, Vol. IV, No. 194, 19 March 1836). Many of

167

Carleton's stories were reprinted in the *Dublin Penny Journal*, by Hardy and by its previous editors, both with and without permission. The arrangements were not always harmonious. The extracts from 'The Landlord and Tenant' on 7th and 14th July 1832 were the cause of a three-sided battle between the then proprietors of the *Dublin Penny Journal*, Carleton (who first gave them permission to publish and then retracted it, claiming copyright), and Hardy (who was then editing the *National Magazine*, in which the story had first appeared). Despite such disputes, Carleton benefited from having his work reprinted in the *Dublin Penny Journal*, *Chambers's Journal*, the *Belfast Guardian* and other magazines and newspapers. Although they did not commission or pay for original stories as the *Dublin University Magazine* did, they publicised his name to an even wider audience in Ireland and abroad than it could command. This helped sales – indeed, the extract often concluded with an exhortation to the reader to go and buy the book for himself. Philip Dixon Hardy once again sets out the advantages for the author, and the pifalls for the editor:

In our first number we took the liberty of giving a story from Lover's Legends, with a notice of the book, which to our *certain* knowledge induced more than one person to inquire after it; in our second and third numbers we have presented an abridgment of the "Landlord and Tenant"; and for both of these high and mighty offences we have been persecuted by a species of petty annoyance, and "*the Law*" is hung over us, like the sword of Damocles threatening to nip asunder the slender thread of our Penny existence! (*Dublin Penny Journal*, Vol. I, No. 3, 21 July 1834, p.24)

Extracts from Carleton's stories appeared in magazines and newspapers through the 1830s and early 1840s, often just after publication of a new novel or collection. It became more general, however, to preface them with a critical notice, and to give the extract as an illustration of it. From the mid-forties, anthologies of Irish literature began to appear with somewhat oppressive regularity: even more oppressively, their contents were monotonous permutations of the same pieces by Lover, Carleton, Mrs. Hall, Father Prout, Mangan, Davis, Ferguson. By the 1880s and 1890s, new material from the writers of the Irish Literary Renaissance swelled the coffers – or Casquets, or Cabinets, or Treasuries – of Irish Literature. But amongst all these one's heart sinks to see Carleton represented again and again by his poems, 'A Sigh for Knockmany' and 'Sir Turlough, or the Churchyard Bride', rather than his prose.

W. B. Yeats, who did make a representative selection of Carleton's prose in his anthology of *Representative Irish Tales* (1891) and in *Irish Fairy and Folk Tales* (1895), found Carleton's books impossible to buy in the Dublin bookshops, and difficult even to borrow. This may explain why the same jaded extracts keep reappearing in the anthologies, borrowed no doubt from their predecessors.

The taste for snatches of poetry and prose in anthologies seems to have diminished in the twentieth century, and any publishing effort that has gone into Carleton's work has given us the stories in full, or whole books in facsimile, forms of republication that convey the curious strength of his work better than any collection of *Shamrock Leaves Gleaned in the Fertile Field of Irish Literature*.

A note on this section
In this section will be found, in chronological order, reprintings of Carleton's work, in full or abridged, in magazines, newspapers or anthologies. (Where an extract is accompanied by a substantial piece of criticism, it will be found in the Criticism section).

In the case of early reprints, when stories appeared in several magazines within a short time, this should make clear which were 'first appearances' and which were reprints. The list may also spare readers the disappointment, which I have often experienced, of discovering an unknown Carleton tale which is in fact an extract from a longer work (as, for example, 'The Piano Thirty', published in the *Dublin Penny Journal*, which is a passage from 'Alley Sheridan'.

'Anthology' here signifies a collection of pieces from several authors. When reprints of Carleton stories appear with the work of others, as in *Representative Irish Tales*, edited by W. B. Yeats, the book appears in this section. (When the book contains stories by Carleton alone, it is classified as an edition of his work, and will be found in the Bibliography section – as when the Carleton stories from *Representative Irish Tales* are published as Carleton's *Irish Tales* [85a]. When his stories appear with those of others in their *first* book publication, as in *Tales of Ireland* with Mrs. Hall and Samuel Lover, the book is classified as an edition of his work, and appears in the Bibliography section.)

I give the bibliographical details of noteworthy and available anthologies because many are themselves of bibliographical and historical, if not of literary, interest.

CHRONOLOGICAL LIST OF
SUBSEQUENT APPEARANCES

1829

Extract from 'The Station' (from *Christian Examiner*, November 1828). *Belfast Guardian and Constitutional Advocate*, 5 June 1829, p. [4]

Extract from 'The Station'. *Belfast Guardian and Constitutional Advocate*, 3 December 1829, p. [4]

1830

Extract from 'Alley Sheridan' (from *Dublin Literary Gazette*, November). *Belfast Guardian and Constitutional Advocate*, 5 November 1830, p. [4]

Extract from 'The Illicit Distiller; or the Force of Conscience' (from *Christian Examiner*). *Belfast Guardian and Constitutional Advocate*, 14 December 1830, p. [4]

Extract from 'The Illicit Distiller; or the Force of Conscience'. *Belfast Guardian and Constitutional Advocate*, 17 December 1830

1832

'The Landlord and Tenant'. An authentic story. *Dublin Penny Journal*, Vol. I, No. 2, 7 July 1832, pp. 14-16; Vol. I, No. 3, 14 July 1832, pp. 18-20
Includes account of dispute with Carleton about abridging, altering and publishing the story.

'Shane Fadh's Wedding'. *Dublin Penny Journal*, Vol. I, No. 4, 21 July 1832, pp. 29-31

'Tubber Derg, or the Red Well', abridged extracts. *The Schoolmaster, and Edinburgh Weekly Magazine* for 1832

'Larry M'Farland – extract from *Traits and Stories of the Irish Peasantry*', *Chambers's Edinburgh Journal*, Vol. I, No. 27, 4 August 1832, p. 211

'An Irish Dance, from *Traits and Stories of the Irish Peasantry*', *Chambers's Edinburgh Journal*, Vol. I, No. 48, 29 December 1832, p. 382

1833

'The Poor Irish Scholar, abridged from *Traits and Stories of the Irish Peasantry*', *Chambers's Edinburgh Journal*, Vol. II, No. 53, 2 February 1833, pp. 3-5

1834

'The Brothers' (by W) from *Christian Examiner*, March 1830. *Dublin Penny Journal*, Vol. II, No. 79, 4 January 1834, pp. 218-220

'Resurrections of Barney Bradley', *Dublin Penny Journal*, Vol. II, No. 88, 8 March 1834, pp. 285-288

'The Piano Thirty' (from 'Alley Sheridan'), *Dublin Penny Journal*, Vol. II, No. 101, 7 June 1834, pp. 391-392

'An Irish Legend. Sir Turlough, or the Church-Yard Bride'. *Dublin Penny Journal*, Vol. III, No. 106, 12 July 1834, pp. 15-16

1835

'Phil Purcel'. *Dublin Penny Journal*, Vol. III, No. 151, 16 May 1835, pp. 365-368; Vol. III, No. 152, 23 May 1835, pp. 373-376

'Laying a Ghost'. *Dublin Penny Journal*, Vol. IV, No. 169, 26 September 1835, pp. 101-104

'The Two Brothers. An Irish Tale,' "abridged from a tale in the *Dublin University Magazine* for October 1834". *Chambers's Edinburgh Journal*, Vol. IV, No. 198, November 14 1835, pp. 330-332

'Mat Kavanagh' (from 'The Hedge School'). *Dublin Penny Journal*, Vol. IV, No. 180, 12 December 1835, pp. 189-192

'Condy Cullen and the Gauger'. *Dublin Penny Journal*, Vol. IV, No. 181, 19 December 1835, pp. 197-200

1836

'Alley Sheridan'. *Dublin Penny Journal*, Vol. IV, No. 205, 4 June 1836, pp. 389-392; Vol. IV, No. 206, 11 June 1836, pp. 396-400; Vol. IV, No. 207, 18th June, pp. 402-406

1840

'The Irish Fiddler'. *Downpatrick Recorder*, Vol. IV, No. 192, 29 August 1840, p. [4]

1841

'A Legend of Knockmany'. *Chambers's Edinburgh Journal*, Vol. IX, No. 468, 16 January 1841, pp. 409-411

Extract from 'Barney Branagan'. *Chambers's Edinburgh Journal*, Vol. IX, No. 494, 17 July 1841, pp. 203-204

1843

'Irish Superstitions – Ghosts and fairies'. *Ulster General Advertiser*, Vol. I, No. 25, 18 February 1843, p. [4]

'Shane Fadh's Wedding'. *Ulster General Advertiser*, Vol. II, No. 30, 25 March 1843, p. [4]
Continued Vol. II, No. 31, 1 April 1843, p. [4]

'The Piano Thirty'. Extract from *Alley Sheridan*, *Ulster General Advertiser*, Vol. I, No. 36, 6 May 1843, p. [4]

1845

[Anthology:] *The Ballad Poetry of Ireland*, edited by Charles Gavan Duffy, 1845 (1 vol., pp. 244)
Includes Carleton's 'Sir Turlough, or the Churchyard Bride', pp. 50-57

Fortieth edition, Dublin and London, Duffy, 1874 (1 vol., pp. 244)
THE | [Gothic:] **Ballad Poetry of Ireland.** | EDITED BY | THE HON. CHARLES GAVAN DUFFY. | [Irish script:] "Bolg an Dána | [short rule] | FORTIETH EDITION. | [short rule] | DUBLIN: | PUBLISHED BY JAMES DUFFY & SONS, | 15 WELLINGTON-QUAY, | AND 22 PATERNOSTER-ROW, LONDON. | 1874.

1846

[Anthology:] *The Book of Irish Ballads*, edited by D. F. M'Carthy, Dublin, London, Duffy etc., 1846 (1 vol., pp. [x] + [11-252])
[Gothic:] **The Book** | OF | **Irish Ballads.** | EDITED BY | D. F. M'CARTHY. | DUBLIN: | PUBLISHED BY JAMES DUFFY, | 10, WELLINGTON QUAY. | LONDON: SIMPKIN,

MARSHALL AND CO., | STATIONERS' HALL COURT. | 1846.

Includes Carleton's 'A Sigh for Knockmany', pp. 151-152

A New Edition, Dublin, London, Duffy, 1869 (1 vol., pp. [x] + [11-256])

THE BOOK | OF | IRISH BALLADS. | EDITED BY DESMOND FLORENCE MAC-CARTHY, M.R.I.A. | AUTHOR OF DRAMAS AND AUTOS | FROM THE SPANISH OF CALDERON, ETC. | A NEW EDITION, | REVISED AND CORRECTED, | WITH ADDITIONAL POEMS AND A PREFACE. | DUBLIN: | JAMES DUFFY, 15 WELLINGTON-QUAY; | AND | 22, PATERNOSTER-ROW, LONDON. | 1869

Includes Carleton's 'A Sigh for Knockmany', pp. 146-147

Another edition, Dublin, Duffy, n.d.

t.p. has '[Gothic] **Dublin:** | JAMES DUFFY AND CO., LIMITED, | 15 WELLINGTON QUAY.', n.d.

1848

[Anthology:] *Half Hours with the Best Authors*, by Charles Knight, London, Knight, n.d. [1848] (4 vols., pp. iv + [586]; iv + 532; iv + [556]; [vi] + 590]

HALF-HOURS | WITH | THE BEST AUTHORS. | SELECTED AND ARRANGED, WITH SHORT BIOGRAPHICAL AND CRITICAL NOTICES, | BY CHARLES KNIGHT. | [short rule] | ILLUSTRATED WITH PORTRAITS. | [short rule] | IN FOUR VOLUMES. | VOL [I.] | LONDON: | CHARLES KNIGHT, LUDGATE STREET.

Includes Carleton's 'An Irish Village', from 'The Hedge School', Vol. III, pp. 275-279

Another edition, 1888

1849

[Anthology:] *The Irishman at Home*, Dublin, McGlashan, 1849 (1 vol., pp. [302])

THE IRISHMAN AT HOME: | CHARACTERISTIC SKETCHES | OF | THE IRISH PEASANTRY. | WITH ILLUSTRATIONS ON WOOD. | DUBLIN: | JAMES McGLASHAN, 21 D'OLIER-ST. | LONDON: W. S. ORR & Co.

Contains Carleton's 'The Gauger Captured' and 'The Gauger Outwitted'.
Sadleir No. [505]

1854

[Anthology:] *Shamrock Leaves*, Boston, Donahoe, n.d. [1854] (1 vol., pp. [320]

[Within rule frame:] SHAMROCK LEAVES; | GLEANED IN THE | FERTILE FIELD OF IRISH LITERATURE: | BEING | TALES AND STORIES OF IRELAND, | SELECTED FROM THE MOST | POPULAR AUTHORS. | [short rule] | "If they found a plot of water-cresses or SHAMROCKS, there they flocked as to a FEAST | for the time." – SPENCER'S [*sic*] FAIRY QUEEN. | [short rule] | BOSTON: | PUBLISHED BY PATRICK DONAHOE, | 23 FRANKLIN STREET.

Includes Carleton's 'Ned M'Keown' (pp. 15-22); 'The Three Tasks' (51-89); 'Confessions of a Reformed Ribbonman' (90-113); 'Neal Malone' (140-155); 'Tubber Derg' (156-171); 'Poor Scholar' (207-259); 'The Two Brothers' (293-219)
Sadleir No. [205]

1855

[Anthology:] *The Ballads of Ireland*, edited by Edward Hayes. London, Edinburgh and Dublin, Fullarton, 1855 (2 vols., pp. viii + [420]; [420])

[within rule frame:] THE | BALLADS OF IRELAND. | COLLECTED AND EDITED | BY EDWARD HAYES. | VOLUME [I.] | [engraving of group of people, horse and cart] | The Emigrants – p. 308. | A. FULLARTON & CO. | LONDON, EDINBURGH, AND DUBLIN. | 1855.

Includes Carleton's 'Sir Turlough, or the Church Yard Bride', Vol. II, pp. 94-100

Fourth Edition, Edinburgh, London, New York, Fullarton (2 vols., pp. viii + [420]; [420])

THE | BALLADS OF IRELAND; | COLLECTED AND EDITED, | BY EDWARD HAYES. | FOURTH EDITION. | VOL. [I.] | A. FULLARTON & CO., | EDINBURGH AND LONDON. | FULLARTON, MACNAB & Co., NEW YORK

1868

[Anthology:] *The Poets and Poetry of Ireland*, notes by Hardiman, Lover, D. F. M'Carthy, New York, Farrell, 1868 (1 vol., pp. 12 + [4] + 300)

[within double rule frame:] THE | POETS AND POETRY | OF | IRELAND: | WITH | NUMEROUS NOTES | BY | J. HARDIMAN, M.R.I.A., SAMUEL LOVER, AND D. F. McCARTHY, | PROFESSOR OF POETRY, UNIVERSITY OF IRELAND. | [Gothic:] **The Illustrations** | BY | WILLIAM J. HENNESSY, MACLISE, H. DOYLE, | AND OTHER EMINENT ARTISTS. | [circular vignette of bird, trees, lake] | NEW YORK: | T. FARRELL & SON, | 107 FULTON STREET.

Includes Carleton's 'Sir Turlough, or the Churchyard Bride', pp. 285-288 and 'A Sigh for Knockmany', p. 288, with biographical memoir pp. 283-284

1872

[Anthology:] *The Casquet of Literature*, edited by Charles Gibbon, London, Blackie, 1872/3 (4 vols., pp. viii + 400 + 400 + [4]; viii + 384 + 4; viii + 384 + [2]; [xxiv] + 368 + [4])

THE CASQUET | OF | LITERATURE: | BEING | A SELECTION IN POETRY AND PROSE | FROM THE WORKS OF THE MOST ADMIRED AUTHORS. | EDITED, | WITH BIOGRAPHICAL AND LITERARY NOTES, | BY CHARLES GIBBON, | AUTHOR OF "ROBIN GRAY," "FOR LACK OF GOLD," ETC. | VOL. [I] | [Blackie device] | LONDON: | BLACKIE & SON, PATERNOSTER BUILDINGS, E.C.; | GLASGOW AND EDINBURGH. | 1872.

[Vols. III and IV have '1873.']

Includes Carleton's 'Ned M'Keown' (Vol. II, pp. 148-150) and 'The Ribbonman' (Vol. IV, pp. 289-297).

1875

[Anthology:] *Little Classics*, Vol. V, Boston, Osgood, 1875 (1 vol., pp. 218)

[Within rule frame:] [Gothic:] **Fifth Volume** | [short rule] | LITTLE CLASSICS. | EDITED BY | ROSSITER JOHNSON. | LAUGHTER. | A CHRISTMAS CAROL. — THE HAUNTED CRUST. — A DISSERTATION UPON ROAST | PIG — THE TOTAL DEPRAVITY OF INANIMATE THINGS. — THE SKEL- | ETON IN THE CLOSET. — SANDY WOOD'S SEPULCHRE. — A | VISIT TO THE ASYLUM FOR AGED AND DECAYED | PUNSTERS. — MR. TIBBOT O'LEARY, THE | CURIOUS. — NEAL MALONE. | BOSTON: | JAMES R. OSGOOD AND COMPANY | 1875.

Includes Carleton's 'Neal Malone', pp. 188-218.

Another edition, Boston, Houghton, Mifflin and Company, n.d. (The Riverside Press)

Another edition, Boston, Houghton, Mifflin, n.d.

1879

[Anthology:] *The Cabinet of Irish Literature*, edited by Charles A. Read, London, Glasgow, Edinburgh, Dublin, Blackie 1879/80 (4 vols., pp. viii + 336 + 4; viii + 336 + 4; [viii] + 336 + 4; x + 336 + *4*)

THE CABINET | OF | IRISH LITERATURE: | SELECTIONS FROM THE WORKS OF THE | CHIEF POETS, ORATORS, AND PROSE WRITERS | OF IRELAND. | WITH BIOGRAPHICAL SKETCHES AND LITERARY NOTICES, | BY CHARLES A. READ, F.R.H.S., | Author of "Tales and Stories of Irish Life," "Stories from the Ancient Classics," &c. | Vol. [I.] | [Blackie device] | LONDON: BLACKIE AND SON, OLD BAILEY; | GLASGOW, EDINBURGH, | AND 89 TALBOT STREET, DUBLIN. | 1879

Vol. III has '1880.'

Vol. IV has 'Vol. IV. | BY T.P. O'CONNOR, M.A.' and '1880.'

Vol. III includes note on Carleton, pp. 213-217; 'The Miser on His Son's Love' (from 'Fardorougha the Miser'), pp. 217-228; 'A Love Scene in a Cabin' (from 'Phelim O'Toole's Courtship') pp. 228-231

New Edition, 'Revised and greatly Extended' by Katharine Tynan Hinkson, London, Gresham, 1902; (4 vols., pp. 2 + [4] + [xxxvi] + [312] + 8; [x] + 324 + 8; viii + 348 + 8; [x] + 372 + 8)

The | Cabinet of Irish Literature | Selections from the Works of | The Chief Poets, Orators, and Prose Writers | of Ireland | With Biographical Sketches and Literary Notices by | CHARLES A. READ, F.R.H.S. | Author of "Tales and Stories of Irish Life" "Stories from the Ancient Classics" &c. | NEW EDITION | Revised and greatly Extended by | KATHARINE TYNAN HINKSON | Author of "Poems" "The Dear Irish Girl" "She Walks in Beauty" "A Girl of Galway" &c. | Volume [I] | LONDON | THE GRESHAM PUBLISHING COMPANY | 34 SOUTHAMPTON STREET, STRAND | 1902

Vol. III includes a Notice of William Carleton (pp. 1-4); 'The Miser on his son's Love' (pp. 4-10) and 'The Miser goes matchmaking' (pp. 10-15) (from *Fardorougha the Miser*) and 'Sir Turlough, or the Churchyard Bride' (pp. 15-17).

Another edition, 1906.

Another edition, n.d.

1880

[Anthology:] *Penny Readings for the Irish People*, Dublin, Sullivan, n.d. [1880]; (3 vols, pp. 32 + 32 + 32 + 32 + 32 + 32 + 32 + 32 + 32 + 32 + 32 + 32; 380; 380)
PENNY READINGS | FOR | THE IRISH PEOPLE. | [short rule] | CONDUCTED BY | [Gothic:] The Editors of the "Nation." | [short rule] | VOL. [I.] | [short rule] | DUBLIN: | PUBLISHED BY A.M. SULLIVAN, | 90 MIDDLE ABBEY-STREET.

A part-work, bound in 3 volumes. Vol. I includes Carleton's 'The Irish Dancing Master' No. 4, pp. 17-27; 'The Irish Fiddler' No. 8, pp. 6-11; Vol. II includes 'An Irish Eviction' (from *Valentine*

M'Clutchy) pp. 52-60; 'The Poor Scholar' pp. 115-123; Vol. III includes 'A Sigh for Knockmany' (pp. 211-212).

1882

[Anthology:] *Irish Pleasantry and Fun*, Dublin, Gill, 1882 (1 vol., pp. [4] + 380)

IRISH | PLEASANTRY AND FUN | A SELECTION OF | THE BEST HUMOROUS TALES | BY | CARLETON, LOVER, LEVER | AND OTHER POPULAR WRITERS. | [Gothic:] **With Sixteen Coloured Illustrations** | BY J.F. O'HEA | DUBLIN | M. H. GILL AND SON, 50, UPPER SACKVILLE STREET. | 1882.

First published as part-work.

Contains Carleton's 'Barney Bradley's Resurrection' (pp. 138-149); 'The Bewitched Pudding' (pp. 357-362); 'Condy Cullen and the Gauger' (pp. 319-323); 'Corny Keho's Birth and Christening' (pp. 219-227); 'Denis O'Shaughnessy's Story of Luther' (pp. 376-379); 'The Gauger Outwitted' (pp. 1-4); 'How Peter Connell took the Pledge' (pp. 244-252); 'An Irish Wake' (pp. 166-171); 'Laying a Ghost' (pp. 265-269); 'Mat Kavanagh, the Hedge Schoolmaster', abridged from 'The Hedge School' (pp. 34-46); 'Phil Purcel, the Pig Driver' (pp. 95-102); 'The Pugnacious Tailor' (pp. 291-296); 'Riches in Spite of Ill-luck', abridged from 'Barney Branagan' (pp. 188-202); 'Shane Fadh's Wedding' (pp. 60-71); 'The Three Tasks' (pp. 122-134); 'The Three Wishes' (pp. 333-342).
S. J. Brown No. 54, though he gives the first edition as 1892.

1886

†[Anthology:] *Weird Tales by Irish Authors*. Nuggets for Travellers, London, Dent, 1886-1895. Vol. I, 1886, includes Carleton's 'The Lianhan Shee'.

1887

[Anthology:] *The Poetry and Song of Ireland*, edited by John Boyle O'Reilly. New York, Gay, n.d. [1887] (1 vol., pp. xxviii + [9-814])

THE | [decorative caps:] | Poetry | AND | Song | OF | IRELAND. | WITH | BIOGRAPHICAL SKETCHES OF HER POETS, |

COMPILED AND EDITED | BY | JOHN BOYLE O'REILLY. | [. . .] | NEW YORK: | GAY BROTHERS & CO., | 30, 32, 34 READE STREET
Includes Carleton's 'Sir Turlough or the Church Yard Bride', pp. 695-697; 'A Sigh for Knockmany', p. 698, and biographical sketch, p. 11.

1888

[Anthology:] *Fairy and Folk Tales of the Irish Peasantry/Irish Fairy and Folk Tales/Irish Folk Stories and Fairy Tales/Fairy and Folk Tales of the Irish Peasantry*, edited by W.B. Yeats, London, New York, Toronto, Walter Scott, Whittaker, Gage, 1888 (1 vol., pp. xx + 326) (Camelot Series)

FAIRY AND FOLK TALES | OF THE IRISH PEASANTRY: | EDITED AND SELECTED BY | W.B. YEATS. | LONDON | WALTER SCOTT, 24 WARWICK LANE | NEW YORK: THOMAS WHITTAKER | TORONTO: W.J. GAGE AND CO. | 1888

Includes Carleton's 'Frank Martin and the Fairies', pp. 5-9; 'Paddy Corcoran's Wife', pp. 33-35; 'The Fate of Frank M'Kenna', pp. 149-155; 'The Pudding Bewitched', pp. 198-213; 'The Three Wishes', pp. 252-278; 'A Legend of Knockmany', pp. 285-299.
Wade No. 212.

Irish Fairy and Folk Tales, London, Walter Scott, n.d. (1 vol., pp. [xx] + 326) [1893]

IRISH | FAIRY AND FOLK TALES | SELECTED AND EDITED, | WITH INTRODUCTION, | BY W.B. YEATS. | TWELVE ILLUSTRATIONS BY JAMES TORRANCE. | LONDON: WALTER SCOTT, LTD. | 24 WARWICK LANE.

Wade No. 223.

Irish Fairy Tales, London, Walter Scott, n.d. (1 vol., pp. xviii + 326)

[red:] IRISH | FAIRY TALES | [publisher's device] | EDITED BY W.B. YEATS | WITH TWELVE FULL- | PAGE ILLUSTRATIONS BY | JAMES TORRANCE. | [publisher's device] | LONDON | WALTER SCOTT, LTD. | PATERNOSTER SQ.
Wade No. 223A.

[Another edition:] [within decorative border:] Irish Fairy Tales | SELECTED AND EDITED BY | W. B. YEATS | . | SEVEN ILLUSTRATIONS BY JAMES TORRANCE | [Gothic:] **London and Felling-on-Tyne** | THE WALTER SCOTT PUBLISHING CO., LTD. | NEW YORK: 3 EAST 14TH STREET

[Australian edition:] *Irish Fairy Tales*, Melbourne, Sydney, Adelaide, Cole, n.d. (1 vol., pp. xvii + 326)

IRISH FAIRY TALES | [ornamental rule] | Edited by | W. B. Yeats | [ornamental rule] | E. W. Cole, BOOK ARCADE, MELBOURNE. | 333 GEORGE STREET, [vertical rule] 67 Rundle Street, | SYDNEY. [vertical rule] ADELAIDE., | VICTORIA LIBRARY.

[Another edition:] *Irish Fairy and Folk Tales*, edited by W. B. Yeats, London and New York, Scott, Scribner, 1895 (1 vol., pp. xviii + [2] + 326)

IRISH | FAIRY AND FOLK | TALES | SELECTED AND EDITED, | WITH INTRODUCTION BY W.B. YEATS. | TWELVE ILLUSTRATIONS BY JAMES TORRANCE. | LONDON | WALTER SCOTT, LTD, PATERNOSTER SQUARE | CHARLES SCRIBNER'S SONS, | 154-157 FIFTH AVENUE, NEW YORK | 1895
Wade No. 224

Reprinted [1907], t.p. as 1895, except publishers' lines 'THE WALTER SCOTT PUBLISHING CO., LTD. | PATERNOSTER SQUARE, LONDON, E.C. | CHARLES SCRIBNER'S SONS | 597 FIFTH AVENUE, NEW YORK

Another edition, London, Felling-on-Tyne, New York as above except publishers' lines: '[Gothic:] **London and Felling-on-Tyne:** | THE WALTER SCOTT PUBLISHING CO. LTD., | NEW YORK: 3 EAST 14TH STREET.

[American edition] New York, Carlton House (1 vol., pp. viii + 344)

IRISH FAIRY AND FOLK TALES | EDITED BY W.B. YEATS | [device] | NEW YORK | CARLTON HOUSE
Wade No. 212B

[American edition] New York, Boni and Liveright, n.d. [1918] (1 vol., pp. xviii + 354) (Modern Library)

IRISH FAIRY AND FOLK TALES | [short rule] | EDITED BY
W.B. YEATS | [short rule] | [device] | [short rule] | BONI AND
LIVERIGHT, INC. | [short rule] | PUBLISHERS NEW YORK
Wade No. 213. Modern Library No. 44

[American edition], as *Irish Fairy and Folk Tales*, New York, Burt,
n.d. (1 vol., pp. xvi + 416) [1902]

IRISH FAIRY | AND FOLK TALES | EDITED AND SELECTED
| BY W.B. YEATS | [vignette] | PROFUSELY ILLUSTRATED |
A.L. BURT COMPANY, | PUBLISHERS, NEW YORK.
Wade No. 212A

[American edition] New York, Modern Library (Random House),
n.d. (1 vol., pp. xviii + 2 + 352)

[in double rule frame] IRISH | FAIRY | AND | FOLK | TALES |
EDITED BY | W.B. YEATS | THE | MODERN LIBRARY |
NEW YORK | [device]
Wade No. 213

[American edition] *Irish Folk Stories and Fairy Tales*, New York,
Grosset & Dunlap, n.d. [1957] (1 vol., pp. xviii + 298)

IRISH FOLK STORIES | AND | FAIRY TALES | edited by |
William Butler Yeats | Grosset's Universal Library | Grosset &
Dunlap · New York
Wade No. 213A

[American edition:] *Irish Folk Tales*, Limited Editions Club,
Connecticut, 1973 (1 vol., pp. xx + 412)

[dark green:] irish | folk | tales, | *Edited by* William Butler Yeats |
Illustrated by Rowel Friers | *Printed for the Members of* | The
Limited Editions Club | Avon, Connecticut · 1973

Fairy and Folk Tales of Ireland, Gerrards Cross, Colin Smythe,
1973 (1 vol., pp. xix + [3] + [390])

FAIRY AND FOLK | TALES OF IRELAND | edited by | W. B.
Yeats | *with a foreword by* | Kathleen Raine | [publisher's device]
|COLIN SMYTHE | GERRARDS CROSS | 1973

Macmillan, New York, bought 2110 copies of the Smythe printing with their imprint on title [The Macmillan Company / New York, New York], verso and spine. Reprinted by Macmillan in 1975.

Fairy and Folk Tales of Ireland, Gerrards Cross, Colin Smythe, 1977 (1 vol., pp. [2] + xxvi + 390 + [6])

FAIRY AND FOLK | TALES OF IRELAND | edited by | W.B. Yeats | *with a foreword by* | Kathleen Raine | *and a list of sources by* | Mary Helen Thuente | [Publisher's device] | COLIN SMYTHE | GERRARDS CROSS | 1977

Reprinted by Pan books, 1978, 1979, 1981, 1984:

edited by | W. B. Yeats | Fairy and Folk Tales | of Ireland | with a foreword by Kathleen Raine | and a list of sources by Mary Helen Thuente | [rule] | PICADOR | [rule] | published by Pan Books

[American edition:] *Fairy and Folk Tales of Ireland*, edited by W. B. Yeats with a foreword by Benedict Kiely. New York, Macmillan, 1983.

1891

[Anthology:] *Representative Irish Tales*, edited by W.B. Yeats. New York and London, Putnam [1891] (2 vols., pp. [4] + vi + 340; [6] + iv + 356)

[within rule frame, on yellow] REPRESENTATIVE | IRISH TALES | COMPILED, WITH AN INTRODUCTION AND NOTES | BY | W.B. YEATS | [short rule] | [FIRST SERIES] | [short rule] | ['Knickerbocker Nuggets' device] | NEW YORK AND LONDON | G.P. PUTNAM'S SONS | THE KNICKERBOCKER PRESS

Vol. II has 'SECOND SERIES' for 'FIRST SERIES'.

Carleton stories are: 'Wildgoose Lodge'; 'Condy Cullen'; 'The Curse' (from 'The Party Fight and Funeral'); 'The Battle of the Factions'.
Wade No. 215.

The Carleton stories and introductory article were later published separately as *Carleton's Irish Tales* [85a].

Another edition, New York and Dublin, Putnam, n.d. (2 vols., pp. [*4*] + vi + 340; [*6*] + iv + 356)

[Within double rule panel] REPRESENTATIVE | IRISH TALES | COMPILED WITH AN INTRODUCTION AND | NOTES BY | W.B. YEATS | [FIRST] SERIES | [short decorative rule] | NEW YORK AND LONDON | G.P. PUTNAM'S SONS | THE KNICKERBOCKER PRESS

Another edition, Gerrards Cross, Colin Smythe, 1979 (1 vol., pp. 364)

REPRESENTATIVE | IRISH TALES | Compiled, with an Introduction and Notes | by | W.B. Yeats | and a Foreword by | Mary Helen Thuente | [publisher's device] | COLIN SMYTHE | GERRARDS CROSS 1979

1892

[Anthology:] *Celtic Fairy Tales*, edited by Joseph Jacobs, London, Nutt, 1892 (1 vol., pp. [xxx] + [268])

CELTIC | Fairy Tales | *SELECTED AND EDITED BY* | JOSEPH JACOBS | EDITOR OF "FOLK-LORE" | *ILLUSTRATED BY* | JOHN D. BATTEN | [vignette of leprechaun and jug] | LONDON | DAVID NUTT, 270 STRAND | 1892

Includes Carleton's 'A Legend of Knockmany', pp. 156-168.

Another edition (facsimile reprint), London, Muller, 1972 (1 vol., pp. [xxx] + [268])

CELTIC | Fairy Tales | SELECTED AND EDITED BY | JOSEPH JACOBS | ILLUSTRATED BY JOHN. D. BATTEN | [vignette of seated Roman soldier, woman] | A FACSIMILE EDITION | PUBLISHED BY FREDERICK MULLER LTD

1894

[Anthology:] *The Humour of Ireland*, edited by D.J. O'Donoghue. London, Walter Scott, 1894 (1 vol., pp. xx + 434 + 10)

THE | HUMOUR OF IRELAND | SELECTED, WITH INTRO- | DUCTION, BIOGRAPHICAL | INDEX AND NOTES, BY |

D.J. O'DONOGHUE: THE | ILLUSTRATIONS BY | OLIVER PAQUE | [spiral device at r.h.s.] | LONDON WALTER SCOTT | 1894 LTD

Includes Carleton's 'Giving Credit', pp. 190-197 (from 'The Geography of an Irish Oath')

Another edition, London, Felling-on-Tyne and New York, Walter Scott, 1898

1896

[Anthology:] *Stories by English Authors*, New York, Scribner, 1896 (vol. 5, pp. 180)

STORIES BY | ENGLISH AUTHORS | IRELAND | . . . | THE GRIDIRON . . . By Samuel Lover | THE EMERGENCY MEN. By George H. Jessop | A LOST RECRUIT . . . By Jane Barlow | THE RIVAL DREAMERS By John Banim | NEAL MALONE . . . . William Carleton | THE BANSHEE . . . . Anonymous | NEW YORK | CHARLES SCRIBNER'S SONS | 1896

Includes Carleton's 'Neal Malone', pp. 123-158.

Another edition, New York, Scribner, 1901

Another edition, New York, Scribner, 1903

1899

[Anthology:] *The Universal Anthology.* A collection of the best literature, ancient, mediaeval and modern, with biographical and explanatory notes. Edited by Richard Garnett, Leon Vallée and Alois Brandl. London, Clarke, and New York, Merrill & Baker, n.d. (c. 1899) 33 vols. Vol. I contains Carleton's 'Fin McCoul, a legend of Knockmany', pp. 285-296.

1904

[Anthology:] *Irish Literature: Irish Authors and their Writings in Ten Volumes.* New York, Collier & Son, 1904

[Title Plate] [green, in frame of rosettes, with two wreaths and harp:] [Gothic:] **Irish Literature** | SECTION ONE | Irish Authors and Their | Writings in Ten | Volumes. | VOLUME [II] [Gothic:] **Sir William Francis Butler** | **George Darley** | P. F. COLLIER & SON

Vol. II (Butler-Darley) includes a 'Biographical and Critical Sketch' of Carleton (pp. 469-470) and his 'The Battle of the Factions' (pp. 472-511); 'Shane Fadh's Wedding' (pp. 512-541); 'Condy Cullen and the Gauger' (pp. 541-553); 'The Fate of Frank M'Kenna' (pp. 553-559); 'The Curse' from 'Party Fight and Funeral' (pp. 559-562); 'Paddy Corcoran's Wife' (pp. 562-564).

1906

[Extract:] 'A New Pyramus and Thisbe. (The Battle of Aughrim.) An Unpublished sketch by William Carleton, Author of 'Traits and Stories of the Irish Peasantry'.' From Carleton's unpublished novel *Anne Cosgrave. Blackwood's Magazine*, Vol. CLXXIX, No. MLXXXIV, February 1906, pp. 273-277.

1915

[Anthology:] *The Dublin Book of Irish Verse*, edited by John Cooke. Dublin and London, Hodges Figgis, O.U.P., 1915 (1 vol., pp. [viii] + [804])

The | Dublin Book | Of Irish Verse | 1728 – 1909 | Edited by | John Cooke | Dublin | Hodges, Figgis & Co., Ltd. | London | Henry Frowde, Oxford University Press 1915

Includes Carleton's 'A Sigh for Knockmany', pp. 67-68.

[Anthology:] *A Treasury of Irish Poetry in the English Tongue* edited by Stopford A. Brooke and T. W. Rolleston, London, Smith Elder, 1915 (Third Impression), pp. [lxiv] + 578

A TREASURY | OF | IRISH POETRY | IN THE ENGLISH TONGUE | EDITED BY | STOPFORD A. BROOKE | AND | T. W. ROLLESTON | *THIRD IMPRESSION* | LONDON | SMITH, ELDER, & CO., 15 WATERLOO PLACE | 1915 | All rights reserved

Includes Introductory Notice of Carleton (p. 76) and his 'Sir Turlough' (pp. 77-82) and 'A Sigh for Knockmany' (p. 83).

[Anthology:] *Humours of Irish Life*, introduced by Charles L. Graves. London, Dublin and Belfast, Gresham, 1915 (1 vol., pp. xlviii + [350]) (Phoenix)

HUMOURS OF | IRISH LIFE | *Introduction by* | *Charles L. Graves, M.A.* | ['The Irish Library' device] | *With Portrait Illustrations* | THE GRESHAM PUBLISHING COMPANY LTD. | LONDON DUBLIN AND BELFAST

Includes Carleton's 'The Mad Pudding of Ballyboulteen' (pp. 58-71) and 'The Battle of Aughrim' ('from *Anna [sic] Cosgrave*, an unpublished novel') (pp. 131-138).

[Another edition:] *Humours of Irish Life*. Dublin & London, Talbot Press, Fisher, Unwin (1 vol., pp. xlviii + [350];

[within rule frame:] Every. Irishman's. Library | *General Editors:* Alfred Perceval Graves, m.a. | William Magennis, m.a. Douglas Hyde, ll.d | [double rule] | HUMOURS | OF IRISH LIFE | [fiat lux device] | WITH AN INTRODUCTION | BY CHARLES L. GRAVES, M.A. | [double rule] | [l.h.s. of short vertical rule:] DUBLIN: | The Talbot Press, ltd. | 89 Talbot Street | [r.h.s:] LONDON: | T. Fisher Unwin, Ltd. | 1 Adelphi Terrace

1935

'Carleton's description of his Mother' (from 'General Introduction' to *Traits and Stories of the Irish Peasantry*, 1842 [15a].) *Irish Book Lover*, Vol. XXIII, No. 6, November-December 1935, pp. 142-143

1945

[Anthology:] *Speak of the Devil*, New York, Doubleday, Doran, 1945 (1 vol., pp. [xii] + 334)

Edited by Sterling North & C.B. Boutell | SPEAK OF THE DEVIL. | Garden City, New York | Doubleday, Doran & company, inc. | 1945

Includes Carleton's 'The Three Wishes'.

1961

Great Irish Short Stories, edited by Vivian Mercier (1 vol., pp. 384)

Great Irish | Short Stories | Edited, with an Introduction, | by Vivian Mercier | [Laurel Edition logo]

Carleton's 'The Donagh, or, the Horse-stealers', pp. 74-104.

1971

AN | ANTHOLOGY | OF | IRISH | LITERATURE | EDITED, WITH AN INTRODUCTION, BY | *David H. Greene,* NEW YORK UNIVERSITY | VOLUME II | New York University Press | New York 1971

Includes Carleton's 'The Hedge School' (extract), pp. 322-327

TRANSLATIONS

French:

French translation of three *Traits and Stories of the Irish Peasantry: Romans Irlandais – Scenes de la Vie Champêtre*, Paris, Hetzel, Dentu, 1861 (1 vol., pp. [vi] + [286])

WILLIAM CARLETON | [short rule] | ROMANS | IRLANDAIS | SCÈNES DE LA VIE CHAMPÊTRE | TRADUITES PAR | M. LÉON DE WAILLY | [Hetzel device] | PARIS | COLLECTION HETZEL | E. DENTU, LIBRAIRE | Palais-Royal, Galerie d'Orleans, 13 et 17 | [short rule] | 1861

Contains: 'William Carleton' (by Léon de Wailly); 'L'ambition au Village' ('Going to Maynooth'); 'Les Trois Epreuves' ('The Three Tasks'); 'Wildgoose Lodge'.

French translation of *The Evil Eye: Le Mauvais Oeil*, Paris, Leipzig, Tournai, Laroche, Kittler, Casterman, 1865 (1 vol., pp. [330])

LE MAUVAIS OEIL | ou le Spectre Noir | Par William CARLETON | SUIVI DE | CELA SEULEMENT. | [short rule] | TRADUCTION DE L'ANGLAIS. | [short decorative rule] | [on l.h.s. decorative cross:] PARIS | LIBRAIRIE DE P.-M. LAROCHE, | Rue Bonaparte, 66. | [on r.h.s. of cross:] | LÉIPZIG | L. A. KITTLER, COMMISSIONNAIRE, | Querstrasse, 34. | H. CASTERMAN | TOURNAI | 1865

Contains *Le Mauvais Oeil*; *Cela Seulement* (anonymous).

Valentine M'Clutchy was translated and published in serial form in *L'Univers* (Paris) as *Les Chroniques de Château-Cumber, ou l'agent d'un landlord irlandais*, from 27 June 1845 (No. 970) to 24 October 1845 (No. 1071).

German:

Traits and Stories of the Irish Peasantry was translated into German as *Skizzen und Erzählungen aus dem Leben des Irischen Landvolks.* Leipzig, H. Roberts, 1837 (3 vols.)

Irish:

Irish translation of *Fardorougha the Miser: Feardorcha Truaillidhe,* Dublin, Oifig díolta Foillseacháin Rialtais, 1933 (1 vol., pp. 412)

Feardorcha Truailldhe | *i.* | WILLIAM CARLETON | do scríobh sa Bhéarla bhunaidh | Sean Mac Maoláin | d'aistrigh go gaedhilg | LE CEANNACH DÍREACH Ó | OIFIG DÍOLTA FOILLSEACHÁIN RIALTAIS | 5 SRÁID THOBAIR PHÁDRAIG, BAILE ÁTHA CLIATH, C.2. | NÓ TRÉ AON DÍOLTÓIR LEABHAR | 1933

Irish translation of *The Black Prophet: An Faidh Dubh*, Dublin, Oifig an tSolathair, 1940 (1 vol., pp. [570])

An Fáid Dub | Séamus O Ceallaiġ | a rinne an leagan gaedilge | Oifig an tsolátair | baile áta cliat

CRITICISM OF CARLETON'S WORKS

INTRODUCTION

Carleton's books were extraordinarily widely reviewed. A glance through this section will show that they were greeted promptly on publication by the great British and Irish journals such as the *Athenaeum, Blackwood's* and the *Dublin University Magazine*, and also, more surprisingly, by provincial papers from the *Truro Advertiser* to the *Monmouthshire Beacon* to the *Edinburgh Schoolmaster*. Carleton was well aware of the power of the press to boost his sales. His preface to the first edition of the Second Series of *Traits and Stories of the Irish Peasantry* noted that the First Series had been sold 'without puff' (that is, without trade advertising) and that its success had been entirely due to the 'Reviewers, Periodicals and the Press in general', whom he thanked for their favourable notices of his efforts. He declared that 'it was impossible to bestow greater praise on any book of the kind' and naturally hoped that they would praise the Second Series yet more highly.

From the first, anonymous, series, all critics joined in praising the authenticity of his writing. It was the time of great interest in 'national characteristics' and semi-anthropological studies of local customs from Pembrokeshire to Peru, and Carleton's Irish observations suited the critics' taste exactly in that respect. The *Athenaeum* describes those among whom 'the rules and habits of modern society prevail' as being 'athirst' for details of 'less fortunate, less civilised beings': Carleton was able to supply such details about the Irish in profusion. It is worth noting that whereas English critics accept one Irish 'type', some Irish reviewers take him to task for lack of variety, and for depicting only Northern Irish characters and dialect. British and Irish alike delight in describing him in such terms as 'the Irish Scott' or 'the Irish Burns', or 'The Crabbe of Prose'. From the beginning of his career he was praised by most reviewers for delineating the 'light and shade of Irish character', although some objected to the coarseness of the 'shady' side. His blending of 'humour and pathos' is almost universally mentioned.

In the early days, the critics were divided on questions of religion.

Carleton's treatment of priests offended not only the Catholic magazines, but others such as the Protestant-owned *Dublin Literary Gazette*; on the other hand, *Fraser's Magazine* agreed with him that it is 'the doctrines of the Romish Church that debase and depress the natural character of Ireland'.

It is doubtful if the novice Carleton paid much attention to critics' suggestions. He did not, for example, moderate his anti-clerical passages until ten years after the reviewers had advised him to do so. Far from cutting out 'mock oaths' as several critics of the First Series suggested, he wrote an essay on them for the Second Series. He did respond when critics in the late 1830s asked 'Why does not this gentleman write a novel?', by producing *Fardorougha the Miser*.

At the height of Carleton's fame, in the 1840s, his work was praised for promoting understanding of his country and countrymen: British critics thought it would be of practical use towards solving the 'Irish problem'; the *Dublin University Magazine* claimed that he could 'set the Irish character right with the world'.

The most unexpected batch of criticism in this section is that concerned with his play 'Irish Manufacture; or Bob McGawley's Project'. Newspapers of 1841 abound in praises of the play, reviews of performances, synopses of the plot, congratulations to the author, announcements of his benefit night, and later even the Prologue, verbatim (*The Nation*, 18 December 1858, p. 245). Carleton's successful play dealt with a subject of great current interest, that of supporting native Irish products. In the 1840s and 1850s the most fulsome praise for Carleton came from the *Nation*. He was their native Irish success, and they admired particularly any novel with a 'message' for the people of Ireland such as *Parra Sastha*. As Carleton's literary output diminished in the 1860s, interest in him naturally declined. There was a flurry of obituaries on his death in 1869, and thereafter the most noticeable cluster of articles about him comes in the 1880s when Yeats was anthologising and reviewing his work, and again in 1896, when D.J. O'Donoghue's edition of *Traits and Stories of the Irish Peasantry* and his *Life of William Carleton* appeared. The twentieth century has produced little substantial criticism of Carleton, apart from Benedict Kiely's biography *Poor Scholar* (1947), and most recently, Robert Lee Wolff's *Willam Carleton, Irish Peasant Novelist* (1979).

The very wide range of Carleton criticism shows him to have been a much more authoritative and popular writer than has perhaps been realised. And although the critical opinions of the book reviewer of the *Bristol Mercury* or the *Hull Rockingham* may not be of vital importance to our judgment of Carleton today, these multiple opinions are worth recording *because of* their multiplicity. That Carleton's work could generate such interest in the British provinces reveals that he was writing very much to the taste of the time, and that he was considered a writer of influence and importance, outside as well as inside Ireland.

A note on this section.
Criticism is listed chronologically; all items, including books and reviews, are grouped under the year of their appearance. The index shows the years in which any book was reviewed.

I have included a few very brief reviews because they are mentioned in such reference books as Hayes's *Irish Manuscript Sources,* but have noted that they *are* brief, to save others the disappointment of hunting them up. I have not attributed authors to anonymous reviews, partly because existing attributions often conflict, partly because of the difficulty of tracking down possibly minor reviewers on very little evidence, and chiefly because it seemed sufficiently important to establish the critical opinions of the magazines themselves.

Sometimes a review which is quoted in a publisher's advertisement turns out, when found, not to be a review of a Carleton book, but, say, a criticism of the current *Dublin University Magazine*, which briefly refers to a Carleton serial. I have entered such reviews with a note to that effect.

When a newspaper or magazine lacks pagination I have located page references as precisely as possible as: p. [4], or omitted.

Newspapers and periodicals are published in London unless otherwise indicated.

CHRONOLOGICAL LIST OF CARLETON CRITICISM

1829

Review of *Father Butler. The Lough Dearg Pilgrim. Dublin Family Magazine*, Vol. I, No. 3, June 1829, p. 207

1830

Review of *Traits and Stories of the Irish Peasantry* [First Series]. *Dublin Literary Gazette, or Weekly Chronicle of Criticism, Belles Lettres, and Fine Arts,* Vol. I, No. 14, 3 April 1830, pp. 211-212

Second notice of *Traits and Stories. Dublin Literary Gazette,* Vol. I, No. 15, 10 April 1830, pp. 233-234

Brief review of *Traits and Stories* introducing extract. *Belfast Guardian and Constitutional Advocate,* Vol. III, No. 298, 23 April 1830, p. [4]

Review of *Traits and Stories. Athenaeum,* No. 129, 17 April 1830, pp. 226-228

Second notice of *Traits and Stories. Athenaeum,* No. 130, 24 April 1830, pp. 242-245

Review of *Traits and Stories. Edinburgh Literary Journal, or, Weekly Register of Criticism and Belles Lettres,* Vol. III, No. 79, 15 May 1830

Review of *Traits and Stories. Blackwood's Magazine* (Edinburgh), Vol. XXVII, No. 166, May 1830, p. 808

Review of *Traits and Stories. Monthly Review,* Vol. XIV, No. 57, May 1830, pp. 110-123

'Sketches of Irish Manners', review of *Father Butler. The Lough Dearg Pilgrim. Christian Examiner* (Dublin), Vol. X, No. 72, May 1830, pp. 380

Review of *Traits and Stories of the Irish Peasantry. Dublin Monthly Magazine,* Vol. I, No. 5, May 1830, pp. 406-413

Second notice of *Traits and Stories of the Irish Peasantry. Dublin Monthly Magazine*, Vol. I, No. 6, June 1830, pp. 474-482

Review of *Traits and Stories. New Monthly Magazine*, Vol. XXX, No. 115, July 1830, pp. 279-280

'Sketches of Irish Scenery and Manners', a review of *Traits and Stories* [2a] with Otway's *Sketches in the North and South of Ireland*, Mrs. S. C. Hall's *Sketches of Irish Character* and Banim's *The Denounced. National Magazine* (Dublin), Vol. I, No. 2, August 1830, pp. 150-160

'A word or Two about an Irish Book, over our Glass of Whiskey Punch', review of *Traits and Stories. Fraser's Magazine*, Vol. II, No. 9, October 1830, pp. 312-319

1831

Review of *The Little Chimney-Sweep. Christian Examiner* (Dublin), Vol. XI, No. 74, August 1831, p. 632

1832

Announcement of second edition of *Traits and Stories of the Irish Peasantry* [First Series]. *Athenaeum*, No. 221, 21 January 1832, p. 47

Notice of *Traits and Stories of the Irish Peasantry*, Second Edition. *London Literary Gazette; and Journal of Belles Lettres, Arts, Sciences, &c.*, No. 786, 14 April 1832, p. 87

Critical note of *Traits and Stories of the Irish Peasantry*, Second Series (after serialisation of *Tubber Derg*). *The Schoolmaster, and Edinburgh Weekly Magazine* for 1832, p. 94

Review of *Traits and Stories of the Irish Peasantry*, Second Series. *Athenaeum*, No. 266, 1 December 1832, pp. 769-770

Review of *Traits and Stories*, Second Series. *Sunday Times*, 14 December 1832

Review of Vols. II and III of *Traits and Stories*, Second Series. *Athenaeum*, No. 268, 15 December 1832, pp. 806-807

Review of *Traits and Stories*, Second Series, with Harriet Martineau's *Illustrations of Political Economy*, Nos. X and XI, and Ebenezer Elliott's *The Splendid Village, Corn-Law Rhymes, and other Poems. London Literary Gazette &c.*, No. 831, 22 December 1832, pp. 801-804

Review of *Traits and Stories,* Second Series. *Weekly Despatch,* 24 December 1832

Review of *Traits and Stories,* Second Series *Sunday Observer,* 30 December, 1832

1833

Review of *Dublin University Review,* singling out Carleton's *Neal Malone* for praise. *Athenaeum,* No. 272, 12 January 1833, p. 24

'Writers on Irish Character', review of *Traits and Stories of the Irish Peasantry,* Second Series. *Dublin University Magazine,* Vol. I, No. 1, January 1833, pp. 31-41

Review of *Traits and Stories,* Second Series, *University Review and Quarterly* (Dublin), Vol. I, No. 1, January 1833, pp. 40-56

Review of *Traits and Stories,* Second Series. *Belfast Newsletter,* 4 January 1833, p. [1]

Review of *Traits and Stories,* Second Series. *Atlas,* 16 January 1833, p. 23

Review of *Traits and Stories,* Second Series. *Metropolitan Magazine,* Vol. VI, No. 21, January 1833, pp. 8-9

Review of *Traits and Stories,* Second Series. *New Monthly Magazine,* Vol. XXXVII, February 1833 pp. 239-240

Review of *Traits and Stories,* Second Series. *Tait's Edinburgh Magazine,* Vol. II, No. 11, February 1833, pp. 554-572

Review of *Traits and Stories,* Second Series. *Monthly Review,* Vol. I, No. 2, February 1833, pp. 177-189

Review of *Traits and Stories,* Second Series. *Comet* (Dublin), Vol. II, 10 February 1833, p. 334

Review of *Traits and Stories,* Second Series. *Gentleman's Magazine,* Vol. CIII, Part 1, May 1833, p. 443

1834

Review of *Popular Tales and Legends of the Irish Peasantry. Dublin Penny Journal,* Vol. II, No. 94, 9 April 1834, pp. 229-230

Review of *Tales of Ireland. Athenaeum,* No. 350, 12 July 1834, pp. 520-521

'A Polemic Novelist', review of *Tales of Ireland. Irish Monthly Magazine* (Dublin), Vol. III, No. 28, August 1834, pp. 478-483

'Irish Storyists – Lover and Carleton', review of Lover's *Legends and Stories of Ireland,* Carleton's *Tales of Ireland, Traits and Stories of the Irish Peasantry*, First Series, Third Edition and Second Series, Second Edition. *Dublin University Magazine*, Vol. IV, No. 21, September 1834, pp. 298-311

1835

'Sketches in Ireland', review and extract. (*Traits and Stories of the Irish Peasantry*). *Dublin Penny Journal*, Vol. III, No. 150, 16 May 1835, pp. 365-369; (extract concluded Vol. III, No. 151, 23 May 1835, pp. 373-376)

Review of *Traits and Stories of the Irish Peasantry*, 'Fourth Edition'. *Dublin Penny Journal*, Vol. IV, No. 180, 12 December 1835, pp. 189-192

1836

'Irish Tales', review of Carleton and others. *Blackwood's Edinburgh Magazine*, Vol. 39, May 1836, pp. 689-698

1838

'Irish Novels and Irish Novelists', review of books by Maria Edgeworth, Lady Morgan, Banim, Griffin, Lover, and Carleton's *Traits and Stories of the Irish Peasantry. Dublin Review*, Vol. IV, No. 8, April 1838, pp. 495-543.

1839

Review of *Fardorougha the Miser. Dublin Monitor*, Vol. I, No. 105, 9 July 1839, p. [2]

Review of *Fardorougha the Miser. Spectator*, Vol. XII, No. 576, 13 July 1839, p. 730

Review of *Fardorougha the Miser. Athenaeum*, No. 613, 27 July 1839, pp. 563-564

Review of *Fardorougha the Miser. Fermanagh Reporter*, 3 July 1839.

Review of *Fardorougha the Miser. Monthly Review*, Vol. II, No. 4, August 1839, pp. 550-564

Review of *Fardorougha the Miser. Londonderry Sentinel*, 4 August 1839

Review of *Dublin University Magazine* for November 1839, containing criticism of and extract from *Fardorougha the Miser. Belfast Newsletter*, 5 November 1839, p. [1]

1840

'Romanism in Ireland'. Review of *Tales and Stories of the Irish Peasantry* by William Carleton, 1836, with other books. *Quarterly Review*, Vol. LXVII, No. 133, December 1840, pp. 117-171

1841

'Our Portrait Gallery, No XV: William Carleton'. *Dublin University Magazine*, Vol. XVII, No. 97, January 1841, pp. 66-72

Comments on *Dublin University Magazine*'s Carleton 'Our Portrait Gallery'. *Dublin Monitor*, Vol. III, No. 339, 5 January 1841, p. [2]

Brief comments on *Misfortunes of Barney Branagan* in review of *Dublin University Magazine*. *Dublin Monitor*, Vol. III, No. 363, 2 March 1841, p. [3]

'The Dublin Stage', review of Carleton's play 'Irish Manufacture'. *The Warder* (Dublin), 13 March 1841, p. 5

'Theatre Royal' (announcement that Carleton's 'Irish Manufacture' is in rehearsal). *Dublin Monitor*, Vol. III, No. 369, 16 March 1841, p. [2]

'Mr Calcraft's Benefit'. *Saunders's Newsletter* (Dublin), 23 March 1841, p. 1

'Irish Manufacture', report of Carleton's play. *Freeman's Journal* (Dublin), 26 March 1841

'Theatre Royal', review of Carleton's play. *The Pilot*, (Dublin), 26 March 1841

'Theatre Royal', review of 'Irish Manufacture'. *Dublin Monitor*, Vol. III, No. 374, 27 March 1841, p. [2]

'Theatre Royal', review of 'Irish Manufacture'. *The Warder* (Dublin), 27 March 1841, p. 5

'Theatre Royal – Carleton's new play of Irish manufactures', review. *The Pilot* (Dublin), 29 March 1841

[Advertisement:] 'Command night – Irish Manufacture'. *Saunders's Newsletter* (Dublin), 29 March 1841, p. [1]

'Theatre Royal', review of repeat performance of 'Irish Manufacture'. *Dublin Monitor*, Vol. III, No. 375, 30 March 1841, p. [2]

'Theatre Royal – Mr. Carleton's play', review. *Dublin Evening Mail*, 31 March 1841, p. [2]

'Theatricals', about Carleton's play and his benefit night. *The Warder* (Dublin), 10 April 1841, p. 4

Review of *The Fawn of Spring-Vale &c. Dublin Monitor*, Vol. III, No. 387, 27 April 1841, pp. [2-3]

Comments on *Barney Branagan* in review of current *Dublin University Magazine. Dublin Monitor*, Vol III, No. 390, 4 May 1841, p. [2]

'William Carleton', about Carleton's theatrical benefit, with extract from *Dublin Evening Mail. Dublin Monitor*, Vol. III, No. 392, 8 May 1841, p. [2]

(Advertisement:) 'Author's Night. Mr. Carleton's Benefit'. *The Warder* (Dublin), 8 May 1841, p. [1]

(Advertisement:) 'Mr Carleton's Benefit'. Same advertisment as above, with an interesting accompanying address from the Letterpress Printers of Dublin praising Carleton's work and his use of Irish printers and publishers: *Dublin Monitor*, Vol. III, No. 394, 13 May 1841, p. [1]

'Mr. Carleton's Night', notice of Carleton's benefit night. *Dublin Evening Mail*, 12 May 1841, p. [3]

(Advertisement:) From Letterpress printers, *Irishman*, Dublin, 15 May 1841

Review of *The Fawn of Spring-Vale. Athenaeum*, No. 707. 15 May 1841, pp. 385-386

'Theatre Royal', review of Carleton's benefit performance. *Dublin Monitor*, Vol. III, No. 396, 18 May 1841, p. [3]

'Fawn of Springvale and other Tales', review. *The World* (Dublin), 22 May 1841, p. 5

Second review of *Fawn of Springvale*. *The World* (Dublin), 29 May 1841, p. 5

'Carleton's Tales' – review of *Jane Sinclair, The Clarionet,* etc. *Spectator*, Vol. XIV, No. 679, 3 July 1841, p. 643

'Mr Carleton's Tales' – brief review of *The Fawn of Spring-Vale, the Clarionet and other Tales*, introducing an extract. *Chambers's Edinburgh Journal*, No. 494, 17 July 1841, p. 203

'Sketches of Irish Peasantry', review of 14 Irish books including Carleton's *Traits and Stories of the Irish Peasantry*, 'Fourth Edition', *Tales of Ireland* and *Father Butler. The Lough Dearg Pilgrim. Quarterly Review*, Vol. LXVIII, No. 136, September 1841, pp. 336-376

'Recent Irish Fiction', review of *The Clarionet, and other Tales. The Citizen* (Dublin), Vol. IV, No. 24, October 1841, pp. 175-182

1842

'Serials' – brief notice of Part I of *Traits and Stories of the Irish Peasantry. Spectator*, Vol. XV, No. 735, 30 July 1842, p. 739

Review of Part I of *Traits and Stories. Dublin Monitor*, Vol. IV, No. 584, 5 August 1842, pp. [2-3]

Review of partwork *Traits and Stories*, with extract. *Cork Examiner*, Vol. I, No. 147, 5 August 1842, p. [4]

Review of Part I of *Traits and Stories. Kendal Mercury*, No. 430, 6 August 1842, p. [4]

'Literary Criticism. The Magazines' (including *Traits and Stories. Derbyshire Courier*, Vol. XV, No. 771, 6 August 1842, p. 4

'Serials' – brief review of *Traits and Stories. Leeds Intelligencer*, 6 August 1842, p. 6

'Serials' – brief review of *Traits and Stories*, Part I. *Naval and Military Gazette*, No. 500, 6 August 1842, p. 503

Brief review of *Traits and Stories*, Part I. *Gloucestershire Chronicle*, No. CCCCLXXV, 6 August 1842, p. [4]

Brief review of *Traits and Stories*, Part I. *Cheltenham Journal and Stroud Herald*, Vol. XVIII, No. 955, 8 August 1842, p. [4]

'Literary Notices – *Traits and Stories*, Part I'. *Cheltenham Journal*, Vol. XVIII, No. 955, 8 August 1842, p. 4

'Literary Notices. *Traits and Stories*, Part I.' *The Bradford Herald*, Vol. I, No. 32, 11 August 1842, p. 4

'Literature'. Review of *Traits and Stories*, Part I. *The Tyne Pilot*, No. 173, 12 August 1842, p. 4

'Literature'. Review of *Traits and Stories*, Part I. *The Bristol Mercury*, Vol. LIII, No. 2735, 13 August 1842, p. 6

Brief review of *Traits and Stories*, Part I. *Staffordshire Examiner*, Vol. VII, No. 325, 13 August 1842

'Literary Notices – *Traits and Stories*, Part I.' *The Halifax Guardian*, Vol. X, No. 507, 13 August 1842, p. 6

'Literature' – brief review of *Traits and Stories,* Part I. *Berwick Advertiser*, No. 1809, 13 August 1842, p. 2

Review of *Traits and Stories*, Part I. *The Monmouthshire Beacon*, Vol. VI, No. 253, 13 August 1842, p. 4

'The Serials' – brief review of *Traits and Stories*, Part I. *Cambridge Chronicle*, No. 4164, 13 August 1842, p. [4]

Review of *Traits and Stories*, Part I. *The Sheffield Iris*, Vol. 55, No. 2891, 16 August 1842, p. 4

Very brief notice of *Traits and Stories*, Part I. *The West Briton and Cornwall Advertiser*, Truro, Vol. XXXIII, No. 1675, 19 August 1842

Review of *Traits and Stories*, Part I, with extract. *Berwick and Kelso Warder*, Vol. VII, No. 354, 20 August 1842, p. [4]

Review of *Traits and Stories*, Part I. *The Brighton Herald*, No. 1900, 20 August 1842, p. 4

'Notices of New Works' – *Traits and Stories*, Part I. *The Somerset County Gazette*, Vol. VI, No. 294, 20 August 1842, p. 4

'Literary Notices' – *Traits and Stories*, Part I. *The Liverpool Chronicle*, Vol. XVI, No. 864, 20 August 1842, p. 2

'The Review – *Traits and Stories of the Irish Peasantry,* Part I'. *The Hull Rockingham*, No. 1808, 20 August 1842, p. 4

'The Magazines: Carleton's *Traits and Stories of the Irish Peasantry* Part I'. *Birmingham Advertiser*, No. 464, 25 August 1842, p. 4

Review of Part II of *Traits and Stories*. *Dublin Monitor*, Vol. IV, No. 594, 29 August 1842, p. [3]

Brief review of Part II of *Traits and Stories*. *Cork Examiner*, Vol. II, No. 161, 7 September 1842, p. [4]

'The Magazines – Carleton's *Traits and Stories of the Irish Peasantry*, Part II. *The Birmingham Advertiser*, No. 466, 8 September 1842

Review of *Traits and Stories*, Part II. *The Tyne Pilot*, No. 177, 9 September 1842, p. 4

'Serials' – brief review of Part II of *Traits and Stories*. *Spectator*, Vol. XV, No. 741, 10 September 1842, p. 884

Review of *Traits and Stories*, Part II. *The Bristol Mercury*, Vol. LIII, No. 2738, 10 September 1842, p. 6

Review of *Traits and Stories*. *Derbyshire Chronicle*, Vol. VII, No. 348, 10 September 1842, p. 4

Paragraph about 'beautiful reprint of Carleton's *Traits and Stories of the Irish Peasantry*', *Belfast Newsletter*, 13 September 1842, p. 4

Mention of Part II of *Traits and Stories*. *The West Briton and Cornwall Advertiser*, Truro, Vol. XXXIII, No. 1679, 16 September 1842

'Notices of New Works – *Traits and Stories of the Irish Peasantry*, Part II'. *The Somerset County Gazette*, Vol. VI, No. 298, 17 September 1842, p. 4

Brief review of Part II of *Traits and Stories*. *Kendal Mercury*, No. 436, 17 September 1842, p. [4]

Review of *Traits and Stories*. *Felix Farley's Bristol Journal*, Vol. XCVIII, No. 5103, 17 September 1842, p.4

Review of Part II of *Traits and Stories*. *Gloucester Journal*, Vol. CXX, No. 6249, 17 September 1842, p. [4]

'The Review – *Traits and Stories of the Irish Peasantry*, Part II'. *The Hull Rockingham*, No. 1812, 17 September 1842, p. 4

Brief review of Part II of *Traits and Stories*. *Berwick and Kelso Warder*, Vol. VII, No. 359, 24 September 1842, p. [4]

Review of Part II of *Traits and Stories*, with extract. *Berwick Advertiser*, No. 1815, 24 September 1842, p. [2]

Review of *Traits and Stories*, part II. *The Halifax Guardian*, Vol. X, No. 513, 24 September 1842, p. 6

Notice of *Traits and Stories*, Part II. *Cheltenham Journal*, Vol. XVIII, No. 962, 26 September 1842, p. 1

Review of *Traits and Stories*, Part II. *The Sheffield Iris*, Vol. 55, No. 2891, 27 September 1842, p. 4

'Irish Character. – By an Anglo-Hibernian', a review of part-work *Traits and Stories*. *Dublin University Magazine*, Vol. XX, No. 118, October 1842, pp. 422-432

Brief notice of Part III of *Traits and Stories*. *Cork Examiner*, Vol. II, No. 174, 5 October 1842, p. [4]

Review of *Traits and Stories*, Part III. *The Bristol Mercury*, Vol. LIII, No. 2742, 8 October 1842, p. 6

Brief notice of Part III of *Traits and Stories*. *Cambridge Chronicle*, No. 4172, 8 October 1842, p. [4]

'Literary Notices: *Traits and Stories of the Irish Peasantry*, Part III'. *The Halifax Guardian*, 15 October 1842, p. 6

'The Magazines', reviewing *Traits and Stories*. *Derbyshire Courier*, Vol. XV, No. 781, 15 October 1842, p. 4

Review of *Traits and Stories*. *The Devonport Telegraph*, Vol. XXXV, No. 1804, 15 October 1842, p. 2

Notice of *Traits and Stories*, Part III. *The Somerset County Gazette*, Vol. VI, No. 302, 15 October 1842, p. 4

Review of *Traits and Stories*. *The Sheffield Iris*, Vol. 55, No. 2900, 18 October 1842, p. 3

Review of *Traits and Stories*. *The Hull Packet*, No. 3018, 21 October 1842, p. 4

Review of *Traits and Stories*, Part III. *The Monmouthshire Beacon*, Vol. VI, No. 263, 22 October 1842, p. 4

Very brief notice of partwork *Traits and Stories*. *Staffordshire Examiner*, Vol. VII, No. 337, 29 October 1842

Review of *Traits and Stories*, Part III. *The Liverpool Journal* Vol. XIII, No. 668, 29 October 1842, p. 6

Review of Part III of *Traits and Stories*. *Berwick Advertiser*, No. 1821, 5 November 1842, p. [2]

'The Magazines', reviewing *Traits and Stories*. *Derbyshire Courier*, Vol. XV, No. 784, 5 November 1842, p. 4

Brief review of Part IV of *Traits and Stories*. *Cork Examiner*, Vol. II, No. 188, 9 November 1842, p. [4]

'Carleton's Irish Tales (Part IV)'. *Salopian Journal*, Vol. XLIX, No. 2549, 9 November 1842, p. 4

Notice of *Traits and Stories of the Irish Peasantry*, Part IV. *The Somerset County Gazette*, Vol. VI, No. 309, 12 November 1842, p. 4

Review of partwork *Traits and Stories*, New Series. *Downpatrick Recorder*, Vol. VI, No. 308, 19 November 1842, p. [4]

Review of Part IV of *Traits and Stories*, with extract. *Berwick Advertiser*, No. 1823, 19 November 1842, p. [2]

Notice of *Traits and Stories*, Part IV. *Cheltenham Journal*, Vol. XIX, 28 November 1842, p. 4

'The Serials', reviewing *Traits and Stories*. *Derbyshire Courier*, Vol. XV, No. 789, 10 December 1842, p. 4

Review of *Traits and Stories*. *Derbyshire Chronicle*, Vol. VII, No. 364, 10 December 1842, p. 4

Notice of *Traits and Stories*, Part V. *The Somerset County Gazette*, Vol. VI, No. 313, 10 December 1842, p. 4

Brief review of Part V of *Traits and Stories*. *The West Briton and Cornwall Advertiser*, Truro, Vol. XXXIII, No. 1692, 16 December 1842

Review of parts III, IV and V of *Traits and Stories*. *The Berwick & Kelso Warder*, Vol. VII, No. 371, 17 December 1842, p. [4]

Notice of *Traits and Stories*, Part IV. *The Halifax Guardian*, Vol. XI, No. 525, 17 December 1842, p. 6

Brief review of Part V of *Traits and Stories*, with extract. *Berwick Advertiser*, No. 1828, 24 December 1842, p. [2]

Brief notice of first five numbers of *Traits and Stories*. *Kendal Mercury*, No. 450, 24 December 1842, p. [4]

'*The Review: Traits and Stories of the Irish Peasantry*, Part V. *The Hull Rockingham*, No. 1826, 24 December 1842, p. 4

1843

Brief review of Part VI of *Traits and Stories. Cambridge Chronicle and Journal*, No. 4185, 7 January 1843, p. [4]

Review of partwork *Traits and Stories. Cambridge Advertiser*, 11 January 1843

Brief notice of Part IX of *Traits and Stories. Dublin Monitor*, Vol. V, No. 687, 3 April 1843, p. [2]

'The persecution of slander', review of *The Edinburgh Review* and Borrow's *Bible in Spain*, containing an attack on partwork *Traits and Stories. Dublin Review*, Vol. XIV, No. 28, May 1843, pp. 443-480

Brief review of 'last number of Vol. I' of *Traits and Stories. Dublin Monitor*, Vol. V, No. 1023, 3 July 1843, p. 2

Brief notice of Part XVI of *Traits and Stories. Dublin Monitor*, Vol. V, No. 1062, 2 October 1843, p. 2

Brief notice of Part XVII of *Traits and Stories. Cambridge Chronicle and Journal*, No. 4233, 9 December 1843

1844

Brief review of Part XIX of *Traits and Stories. Dublin Monitor*, Vol. VI, No. 1150, 12 January 1844, p. [2]

'Carleton's Traits and Stories: New Edition', review. *Dublin University Magazine*, Vol. XXIV, No. 141, September 1844, pp. 268-282.

Review of *Traits and Stories*, with extract from the *Dublin University Magazine*'s review of the book. *Dublin Monitor*, Vol. VI, 2 September 1844, p. [2]

Review of *Traits and Stories. The Nation* (Dublin) 12 October 1844, p. 11

1845

Review of *Valentine M'Clutchy. Athenaeum*, No. 898, 11 January 1845, pp. 38-39

Review of *Valentine M'Clutchy. The Nation* (Dublin), 11 January 1845, pp. 219-220

Review of *Valentine M'Clutchy. The Spectator*, Vol. XVIII, No. 863, 11 January 1845, pp. 41-42

Review of *Valentine M'Clutchy. The World* (Dublin), Vol. V, No. 242, 18 January 1845, p. 6

'Resumed' review of *Valentine M'Clutchy. The World* (Dublin), Vol. V, No. 243, 18 January 1845, p. 8

Second review of *Valentine M'Clutchy. The Nation* (Dublin), 25 January 1845, pp. 251-252

Review of *Rody the Rover. The Vindicator* (Belfast), 17 April 1845, p. 4

'The Irish Peasantry', review of *Tales and Sketches illustrating the Irish Peasantry. The Nation* (Dublin) 12 July 1845, p. 650

'Ballad Poetry of Ireland' including Carleton's poetry. *The Nation* (Dublin), 2 August 1845, p. 698

Review of *Art Maguire. The World* (Dublin), Vol VI, No. 268, 2 August 1845, p. 8

Review of *Rody the Rover. The Nation* (Dublin), 13 September 1845, p. 795 (includes a reprint of criticism from the *Freeman's Journal*)

Review of *Art Maguire; or, The Broken Pledge. Dublin Review*, Vol. XIX, No. 57, September 1845, pp. 272-273

Review of *Rody the Rover. The World* (Dublin), Vol. VI, No. 275, 20 September 1845, p. 8

Review of *Rody the Rover. The Spectator*, Vol. XVIII, No. 900, 27 September 1845, pp. 929-930

Review of *Rody the Rover. Irish Union Magazine* (Dublin), Vol. II, No. 8, October 1845, pp. 158-159

'Sea-side Reading', including review of *Valentine M'Clutchy. Fraser's Magazine*, Vol. XXXII, No. 191, November 1845, pp. 568-571

'The didactic Irish novelists – Carleton, Mrs. Hall', review of *Art Maguire, Rody the Rover, Parra Sastha* and Mrs. Hall's *The Whiteboy. Dublin University Magazine*, Vol. XXVI, No. 156, December 1845, pp. 737-752

1846

'Habits and character of the peasantry' (based on Carleton's *Tales and Sketches of the Irish Peasantry*, Duffy, 1845). In *Literary and Historical Essays* by Thomas Davis, Dublin, Duffy, 1846, pp. 208-215.

Reprinted in *The Prose Writings of Thomas Davis* ed. T. W. Rolleston, London, Walter Scott, 1891 (Camelot Series); in *Thomas Davis. Selections from his Prose and Poetry*, ed. T. W. Rolleston, London, Dublin and Belfast, Gresham, 1914 (Irish Library), etc. Centenary edition, Dundalk, Tempest, 1914, edited by D.J. O'Donoghue, has another Carleton piece (see 1914)

Review of *Rody the Rover*. *Athenaeum*, No. 955, 14 February 1846, pp. 167-168

Review of Duffy's 'Library of Ireland' series, including *Rody the Rover, Paddy-go-Easy*, and the Carleton piece in Thomas Davis's *Essays*. *Athenaeum*, No. 975, 4 July 1846, pp. 679-680

1847

Review of *The Black Prophet. Belfast People's Magazine*, Vol. I, No. 3, 1 March 1847, pp. 64-67

Review of *The Black Prophet* etc. *Athenaeum*, No. 1011, 13 March 1847, pp. 278-279

Review of *The Black Prophet. Howitt's Journal*, Vol. I, No. 17, 24 April 1847, pp. 236-237.

1848

Review of *The Emigrants of Ahadarra*. *Athenaeum*, No. 1061, 26 February 1848, pp. 208-209

Introduction to and review of *The Evil Eye*, which starts on p. 13 of the magazine. *The Irish Tribune* (Dublin), Vol. I, No. 1, 10 June 1848, p. 11

Paragraph quoting from *Evening Post* about Carleton's pension. *Irish Tribune* (Dublin), Vol. 1, No. 4, 1 July 1848, p. 56

'Answers to correspondents'. Statement that Carleton only a contributor to, not proprietor of, the paper. *Irish Tribune* (Dublin), Vol. 1, No. 5, 8 July 1848, p. 72

'Mr William Carleton's Literary Pension' (support for). *Dublin Evening Post*, 11 July 1848, p. 3

1849

Review of *The Tithe Proctor*. *Athenaeum*, No. 1121, 21 April 1849, pp. 403-404

1851

'The Irish Stage' contains two fleeting references to Carleton. *Duffy's Fireside Magazine* (Dublin), Vol. II, No. 13, November 1852, pp. 277-281

1852

'Carleton's *Squanders of Castle Squander.*' *Spectator*, Vol. XXV, No. 1253, 3 July 1852, pp. 638-9

Article about Carleton by Patrick Murray, Professor of Theology at Maynooth. *Edinburgh Review*, Vol. XCVI, October 1852, pp. 384-403

Review of *Red Hall*. *Athenaeum*, No. 1307, 13 November 1852, pp. 1236-1237

Review of *Red Hall*. *Spectator*, Vol. XXV, No. 1273, 20 November 1852, p. 1119

'Gossip', mentioning Carleton's denial that he is about to emigrate to Canada. *Athenaeum*, No. 1419, 6 January 1855, p. 20

Letter of William Carleton to the Dublin papers explaining his 'defiant lines' about emigration. *Athenaeum*, No. 1421, 20 January 1855, p. 83

Review of *Willy Reilly and his dear Colleen Bawn*. *Spectator*, Vol. XXVIII, No. 1399, 21 April 1855, p. 415

Review of *Willy Reilly and his dear Colleen Bawn*. *Athenaeum*, No. 1436, 5 May 1855, p. 519

1856

'The Dramatic Writers of Ireland', No. XI, includes Carleton's 'Irish Manufacturer' [*sic*]. *Dublin University Magazine*, Vol. XLVII, No. 279, March 1856, pp. 359-374

1857

Review of *Willy Reilly*. *The Nation* (Dublin), 25 April 1857, p. 554

Review of *The Black Baronet*. *The Nation* (Dublin), 12 December 1857, p. 334

Review of *The Black Baronet*. *General Advertiser* (Dublin), 12 December 1857, p. 2

Review of *The Black Baronet*. *Impartial Reporter* (Enniskillen), 17 December 1857, p. 2

1858

Review of *The Black Baronet*. *Athenaeum*, No. 1580, 6 February 1858, pp. 177-178

1860

Review of *The Evil Eye*. *Duffy's Hibernian Magazine* (Dublin), Vol. I, No. 4, October 1860, pp. 169-176

Review of *The Evil Eye*. *Athenaeum*, No. 1725, 17 November 1860, p. 669

1861

'National Tintings. No. II: William Carleton'. *Illustrated Dublin Journal*, No. 9, 2 November 1861, pp. 129-132

1869

(Carleton died on 30 January 1869, and press interest in him was briefly revived)

'Death of William Carleton'. *Express*, 1 February 1969, p. [3]

'Death of William Carleton'. *Freeman's Journal* (Dublin), 1 February 1869. (Reprinted *Galway Vindicator and Connaught Advertiser*, 3 February 1869; *The Irishman* (Dublin), 6 February 1869, p. 500; *The Nation* (Dublin), 6 February 1869, pp. 390-391

'Death of William Carleton'. *Irish Times* (Dublin), 1 February 1869, p. [2]

Obituary notice of William Carleton. *Cork Examiner*, 1 February 1869

2-line notice of Carleton's death. *Irish Builder* (Dublin), No. 186, 1 February 1869, p. 37

'The late William Carleton'. *Dublin Evening Post*, 2 February 1869

'Ireland.' *The Times* , 2 February 1869, p. 7. Includes one paragraph on Carleton's death, and erroneous statement that he had been editor of the *Christian Examiner*

'William Carleton, the Irish novelist'. *Daily Telegraph*, 3 February 1869

Obituary notice of William Carleton. *Kilkenny Journal*, 3 February 1869

'Funeral of William Carleton'. *Freeman's Journal*, 4 February 1869

'Funeral of Mr William Carleton'. *Saunders's Newsletter and Daily Advertiser*, 4 February 1869 (reprinted in *Express*, 4 February 1869)

'Funeral of William Carleton'. *Weekly News*, Dublin, 6 February 1869

'Death of William Carleton'. *The Flag of Ireland* (Dublin), Vol. I, No. 23, 6 February 1869, p. 3

Obituary, *The Nation*, 6 February 1969, pp. 390-391

Poem, 'William Carleton, Died, January 30th, 1869', by Speranza (Lady Wilde). *The Nation* (Dublin), 6 February 1869, p. 393

'William Carleton'. *The Shamrock* (Dublin), 13 February 1869, pp. 328-329

'English critics on Carleton'. *The Nation* (Dublin), 13 February 1869, pp. 410-411

'William Carleton, in Memoriam'. *Christian Examiner*, New Series No. VIII, March 1869, pp. 277-281. Contains funeral sermon by Rev. W. Pakenham Walsh.

Letter about Carleton. *The Shamrock* (Dublin), 25 April 1869, p. 498

1871

'The republication of Carleton's "Traits and Stories of the Irish Peasantry" '. *Daily News*, 19 August 1871

'William Carleton'. *Spectator*, Vol. XLIV, No. 2256, 23 September 1871, pp. 1157-1158 (Review of Tegg's 'New Edition' of *Traits and Stories*)

'William Carleton' – memoir in *A Book of Memories of Great Men and Women of the Age, from Personal Acquaintance* by S. C. Hall, London, Virtue, 1871, p. 237

1874

'Records of departed genius. Memoir of William Carleton' by J. R. O'Flanagan. *Now-a-days* (Dublin), Vol. I, 1874, pp. 753-757

1875

Life of William Carleton by J. Savage, New York and Montreal, Sadlier, 1875. Bound with *Valentine M'Clutchy* as one of the ten volumes of Sadlier's *Works of William Carleton*.

1883

'Young Ireland: A batch of "Young Ireland" letters – J. C. Mangan, W. Carleton.' *Irish Monthly* (Dublin), Vol. XI, July 1883, pp. 376-382

1888

'Carleton and Lever – a contrast', by D. J. O'Donoghue. *Young Ireland* (Dublin), 4 August 1888, pp. 135-137, continued 11 August 1888, pp. 172-173

1889

Review of W. B. Yeats's *Fairy and Folk Tales of the Irish Peasantry*, discussing Carleton. *Athenaeum*, No. 3198, 9 February 1889, pp. 174-175

'William Carleton', W. B. Yeats's own (unsigned) review of his collection of *Stories from Carleton*, and Carleton's *The Red-haired Man's Wife. The Scots Observer* (Edinburgh), 19 October 1889. Reprinted in *Uncollected Prose by W. B. Yeats,* Vol. I, ed. John P. Frayne, London, Macmillan, 1970, pp. 142-146

Review of *Stories from Carleton* edited by W. B. Yeats. *The Nation* (Dublin), 28 December 1889, p. 4

1890

'Carleton as an Irish Historian'. Letter from W. B. Yeats about the review of his *Stories from Carleton* (28 December 1889). *The Nation*

(Dublin), 11 January 1890. Reprinted in *Uncollected Prose by W. B. Yeats*, Vol. I, ed. John P. Frayne, London, Macmillan 1970, pp. 166-169

1895

Very brief notice of Irish Literary Society's benefit concert for Carleton's daughters. *Irish Builder* (Dublin), 15 June 1895, p. 156

'Irish National Literature, I: From Callanan to Carleton'. *The Bookman*, Vol. VIII, No. 46, July 1895, pp.105-107. Reprinted in *Uncollected Prose by W. B. Yeats*, Vol. I, ed. John P. Frayne, London, Macmillan, 1970, pp. 360-364

'New Novels and New Editions' includes review of *Fardorougha the Miser*, Downey. *Literary World*, London, Vol. LII, No. 1356 (N.S.), 25 October 1895, p. 312

1896

(Book:) *The Life of William Carleton*: being his autobiography and letters; and an account of his life and writings, from the point at which the autobiography breaks off. By David J. O'Donoghue, with an introduction by Mrs. Cashel Hoey. London, Downey & Co., 1896. (See Bibliographical section, [84a])

Review of D. J. O'Donoghue's *Life of William Carleton,*, mainly about Carleton. *Athenaeum*, No. 3566, 29 February 1896, pp. 277-278

Review (by W. B. Yeats) of D. J. O'Donoghue's *Life of William Carleton*. *Bookman*, Vol. 9, No. 54, March 1896, pp. 188-189. Reprinted in *Uncollected Prose by W. B. Yeats*, Vol. I, ed. John P. Frayne, London, Macmillan, 1970, pp. 394-397

'William Carleton'. Review of D. J. O'Donoghue's *Life* of Carleton by Eleanor Hull. *Literary World*, London, Vol. LIII, No. 1, 375 (N.S.), 6 March 1896, pp. 216-7

Review of D. J. O'Donoghue's *Life of William Carleton*. *The Spectator*, Vol. 76, No 3534, 21 March 1896, pp. 413-414

'The Real Irishman'. Review of Dent/Macmillan *Traits and Stories of the Irish Peasantry*. *Literary World*, London, Vol. LIII, No. 1, 380 (N.S.), 10 April 1896, pp. 346-7

'New Novels and New Editions' contains brief notice of Vol. II of *Traits and Stories of the Irish Peasantry*. *Literary World*, London, Vol. LIII, No. 1, 382 (N.S.), 24 April 1896, p. 386

Review of D. J. O'Donoghue's *Life of William Carleton*. *Catholic World* (New York) No. 63, May 1896, pp. 273-274

Review of *Traits and Stories of the Irish Peasantry*, edited by D. J. O'Donoghue. *Illustrated London News*, Vol. CVIII, No. 2976, 3 May 1896, p. 558

'Irish Life and Character'. Paragraph reviewing Dent/Macmillan *Traits and Stories of the Irish Peasantry*. *Literary World*, Boston, Vol. XXVII, No. 13, 27 June 1896, p. 204

Review of *Traits and Stories*, edited by D. J. O'Donoghue. *Athenaeum*, No. 3586, 18 July 1896, p. 94

Review of *Traits and Stories*. *Bookman*, Vol. X, No. 60, August 1896, p. 549

1897

'William Carleton: A brilliant Irish Novelist' (by G. Barnett-Smith). *Fortnightly Review*, Vol. 67/61, 1 January 1897, pp. 104-116. Reprinted *Eclectic Magazine* (New York), Vol. 128, No. 3, March 1897, pp. 315-324

1899

Brief review of *The Black Prophet*, edited by D. J. O'Donoghue. *Illustrated London News*, Vol. CXIV, No. 3123, 25 February 1899, p. 272

1903

[Book:] *Irish Life in Irish Fiction* by H.S. Krans, New York, Columbia University Press, Macmillan & Co, 1903, discusses Carleton.

'Carleton' by L. McManus. *The Academy and Literature*, Vol. LXV, No. 1651, 26 December 1903, pp. 719-720

1907

'Saint Patrick and Purgatory Island', by W. A. Henderson. *Journal of the National Literary Society of Ireland* (Dublin), Vol. II, Part I, 1907, pp. 23-38. (Reprinted in *National Literary Society Pamphlets*, 1907)

1911

'Our Scrapbook' mentions Carleton very briefly. *Irish Book Lover* (Dublin), Vol. II, May 1911, p. 156

1914

'Tales and Stories of the Irish Peasantry' in Centenary Edition of *Essays Literary and Historical* by Thomas Davis, Dundalk, Tempest, 1914, pp. 359-361. (This piece was not included in the book until this edition; 'The Irish Peasantry', pp. 356-358 had been entitled 'Habits and Characters of the Irish Peasantry' in the editions from 1846 to 1914.)

1917

'The Prelate, the Pervert and the Professor', by. Rev. E. J. Quigley. *Irish Ecclesiastical Record* (Dublin), Vol. IX, March 1917, pp. 206-214

1918

'Clerical and Catholic types in Carleton', by P. J. Lennox. *Ecclesiastical Review*, Philadelphia, June 1918, pp. 614-631

1919

Brief review of Carleton's *Stories of Irish Life*, edited by Darrell Figgis. *Athenaeum*, No. 4649, 6 June 1919, p. 445

'Every Irishman's Library'. Review of works by Maria Edgeworth, Gerald Griffin, and *Carleton's Stories of Irish Life*. By William Dawson. *Studies*, (Dublin), Vol. VIII, June 1919, pp. 346-349

1920

'Anne Cosgrave (Carleton's 'lost' novel)'. *Irish Book Lover* (Dublin), Vol. XII, August-September 1920, p. 20

1925

'William Carleton, Ulster Novelist' by Cahir Healy. *Impartial Reporter* (Enniskillen), 1 October 1925, p. 5

'More about Carleton. The Clogher Novelist'. *Impartial Recorder* (Enniskillen), 22 October 1925

1929

'A forgotten novelist' by Charles Hooper. *Saturday Review of Literature* (New York), Vol. III, 20 April 1929, p. 932 (Reprinted *Carleton Newsletter* (Gainesville), Vol. II, No. 3, January 1971, pp. 22-23)

1930

(Book:) *Carleton's Country*, by Rose Shaw. Dublin and Cork, Talbot Press, 1930

'A current commentary' – very brief mention of Carleton. *Irish Book Lover* (Dublin), Vol. XVII, May-June 1930, p. 73

1931

'A contrast in public values: the Catholic statesman, the apostate man of letters' by 'Molua'. *Catholic Bulletin* (Dublin), Vol. XXI, June 1931, pp. 583-587

1938

'William Carleton. A portrait of the Artist as Propagandist' by Roger McHugh. *Studies* (Dublin), Vol. XXVII, March 1938, pp. 47-62

'Irish wake games' by Henry Morris. *Béaloideas* (Dublin), Vol. VIII, 1938, pp. 123-141

1946

'Poor Scholar' by Benedict Kiely. *Irish Bookman* (Dublin), Vol. I, August 1946, pp. 20-33 (Reprinted *Carleton Newsletter* (Gainesville), Vol. II, No. 4, April 1972, pp. 28-29)

1947

(Book:) *Poor Scholar; A study of the works and days of William Carleton*, by Benedict Kiely. London, Sheed & Ward, 1947. New York, Sheed & Ward, 1948. Reprinted Dublin, Talbot Press, 1972

Brief reply in 'Notes and Queries'. *Irish Booklover* (Dublin), Vol. XXX, November 1947, p. 66. (Question inserted in Vol. XXX, February 1947, p. 39)

1948

Review of Benedict Kiely's *Poor Scholar*. *Irish Ecclesiastical Record* (Dublin), Vol. LXX, January 1948, pp. 92-94

'Otway's magic mountain' by Benedict Kiely. *The Bell* (Dublin), Vol. XV, No. 4, January 1948, pp. 53-60

'Ghosts of famous Irish writers' by P. O'Donnell. *The Bell* (Dublin), Vol. XV, No. 5, February 1948, pp. 1-2

1949

Review of Benedict Kiely's *Poor Scholar*. *Dublin Magazine*, Vol. XXIV (New Series), No. 2, April-June 1949, pp. 74-75

1950

'The Burning of Wildgoose Lodge' by T. G. F. Paterson. *County Louth Archaeological Journal* (Dundalk), Vol. XII, No. 2, 1950, pp. 159-180. (Reprinted as pamphlet, 1972)

1952

'Tribute to William Carleton', by John Montague. *The Bell* (Dublin), Vol. XVIII, No. 1, April 1952, pp. 13-20

1959

(Book:) *The Irish Novelists 1800-1850* by Thomas Flanagan, New York, Columbia University Press, 1959

1961

'William Carleton and his neighbours' by Sam Hanna Bell. *Ulster Folklife* (Belfast), Vol. VII, 1961, pp. 37-40

1962

Review of *The Courtship of Phelim O'Toole*. *Kilkenny Magazine*, No. 7, Summer 1962, pp. 69

'William Carleton writes to Rev. Dr. Murray'. *Clogher Record*, Vol. IV, No. 3, 1962, pp. 208-211

1966

'William Carleton and the Irish people', by André Boué. *Clogher Record*, Vol. VI, No. 1, 1966, pp. 66-70

(Dissertation:) 'Realistic accounts of the Irish peasantry in four novels of William Carleton.' Eileen S. Ibarra. Gainesville (University of Florida), 1969

1970

'William Carleton: an Introduction' by Eileen S. Ibarra. *Eire-Ireland*, St. Paul, Minnesota, Vol. V, No. 1, Spring 1970, pp. 81-86

The Carleton Newsletter (Gainesville, Florida), Vol. I, No. 1, 4 July 1970 – Vol. V, No. 2, 4 April 1975, contains checklists of Carleton holdings, reprints of articles about Carleton and a few original articles. All articles are listed below in the chronological order of their first publication.

'The death of William Carleton' by Terence Brown. *Hermathena* (Dublin), Vol. CX, 1970, pp. 81-85. (Reprinted *Carleton Newsletter* (Gainesville), Vol. II, No. 2, October 1971, pp. 12-13)

'Carleton in Louth' by Daniel J. Casey. *County Louth Archaeological and Historical Journal* (Dundalk), Vol. XVII, No. 2, 1970, pp. 96-106

'William Carleton, máistir scoile', by Séamas Ó Saothraí. *Díolaim Iriseora*, Dublin, Foilseacháin Náisiúnta Teo, 1970 (1971)

'An introduction to a research proposal . . . Views of nineteenth-century Irish peasantry: An examination of the life and works of William Carleton' by Daniel J. Casey. *Carleton Newsletter* (Gainesville), Vol. I, No. 1, 4 July 1970, p. [3]

'Paddy's ruse and Anna's revenge: Carleton's "Essay on Irish Swearing" ', by Grace Eckley. *Carleton Newsletter* (Gainesville), Vol. I, No. 1, 4 July 1970, pp. [5-6]

'Folktales in Carleton's "The Three Tasks"' by Eileen S. Ibarra. *Folklore Society Bulletin*, Tennessee, Vol. XXXVI, No. 3, September 1970, pp. 66-71

'Carleton's characterisation of women' by C. George Denman. *Carleton Newsletter* (Gainesville), Vol. I, No. 2, 4 October 1970, pp. 10-11

'The Evil Eye and the English pre-Romantic Gothic novels', by William R. Jones. *Carleton Newsletter* (Gainesville), Vol. I, No. 2, 4 October 1970, pp. 12-14

1971

'William Carleton and the picaresque novel: the Irish peasant and the Spanish picaro', by Eileen S. Ibarra. *Carleton Newsletter* (Gainesville), Vol. I, No. 4, 4 April 1971, pp. 3-4

'The Comic Character of Fin M'Coul' by E. S. Ibarra. *Folklore*, Vol. 82, Autumn 1971, pp. 212-215

'Lough Derg's infamous pilgrim' by Daniel J. Casey. *Clogher Record*, Vol. VII, No. 3, 1971-72, pp. 449-479. [Edited reprint in *Carleton Newsletter* (Gainesville), Vol. III, No. 1, 4 July 1972, whole issue]

'Man of the soil; an assessment of the nineteenth-century novelist, William Carleton' by Terence Brown. *Hibernia* (Dublin), 17 December 1971, p. 20

'The Poor Scholar: the oral style of William Carleton' by H. J. O'Brien. *Aquarius* (Benburb) No. 4, 1971, pp. 74-82

1972

'Carleton and Columcille' by Maureen O'Rourke Murphy. *Carleton Newsletter* (Gainesville), Vol. II, No. 3, 4 January 1972 (dated 1971) pp. 19-22

'The Irish priest and his niece: Carleton's work?' by Eileen S. Ibarra. *Carleton Newsletter* (Gainesville), Vol. II, No. 4, 4 April 1972, pp. 26-27

'Influence of old Irish beliefs on Carleton' by Steven Emery. *Carleton Newsletter* (Gainsville), Vol. II, No. 4, 4 April 1972, pp. 30-31

'William Carleton and Charles Lever' by Robert L. Meredith. *Carleton Newsletter* (Gainesville), Vol. III, No. 2, 4 Oct. 1972, pp. 11-14

1973

'Valentine M'Clutchy, the Irish Agent: A novel of Orange Terrorism in Early Nineteenth Century Northern Ireland' by Eileen S. Ibarra. *Carleton Newsletter* Vol. III, No. 3, January 1973, pp. 21-22

'The Tithe Proctor – a Revaluation' by William Bradley. *Carleton Newsletter,* Vol III, No. 4, 4 April 1973, pp. 28-30

(Dissertation:) 'William Carleton 1794-1869. Romancier Irlandais.' André Boué. Paris, 1973

'Four letters from William Allingham to William Carleton' by Alan Warner. *Carleton Newsletter*, Vol. IV, No. 1, July 1973, pp. 2-3

Review of Carleton's *The Black Prophet* by Eileen Ibarra. *The Carleton Newsletter*, Vol. IV, No. 1, July 1973, pp. 6-7

1974

'Wildgoose Lodge: the evidence and the Lore' Part I, by Daniel J. Casey. *County Louth Archaeological and Historical Journal* (Dundalk), Vol. XVIII, No. 3, 1974, pp. 140-164. Part II, Vol. XVIII, No. 4, 1975, pp. 140-164

'Violence in the fiction of William Carleton' by Nancy Eyles Burbash. *Carleton Newsletter*, Vol. IV, No. 3, 4 January 1974, pp. 20-23

'William Carleton'. *Irish Democrat*, February 1974. Reprinted *Carleton Newsletter*, Vol. V, No. 2, 4 April 1975, p. 15

'Dramatic qualities in Carleton's fiction' by William A. Dumbleton. *Carleton Newsletter*, Vol. IV, No. 4, 4 April 1974, pp. 27-31

'Carleton: a perception of Irish reality' by P. Barlow, C. McClellan and D. Sullivan. *Education Times* (Dublin), 11 April 1974, p. 7

'The dark side of Carleton' by Anthony Cronin. *Irish Times*. 5 April 1974

'John Eglinton and William Carleton: the search for a prose model for the Irish literary revival' by Mary E. Bryson. *Carleton Newsletter* (Gainesville) Vol. V, No. 1, 4 October 1974, pp. 4-6

'Carleton in a new format' by James O'Brien. *Carleton Newsletter*, Vol. V, No. 1, 4 October 1984, pp. 6-7

'Attitudes to nationality of four nineteenth-century novelists' by Mary Buckley. *Journal of the Cork Historical and Archaeological Society*, Vol. 78, No. 227, 1974, pp. 27-34

(Dissertation:) 'The scope and quality of William Carleton's presentation of Irish peasant life and character in his novels and stories.' William Bradley. University of London, 1974

1975

Review of *Tubber Derg, Denis O'Shaughnessy, Phelim O'Toole's Courtship and Neal Malone. Carleton Newsletter* (Gainesville), Vol. V, No. 1, January 1975, pp. 6-7

Review of *Tubber Derg, Denis O'Shaughnessy, Phelim O'Toole's Courtship and Neal Malone*, by Ralph W. Hyde. *Tennessee Folklore Society Bulletin*, Vol. XLI, No. 1, March 1975. Reprinted *Carleton Newsletter* Vol. V, No. 2, 4 April 1975

'Yeats and Carleton'. Eileen Sullivan. *Carleton Newsletter* (Gainesville), Vol. V, No. 2, 4 April 1975, pp. 12-14

'William Carleton: a Monaghan view' by John Nemo. *Carleton Newletter* (Gainesville), Vol. V, No. 2, 4 April 1975, pp. 11-12

'Carleton and the Count' by Daniel J. Casey. *Seanchas Ard Mhacha* (Armagh), Vol. VIII, No. 1, 1975-76, pp. 7-22

1976

(Book:) *Studies in the short stories of William Carleton* by Margaret Chesnutt. Goteburg, Acta Universitatis Gothoburgensis (Gothenburg Studies in English, 1976)

1977

'An introduction to William Carleton' by Margaret Chesnutt. *Moderna Språk*, Vol. LXXI, 1977, pp. 25-36

'William Carleton: Artist of Reality' by Eileen Sullivan. *Eire-Ireland*, St. Paul, Minnesota, Vol. XII, No. 1, Spring 1977, pp. 130-140

Review of Margaret Chesnutt's *Studies in the short stories of William Carleton* by Daniel J. Casey, *Eire-Ireland*, Vol. XII, Winter, 1977, pp. 142-143

(Dissertation:) 'William Carleton in Text and Context – a comparative study of *Traits and Stories of the Irish Peasantry*'. Barbara Hayley, University of Kent at Canterbury, 1977

1978

(Book:) *William Carleton Romancier Irlandais (1794-1869)* by André Boué, Paris, Publications de la Sorbonne, Imprimerie Nationale, 1978

1979

(Book:) *William Carleton, Irish Peasant Novelist. A Preface to his Fiction* by Robert Lee Wolff. New York and London, Garland Publishing Inc., 1979

'Voice and audience in the early Carleton' by Colin Meir. *Études Irlandaises*, Villeneuve-d'Ascq, New Series No. 4, December 1979, pp. 271-286

Review of André Boué's *William Carleton, Romancier Irlandais* by Patrick Rafroidi, *Études Irlandaises*, Villeneuve-d'Ascq, New Series No. 4, December 1979, pp. 374-376

1980

Review of Robert Lee Wolff's *William Carleton, Irish Peasant Novelist* by Daniel J. Casey. *Éire-Ireland*, St. Paul, Minnesota, Vol. XV, No. 3, Fall, 1980, pp. 148-150

1981

'Three Roads out of Clogher: a study of nineteenth-century Ireland in the life of William Carleton', by Daniel J. Casey. *Clogher Record*, Vol. IX, No. 3, 1981, pp. 392-404

'The Carleton Canon; additions and subtractions', by Brian Earls. *Studia Hibernica*, Dublin, No. 21, 1981 (published 1983), pp. 95-125

1982

Review of Robert Lee Wolff's *William Carleton. Irish Peasant Novelist* by Maureen Waters. *Irish Literary Supplement*, New York, Vol. I, No. 1, Spring 1982, p. 13

1983

'The Gaelic Background of Carleton's *Traits and Stories*' by Cathal O Háinle, *Éire-Ireland*, St. Paul, Minnesota, Vol. XVIII, No. 1, Spring 1983, pp. 6-19

(Book:) *William Carleton* by Eileen A. Sullivan. Boston, Twayne Publishers, 1983

(Book:) *Carleton's Traits and Stories and the 19th Century Anglo-Irish Tradition* by Barbara Hayley. Gerrards Cross, Totowa, New Jersey, Colin Smythe, Barnes & Noble, 1983

'The words of William Carleton' by Benedict Kiely. Review of Barbara Hayley's *Carleton's Traits and Stories*. *Irish Times*, Dublin, 1 October 1983, 'Weekend' p. 5

'Nouvellistes et Romanciers de Carleton à Stephens' by Patrick Rafroidi. Review of Barbara Hayley's *Carleton's Traits and Stories* etc. *Études Irlandaises*, Villeneuve-d'Ascq, New Series No. 8, December 1983, pp. 358-360

'A master of the uproar', review of Barbara Hayley's *Carleton's Traits and Stories* by Patricia Craig. *Times Literary Supplement*, 16 December 1983, pp. 1415-1416

1984

Review of Barbara Hayley's *Carleton's Traits and Stories* by Joseph Dunne. *Irish University Review*, Dublin, Vol. 14, No. 1, Spring 1984, pp. 135-136

Review of Barbara Hayley's *Carleton's Traits and Stories* by Brian Earls. *Studies*, Dublin, Spring 1984, pp. 84-86

'In praise of proper swearing' by Tony O'Riordan. Review of Barbara Hayley's *Carleton's Traits and Stories*. *Sunday Independent*, Dublin, 26 February 1984, p. 16

'Colored Photographs: William Carleton's Contribution to the Short Story Tradition' by Harold Orel. *Éire-Ireland*, St. Paul, Minnesota, Summer 1984, pp. 75-97

Review of Barbara Hayley's *Carleton's Traits and Stories* by Patrick Quigley. *Clogher Record*, Vol. XI, No. 3, 1984, p. 466

'William Carleton: A Divided Tradition' by Maureen Waters. *Canadian Journal of Irish Studies*, Vancouver, B.C., Vol. X, No. II, December 1984, pp. 27-36

Review of Barbara Hayley's *Carleton's Traits and Stories* by W. J. McCormack. *Hermathena*, Dublin, CXXXCII, Winter 1984, pp. 68-71

1985

(Dissertation:) 'Style in the Novels of William Carleton', by Mary Ellen Cohane, Rutgers University

(Book:) *A Bibliography of the writings of William Carleton* by Barbara Hayley. Gerrards Cross, Colin Smythe, 1985

LIBRARIES WITH SIGNIFICANT CARLETON HOLDINGS

The following libraries have significant holdings of publications by William Carleton. I am most grateful to their librarians for the help they have given me, without which I could not have completed this work.

Aberdeen University Library, King's College, Aberdeen, AB9 2UB

Alcuin Library, St. John's University, Collegeville, Minnesota 56321

American Antiquarian Society, 185 Salisbury Street, Worcester, Massachusetts 01609

Amherst College, Amherst, Massachusetts 01002

The Athenaeum, 219 South Sixth Street, Philadelphia, Pennsylvania 19106

City of Baltimore, Enoch Pratt Free Library, 400 Cathedral Street, Baltimore, Maryland 21201

The Belfast Education and Library Board, Central Library, Royal Avenue, Belfast BT1 1EA

Boston Athenaeum, Boston, Massachusetts 02117

Boston Public Library, Boston, Massachusetts 02117

Brown University Library, Providence, Rhode Island 02912

Bryn Mawr College Library, Bryn Mawr, Pennsylvania 19010

University of California, Berkeley, California 94720

University of California, Davis, California 95616

University of California, Los Angeles, California 90024

Case Western Reserve University, Freiberger Library, Cleveland, Ohio 44106

The Center for Research Libraries, 5721 Cottage Grove Avenue, Chicago, Illinois 60637

Chestnut Hill College, Logue Library, Philadelphia, Pennsylvania 19118

The University of Chicago, Joseph Regenstein Library, 1100 East 57th Street, Chicago, Illinois 60637

The Public Library of Cincinnati and Hamilton County, 800 Vine Street, Cincinnati, Ohio 45202

Cleveland Public Library, 325 Superior Avenue, Cleveland, Ohio 44114

Colby College Library, Waterville, Maine 04901

The Library of Congress, Washington, D.C. 20540

Cork City Library, Grand Parade, Cork

Cornell University Libraries, Ithaca, New York 14853

Duke University, William R. Perkins Library, Durham, North Carolina 27706

Edinburgh University Library, George Square, Edinburgh EH8 9LJ

Emory University, Robert W. Woodruff Library for Advanced Studies, Atlanta, Georgia 30322

The University of Florida Libraries, Gainesville, Florida 32601

Furman University Library, Greenville, South Carolina 29613

Gonzaga University, Crosby Library, Spokane, Washington 99258

Haverford College Library, Haverford, Pennsylvania 19041

Harvard University, The Houghton Library, Cambridge, Massachusetts 02138

University of Illinois at Urbana Champaign, Urbana, Illinois 61801

The Historical Society of Pennsylvania, 1300 Locust Street, Philadelphia, Pennsylvania 19107

Indiana University Library, Bloomington, Indiana 47401

The University of Iowa Library, Iowa City, Iowa 52242

National Library of Ireland, Kildare Street, Dublin 2

John Carroll University, Grasselli Library, University Heights, Ohio 44118

Joint University Libraries, Nashville, Tennessee 37203

University of Kansas, Kenneth Spencer Research Library, Lawrence, Kansas 66045

The Royal Borough of Kensington & Chelsea Central Library, London W8 7RX

University of Leeds, Brotherton Library, Leeds LS2 9JT

Lehigh University, Linderman Library, Bethlehem, Pennsylvania 18015

Linen Hall Library, 17 Donegall Square North, Belfast BT1 5GD

Lucy Cavendish College, Cambridge CB3 0BU

The University of Michigan Library, Ann Arbor, Michigan 48109

Michigan State University Library, East Lansing, Michigan 48824

University of Minnesota Libraries, Minneapolis, Minnesota 55455

University of Missouri Library, Columbia, Missouri 65201

The Newberry Library, 60 West Walton Street, Chicago, Illinois 60610

Oberlin College Library, Oberlin, Ohio 44074
The Ohio State University Library, 1858 Neill Mall, Columbus, Ohio 43210
University of Oregon Library, Eugene, Oregon 97403
Oregon State University Library, P.O. Box 1086, Corvallis, Oregon 97330
The Free Library of Philadelphia, Logan Square, Philadelphia, Pennsylvania 19103
University of Pennsylvania, The Charles Patterson Van Pelt Library, Philadelphia, Pennsylvania 19104
The Library Association of Portland, 801 S.W. Tenth Avenue, Portland, Oregon 97205
Queen's University of Belfast, Belfast BT9 5EQ
University of Reading Library, Whiteknights, Reading RG6 2AE
Representative Church Body, Braemor Park, Rathgar, Dublin 14
Royal Irish Academy, Dawson Street, Dublin 2
National Library of Scotland, George IV Bridge, Edinburgh EH1 1EW
Southern Illinois University at Carbondale, Carbondale, Illinois 62901
The Swarthmore College Library, Swarthmore, Pennsylvania 19081
Tacoma Public Library, Tacoma, Washington 98416
Texas Christian University, Mary Coutts Burnett Library, Fort Worth, Texas 76129
Trinity College Library, Dublin 2
University of Ulster Library, Coleraine, Londonderry BT52 1SA
National Library of Wales/Llyfrgell Genedlaethol Cymru, Aberystwyth SY23 3BU
University of Wisconsin, Memorial Library, Madison, Wisconsin 53706
Commonwealth of Virginia State Library, Richmond, Virginia 23219
University of Washington Libraries, Seattle, Washington 98195
The Wistar Institute, 36th Street at Spruce, Philadelphia, Pennsylvania
Xavier University Library, Victory Parkway and Dana Avenue, Cincinnati, Ohio 45207
Yale University Library, New Haven Connecticut 06520

INDEX

This index shows the original periodical publication of stories and novels by reference to the *Original Periodical Publication* section of the bibliography (as, *Neal Malone, Per. Publ. 24*); their appearances in book form, either in collections or alone, by reference to the *Bibliography* section (as, [8a], [12a], [15a-l] . . .); any reviews or critical articles are placed by year, and can be found under those years in the chronological *Criticism* section (as, 'reviewed 1833').

Extracts appear in the Subsequent Printings section. Books and articles on Carleton, and reviews are to be found in the *Criticism* section.

'Abduction, The': see Alley Sheridan

'Abduction of Mat Kavanagh, The': see 'The Hedge School'

Alley Sheridan and other Stories: [45a-b]

'Alley Sheridan, or the Runaway Marriage': *Per. Publ. 15*; [9a-b]; [13a-j] (as 'The Abduction'); [45a-b] (as 'Alley Sheridan, or the Irish Runaway Marriage')

Amusing Irish Tales: [77a-c]

Anne Cosgrave: extract 1906, reviewed 1920

'Around Ned's Fireside, or the Story of the Squire' (extract from 'Ned M'Keown'): [77a-c]

'Art Maguire, or, the Broken Pledge': *Per. Publ. 2* (as 'The Broken Oath'); [19a-g], [29a], [76a-h]; reviewed 1845

Art Maguire, or, the Broken Pledge, and the Lives of Curran and Grattan: [29a]

Autobiography of William Carleton: [91a] (see also *Life of William Carleton* [84a-b])

'Barney Bradley': see 'The Resurrections of Barney Bradley'

Barney Brady's Goose, The Hedge School, The Three Tasks, and other Irish Tales: [52a-e], [68a]

'Barney Brady's Goose; or, Dark Doings at Slathbeg': *Per. Publ. 33*; [18a-h], [43a-b], [46a-g], [52a-e], [77a-c] [. . . Mysterious Doings . . .]; [79a]

'Barney Branagan': see 'The Misfortunes of Barney Branagan'

Barney Branagan, Fawn of Spring Vale, Barney Bradley, and other Tales: [26a]

'Barney M'Haigney, the Irish Prophecy Man': *Per. Publ. 51* (as 'The Irish Prophecy Man'); [18a-h], [77a-c]

'Battle of the Factions': [2a-f], [15a-n], [22a], [37a], [58a-d], [59a], [60a-b], [61a], [62a-e], [63a], [64a], [68a-d], [76a-i], [83a-b], [86a], [87a], [90]

Battle of the Factions and other Tales of Ireland, The: [22a]

'Black-and-all-Black. A Legend of the Padereen Mare': *Per. Publ. 61*

Black Baronet, The: see *Red Hall or the Baronet's Daughter*

Black Prophet, The: Per. Publ. 56; [25a-k], [76a-i]; reviewed 1847; Irish translation

'Bob Pentland; or, The Gauger Outwitted': *Per. Publ. 39*; [18a-h], [51a-c], [77a-c], [88a-d]

'Broken Oath, The': see 'Art Maguire, or the Broken Pledge'

'Brothers, The': *Per. Publ. 12*; [8a-b], [12a]

'Buckramback, the Country Dancing-Master': *Per. Publ. 37* (as 'The Country Dancing Master'); [18a-h], [51a-c], [77a-c]

Carleton, William, articles about: 1841, 1848, 1851, 1852, 1855, 1861, 1869, 1874, 1883, 1888, 1889, 1890, 1895, 1896, 1897, 1911, 1917, 1920, 1929, 1930, 1931, 1938, 1946, 1948, 1949, 9152, 1961, 1962, 1966, 1970, 1971, 1972, 1973, 1974

Carleton, William, books about: 1930, 1947, 1959, 1976, 1977, 1979

Carleton's Irish Tales, ed. W. B. Yeats: see *Irish Tales*

Carleton's Stories of Irish Life, ed. Figgis [88a-d]; reviewed 1919

'Castle Cumber Correspondence, The': *Per. Publ. 54*

to Maynooth'); [65a]; [72a-d], [76a-i] (as 'Going to Maynooth'); [83a-b]; [87a] (as 'Going to Maynooth'); [88a-d], [90a], [93a]; [96a] (as 'Denis O'Shaughnessy')

Denis O'Shaughnessy Going to Maynooth etc., ed. Harmon [93a]

'Dick M'Grath. A Sketch of living character': *Per. Publ. 7*

Dominick, the Poor Scholar: [74a-d], and see *The Poor Scholar*

'Donagh, or the Horse Stealers, The': *Per. Publ. 17*; [4a-d], [5a]; [13a-j] (as 'The Horse Stealers'); [15a-l], [22a], [39a], [45a-b], [58a-e], [59a-b], [60a-b], [61a-c], [62a-e], [63a], [64a], [66a-d], [76a-h], [81a], [83a-b], [87a]

'Double Prophecy, or, Trials of the Heart, The': *Per. Publ. 71*; [48a]

'Dream of a Broken Heart, The': *Per. Publ. 25*; [8a-b], [12a]

'Dublin University Magazine and Mr. Lever, The': *Per. Publ. 53*

'Ellen Duncan': [56a-b], [76a-i] (attrib. to Carleton but by 'Denis O'Donoho')

Emigrants of Ahadarra, The: [30a-b]; [30c-d] (as *The Emigrants*); [30e-g], [76a-i]; reviewed 1848

'Essay on Irish Swearing, An': [4a-d], [6a], [39a], [61a-e], [62a-e], [65a], [83a-b], [94a]; see also 'The Geography of an Irish Oath'

'Evil Eye; a tale of Mystery, The': *Per. Publ. 60*; reviewed 1848

Evil Eye, or the Black Spectre, The: [47a-h], [76a-i]; reviewed 1860

Faidh Dubh, An: translation of *The Black Prophet*

'Fair Gurtha; or, the Hungry Grass': *Per. Publ. 67*

'Fair of Emyvale, The': *Per. Publ. 63*; [50a], [54a], [63a]

Fardorougha the Miser: Per. Publ. 31; [11a]; [11b] (as *The Miser*); [11c-n], [76a-i]; reviewed 1839; Irish translation

'Fate of Frank M'Kenna, The': *Per. Publ. 40* (as 'Irish Superstitions – Ghosts and Fairies'): [18a-h], [51a-c]

'Father Butler': *Per. Publ. 3*; [1a-c], [7a-b]

Father Butler, or Sketches of Irish Manners: [7a-b]

'Irish Legends': see 'Sir Turlough; or, the Churchyard Bride'

Irish Life and Character; or, Tales and Stories of the Irish Peasantry: [79a]

'Irish Manufacture', reviewed 1841, 1856; prologue

'Irish Matchmaker, The': see 'Mary Murray, the Irish Matchmaker'

'Irish Midwife, The': *Per. Publ. 42, 44, 47.* See also 'Rose Moan, the Irish Midwife' and 'Dandy Kehoe's Christening'

'Irish Oath, An': see 'The Geography of an Irish Oath'

Irish Oath and Lianhan Shee, An: [71a-d]

'Irish Prophecy Man, The': see 'Barney M'Haigney, the Irish Prophecy Man'

Irish Life and Character: [79a]

'Irish Rake, The': [18a-h] (from 'Rickard the Rake', *Per. Publ. 32*)

'Irish Shanahus, The': see 'Tom Gressiey, the Irish Senachie'

'Irish Student, The; or, How the Protestant Church was invented by the Devil' (extract from early version of 'Denis O'Shaughnessy going to Maynooth'): [77a-c]

'Irish Superstitions – Ghosts and Fairies': *Per. Publ. 40, 41, 45.* See also 'The Fate of Frank M'Kenna', 'The Rival Kempers' and 'Frank Martin and the Fairies'

Irish Tales, ed. W. B. Yeats: [85a]

Jane Sinclair, Neal Malone &c &c: [33a-b] and see next entry, 'and other Tales'

Jane Sinclair, Neal Malone and other Tales: [33c]. Previous entry, retitled

'Jane Sinclair, or, the Fawn of Spring Vale': *Per. Publ. 30*; [14a,c] (as 'The Fawn of Spring-Vale'); [14b]; [26a] (as 'The Fawn of Spring Vale'); [32a], [33a-c], [56a-b], [76a-i] (as 'Jane Sinclair')

Jane Sinclair; or, the Fawn of Springvale (collection): [56a-b]

Jane Sinclair; or, the Fawn of Spring-Vale; and The Dark Day: [32a]

Jane Sinclair; or, the Fawn of Spring Vale, the Clarionet and other Tales: [14a,c] (as *The Fawn of . . .*); [14b]; reviewed 1841

'Master and Scholar': *Per. Publ. 65*; [50a], [63a]

'Materialist, The': *Per. Publ. 22*

Mauvais Oeil, Le: translation of *The Evil Eye*

Mickey M'Rorey, the Irish Fiddler': *Per. Publ. 36* (as 'The Irish Fiddler'); [18a-h], [43a-b], [46a-g], [51a-c], [77a-c]

'Midnight Hour, The' (poem): *Per. Publ. 5*

'Midnight Mass, The': [4a-d], [6a], [15a-l], [39a], [55a], [58a-e], [59a-b], [60a-b], [61a-e], [62a-e], [63a], [64a], [69a-d], [76a-i], [81a], [83a-b], [87a], [88a-d], [95a]

Midnight Mass, The, and The Station: [69a-d]

'Miller of Mohill, The': *Per. Publ. 72*

Miser, The: see *Fardorougha the Miser*

'Misfortunes of Barney Branagan, The': *Per. Publ. 43*; [14a-c], [26a]; [34a-b], [57a] (as 'Barney Branagan')

'Moll Roe's Marriage; or, the Pudding Bewitched': *Per. Publ. 46*; [18a-h], [52a-e], [79a]

'Neal Malone': *Per. Publ. 24*; [8a-b], [12a], [15a-l], [22a], [33a-c], [52a-e], [58a-e], [59a-b], [60a-b], [63a], [75a-d], [76a-i], [79a], [83a-b], [86a-b], [87a], [88a-d], [93a], [96a]; reviewed 1833

Neal Malone and other Tales of Ireland: [12a]

Neal Malone and Tubber Derg: [75a-d]

Ned M'Keown: [2a-f], [15a-l], [24a], [37a], [58a-d], [59a], [59a], [60a-b], [61a-c], [62a-e], [63a], [64a], [70a-d], [76a-i], [83a-b], [87a], [92a]

Nostalgia; or, Home Sickness: *Per. Publ. 74*

Owen M'Carthy: see *Tubber Derg, or the Red Well*

O'Sullivan's Love, A Legend of Edenmore: *Per. Publ. 58*; [28a]

Parra Sastha, or the History of Paddy Go-Easy and his wife Nancy: [21a-g], [28a]; reviewed 1845, 1846

Party Fight and Funeral, The: [2a] (as *The Funeral, and Party Fight*); [2b-f], [15a-l], [38a], [53a-f], [58a-e], [59a], [60a-b], [61a-c],

Rapparee, The: see *Redmond Count O'Hanlon, the Irish Rapparee*

'Record of the Heart, A': *Per. Publ. 35* (as 'Records of . . .'); [18a-h]

Red-Haired Man's Wife, The: [78a]

Red Hall or the Baronet's Daughter: [36a-b]; [36a-i], [87a-i] (as *The Black Baronet*); reviewed 1852, 1858

Redmond Count O'Hanlon, the Irish Rapparee: *Per. Publ. 70* (as *The Rapparee*); [49a-g], [a]

Representative Irish Tales ed. W. B. Yeats. See *Extracts and Anthologies, 18*

'Resurrections of Barney Bradley, The': *Per. Publ. 27*; [14a-c]; [26a], [33a-c] (as 'Barney Bradley')

'Retrospect, The' (poem): *Per. Publ. 8*

'Retrospections' (poem): Per. Publ. 4

'Rickard the Rake': *Per. Publ. 32*; introduction, *The Irish Rake* [18a-h]

'Rival Kempers': *Per. Publ. 41*; [18a-h], [51a-c]

Rody the Rover; or, the Ribbonman: [20a-f]; [20g] (as *The Life and Adventures of Rody the Rover, the Ribbonman of Ireland*); reviewed 1845, 1846

'Romance of Instinct, The': *Per. Publ. 75*

Romans Irlandais. Scènes de la vie champêtre: translation of *Traits and Stories of the Irish Peasantry*

'Rose Moan, the Irish (Country) Midwife': *Per. Publ. 42, 44, 47*; [18a-h], [21d-g], [77a-c]

'Second Sight and Apparition': see 'Stories of Second Sight and Apparition'

'Sha Dhu': see 'Lha Dhu'

'Shane Fadh's Wedding': [2a-f], [15a-l], [24a], [37a], [58a-d], [59a-b], [60a-b], [61a-c], [62a-e], [63a], [64a], [66a-d], [76a-i], [80a-c], [83a-b], [87a], [90a]

Shane Fadh's Wedding and Other Stories: [66a-d]

Volumes in One'; [59b], Lovell, n.d., 'Various Complete Stories in One Volume'; [60a], Tegg, n.d., 'New Edition' (in one volume); [60b], Worthington, 1875; [61a-c], Routledge, 1877, n.d., n.d., (two 'series'); 'Complete Edition'; [62a-e], Routledge, n.d., (four 'series'), 'Complete Edition'; [63a], Maxwell, Vickers, n.d., 'New Edition' (includes *The Silver Acre* etc.); [64a], Routledge, 1877, 'First Series'; [65a], Routledge, 1877, 'Second Series'; [66a-d], Ward, Lock/Munro/Lovell, n.d., '*Shane Fadh's Wedding and other Stories*'; [67a-d], Ward, Lock/Munro/Lovell, n.d., '*Larry M'Farland's Wake and The Hedge School*'; [68a-d], Ward, Lock/Munro/Lovell, n.d., '*The Party Fight and Funeral and The Battle of the Factions*'; [69a-d], Ward, Lock/Munro/Lovell, n.d., '*The Midnight Mass and The Station*'; [70a-d], Ward, Lock/Munro/Lovell, n.d., '*Phil Purcel the Pig Driver and Other Stories*'; [71a], Ward, Lock/Munro/Lovell, n.d., '*An Irish Oath and Lianhan Shee*'; [72a], Ward, Lock/Munro/Lovell, n.d., '*Going to Maynooth*'; [73a], Ward, Lock/Munro/Lovell, n.d., '*Phelim O'Toole's Courtship and Wildgoose Lodge*'; [74a-d], Ward, Lock/Munro/Lovell, n.d., '*Dominick the Poor Scholar*'; [75a-d], Ward, Lock/Munro/Lovell, n.d., '*Neal Malone and Tubber Derg*'; [83a-b], Dent, 1896, edited by D. J. O'Donoghue, reviewed 1896; [87a], Niccolls, 1911, 'In Four Volumes'; [92a], Mercier, 1973, I, '*Wildgoose Lodge and other Stories*'; [93a], Mercier, 1973, II, '*Denis O'Shaughnessy Going to Maynooth*'; [94a], Mercier, 1973, III, '*Phelim O'Toole's Courtship and other Stories*'; [95a], Mercier, 1973, IV, '*The Party Fight and Funeral*'

'Tubber Derg, or the Red Well': *Per. Publ. 20* (as 'The Landlord and Tenant'); [4a-d], [6a], [13a-j] (as 'Owen M'Carthy'); [15a-l], [40a], [43a-c]; [45a-b] (as 'Owen M'Carthy, or the Landlord and Tenant'); [58a-e], [59a], [60a-b], [61a-c], [62a-e], [63a], [65a], [75a-d], [76a-i], [80a-c], [83a-c], [87a], [96a]

Tubber Derg; Denis O'Shaughnessy; Phelim O'Toole's Courtship and Neal Malone, ed. Ibarra, [96a]

Tubber Derg; or, the Red Well, and other Tales of Irish Life: [43a-b]

Tubber Derg; or, the Red Well, The Party Fight and Funeral, Dandy Kehoe's Christening, and other Irish Tales: [53a-f]

'Utrom Horum? or the Revenge of Shane Roe na Soggarth': *Per. Publ. 68*